JOHN CHARLES BEALES'S RIO GRANDE COLONY

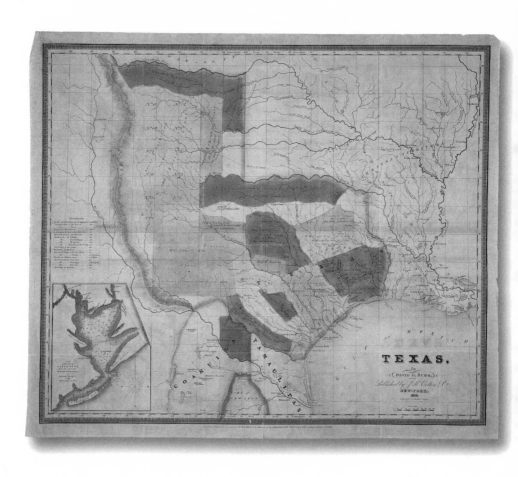

TEXAS,

By

(DAVID H. BURR.)

Published by J. H. Colton & Co.

NEW YORK.

1834.

JOHN CHARLES BEALES'S
RIO GRANDE COLONY

Letters by Eduard Ludecus, a German Colonist,
to Friends in Germany in 1833–1834,
Recounting His Journey, Trials, and
Observations in Early Texas

TRANSLATED AND EDITED
BY LOUIS E. BRISTER

Texas State Historical Association

© Copyright 2008 by the Texas State Historical Association.

Printed in the United States of America.

LIBRARY OF CONGRESS CATALOGING-IN-PUBLICATION DATA

Ludecus, Eduard.
John Charles Beales's Rio Grande Colony: letters by Eduard Ludecus, a German colonist, to friends in Germany in 1833–1834, recounting his journey, trials, and observations in early Texas / translated and edited by Louis E. Brister.
   p. cm.
Includes bibliographical references and index.
ISBN 978-0-87611-234-2 (alk. paper)
   1. Ludecus, Eduard—Correspondence. 2. Pioneers—Texas—Correspondence. 3. Germans—Texas—Correspondence. 4. Colonists—Texas—Correspondence. 5. Beales, John Charles—Friends and associates. 6. Frontier and pioneer life—Texas. 7. Frontier and pioneer life—Rio Grande Valley. 8. Texas—History—To 1846. 9. Rio Grande Valley—History—19th century. 10. Rio Grande Valley—Description and travel. I. Brister, Louis E. (Louis Edwin), 1938– II. Title.
F389.L93A3 2008
976.4'4—dc22   2008005568

    5   4   3   2   1   08   09   10   11   12

Published by the Texas State Historical Association.
Design by David Timmons.

  ∞ The paper used in this book meets the minimum requirements of the American Standard for Permanence of Paper for Printed Library Materials, z39.84—1984.
    Frontispiece: "Map of Texas," created by David H. Burr, 1834. *Courtesy of Center for American History, University of Texas—Austin.*

CONTENTS

ACKNOWLEDGMENTS

My interest in the letters of Eduard Ludecus, in which he recounts his 1833 journey to Texas, began while I was researching the attempt of another German, Johann von Racknitz, to establish a colony near Bastrop in 1832. Von Racknitz brought over two hundred German colonists to Texas, but most died of cholera soon after landing near Brazoria. In 1834, in San Antonio, Ludecus discovered a young survivor of the Racknitz colony, an orphan boy who had been adopted by a Spanish priest.

As I began to read the letters of Ludecus, I became convinced that they contain a wealth of information that should be translated into English and made accessible to American students of Texas history. Ludecus possessed a depth of observation and an unobtrusive style of writing uncommon among German visitors to Texas during the nineteenth century.

A great many people, chief among them archivists in Germany and the U.S., have selflessly assisted me in the preparation of this book. They are listed here in alphabetical order, and not necessarily according to the amount of assistance they rendered in the completion of this project.

The efficient staff at the Center for American History at the University of Texas at Austin has my gratitude for making available to me documents relating to the John Charles Beales grant.

Special thanks are due to Hannelore Bade, curator at the Focke Museum in Bremen, Germany, for providing me with valuable information about the notorious *Vergifterin* [poisoner], Gesche Gottfried.

Harald Baum, curator at the Stadtmuseum Erfurt in Erfurt, Germany, assisted me very generously with valuable information and with his thoughtful suggestions as I was researching the history of Erfurt.

Jane Fitzgerald, archivist of Old Military and Civil Records at the National Archives in Washington, D. C., deserves my special thanks for providing me with valuable information about U. S. maritime law governing the transport of European emigrants to the U. S.

Ed Loch, archivist at the San Antonio Archdiocese in San Antonio, Texas, was an indispensable source of information regarding the history of San Fernando Cathedral in San Antonio. To him I am extremely grateful.

Herr Otto, archivist at the Stadtkirchenamt in Weimar, Germany, assisted me generously in my search for genealogical records about Eduard Ludecus. The information he provided about Ludecus's birth and parents was indispensable to my research.

I am especially indebted to Salle Stemmons for her inspiring interest in my research and in seeing the letters of her ancestor published. She has contributed greatly to my study of Ludecus in a most material way; she shared with me copies of Eduard's sketches of the colony of Dolores, his personal copy of the map of Texas published by Stephen F. Austin, and the results of genealogical research on the Ludecus family done several years ago by a professional genealogist.

Finally, Jerry Weathers and his reference staff at the Alkek Library at Texas State University also deserve a nod of appreciation for their untiring assistance in obtaining materials for my research from other libraries in the U.S.

INTRODUCTION

The foreword to Eduard Ludecus's letters from North America to friends and family in Germany was written by his father, Wilhelm Ludecus, who identifies himself in the book only as *der Herausgeber*, "the editor." However, the elder Ludecus knew details about Eduard Ludecus's life that only a close friend or relative would know. Moreover, the organization and language of the letters bear little evidence of an editor's hand. No doubt, as Wilhelm Ludecus read the letters and prepared to have them published for the German public, his chief concern was his son's safety as the young man traveled in North America. By the time he had read the last letter, however, Wilhelm Ludecus shared his son's concern for other German emigrants who might be lured to colonies in Mexico. To Wilhelm Ludecus (as to most Germans), North America, especially Mexico, was a vast wilderness, a land of opportunity to be sure, but also (for the immigrant) a land of grave hardship and ubiquitous danger. As Wilhelm writes in the foreword, prior to publishing the letters he had read almost everything that had been published at the time about Mexico, but hadn't found much information about Coahuila and Texas, the region where his son proposed to settle.[1] Wilhelm goes on to list all the works he read, beginning with Humboldt's scholarly account of his travels in Mexico in 1803, and to summarize their content. For that and other reasons, his lengthy foreword has not been included in this translation.

LANGUAGE AND STYLE OF LETTERS

On August 7, 1833, while in Bremerhaven awaiting instructions to board ship, Eduard Ludecus began writing the letters intended to record for family and friends his journey to North America. He was not an experienced writer. Hence, the early letters especially, are written in the manner of someone talking. He strings together clause after clause until, at times, one sentence fills a third of a page. It is obvious too that he wasn't writing for a gen-

---

[1] Eduard Ludecus, *Reise durch die Mexikanischen Provinzen Tumalipas, Cohahuila und Texas im Jahre 1834. In Briefen an seine Freunde* (Leipzig: Johann Friedrich Hartknoch, 1837), v.

eral audience, but for specific readers who, he presumed, shared his experience and values. His writing style is rambling as he records his experiences of the day and impressions of his fellow travelers. He begins a new paragraph, for example, not necessarily to introduce a new topic, but to mark his next opportunity to write.

Eduard Ludecus was well educated and had a circle of friends who were equally well educated. Indeed, the letters show a sophistication and familiarity with Greek and Roman mythology, contemporary German literature, and theater (especially the theater in Braunschweig) rarely found in the writings of German immigrants to North America at the time. The organization of the first four or five letters (written in Bremerhaven, aboard ship, and in New York) reveals his inexperience as a writer. He jumps from topic to topic with each new experience. His German also shows a pronounced predilection for French loan words, which were no doubt common to the vernacular speech of Weimar, the cosmopolitan capital of Saxe-Weimar, where Ludecus grew up. The letters he wrote before arriving in Texas are full of French words such as *cafetière, pecuniär, retirade, arretiren, balanciren, bouteille, logiren, kokettiren, trottoir, promeniren,* and *comptoir.* After arriving in Texas, however, he uses fewer expressions borrowed from French and eventually replaces them with the Spanish ones he was assimilating daily. In this manuscript, the spelling of all foreign words and phrases (whether French, English, or Spanish) has been silently corrected and reproduced in italics.

Throughout the narrative, Ludecus abbreviates the names of people he's mentioned earlier. After introducing Dr. J. C. Beales for the first time, for example, he refers to the empresario variously as Dr. Beales, Mr. Beales, Beales, Bls. and Mr. Bls. Each time Ludecus uses an abbreviated form (for the name of Dr. Beales as well as for other persons) the surname has been silently inserted by the translator. Literary, historical, and military figures (who were familiar to Ludecus and his educated contemporaries) enjoyed such name recognition that he usually referred to them only by their surname. For the modern reader their given names have been supplied in brackets and their contributions explained briefly in the notes. In a similar effort to clarify Ludecus's intent, his spelling of names, places, plants, animals, and Indian tribes has been silently corrected. References to the Mexican peso as "piaster" or most frequently as "P" (as in "ten P") have been silently rendered as "peso." Otherwise, words or phrases have been inserted by the translator to clarify or supplement the language Ludecus uses and are enclosed in brackets. The German editor also inserted a few explanatory footnotes throughout the text; these have been translated as well as an integral part of the original German publication.

Many portions of the letters were written in the present tense, for Ludecus was recounting daily, sometimes every two or three days, his most recent experiences. To him they were current experiences and fresh in his memory. Sometimes, when he wanted to relate something he had previously forgotten to include in the narrative, or when he wanted to revisit an event from days earlier, he naturally used the past tense. For the sake of continuity and consistency, therefore, his narrative has been translated for the most part in the past tense. This tense also lends to Ludecus's voice some historical distance from our own time as he recounts his voyage to North America and his experiences in Texas and Mexico just months before the Texan revolt.

Eduard Ludecus did not write the letters about his journey to the Mexican provinces with the same care and attention to stylistic form he might have taken had he been writing in retrospect for publication. At the time he left Germany, he planned to settle on the Missouri River and to record in a series of letters his experiences as a frontier farmer. At first he wished to see his letters published as an entertaining record of a German emigrant's trials and triumphs on the Midwestern frontier. However, in New York he was persuaded by Dr. John Charles Beales to join his colony on the Rio Grande River in Texas. Soon after arriving in Texas, Eduard decided that his experiences as a colonist might serve as a cautionary tale for other Germans contemplating emigration. As he began to realize that Dr. Beales and his lieutenants were not well informed about the land into which they were leading the colonists, he came to believe that his experiences in Texas and Mexico would be invaluable to fellow countrymen who might also be persuaded to join similar colonization enterprises. His narrative, which from time to time addressed the many pitfalls confronting German emigrants coming to settle in Texas or Mexico, gradually took on a pragmatic tone. He began writing less about his own difficulties and disappointments, and more about the experiences of the other colonists, their interactions with one another and with the leaders of the expedition, and about Dr. Beales and his failures as *empresario*. Eduard Ludecus became a much more careful observer of the country in which he and the other colonists were traveling and he began to pay more attention to the people and cultures—Mexican, Anglo, and Native American—he encountered in Texas. Eduard's father, Wilhelm Ludecus, recognized the value of his son's letters and brought them to Johann Friedrich Hartknoch (a prestigious publisher in Leipzig) for publication. Hartknoch was the publisher for such eminent writers as Immanuel Kant, Johann Gottfried Herder, and Johann Georg Zimmermann, and his imprimatur on Eduard's letters was guaranteed to attract the attention of many readers throughout Germany.[2]

---

[2] *Allgemeine Deutsche Biographie*. Historische Commission bei der königlichen Akademie der Wissenschafter. (56 vols., 1875; reprint, Berlin: Duncker and Humblot, 1967), X, 667.

Eduard Ludecus (1807–1879)

Eduard Ludecus—younger son of Wilhelm Ludecus, ducal court secretary and privy councilor at the court of Karl August, Duke of Saxe-Weimar—was born on October 27, 1807.[3] In 1792, before the demise of the Holy Roman Empire of the German Nation in 1806, the family of Johann August Ludecus was ennobled, but family records do not indicate that the appellation "von Ludecus" was ever used by any members of the family.[4] As a member of the upper middle class in Weimar, Eduard Ludecus received a sound education at the Wilhelm-Ernst-Gymnasium, the only secondary school in Weimar for preparing young men to attend the university or to make a career in the world of commerce.[5] The evidence (largely the writings of Eduard Ludecus himself) indicates that he was a typical pupil, but one who was capable of independent thought and who learned his lessons well. In his thirteenth letter Ludecus relates how as a *Tertianer* (ninth grader) he was punished for loafing about in the outdoors when he should have been attending church services.[6] In his sixteenth letter he notes that in Mexico he pronounced the Spanish word *agua* the way his Latin instructor, the assistant principal at the *Gymnasium*, had taught him and he recalls his fear at being examined orally by the school's director on his knowledge of Latin and Greek before an examination committee.[7] In addition, the many references in Ludecus's letters to figures from Greek and Roman mythology and literature leave little doubt about the depth and breadth of his education.

Eduard Ludecus's mother was Louise Amalie Ludecus, née Brückmann, a native of Braunschweig.[8] It was probably through her family's connections in Braunschweig that upon completing his education, Edward was able to launch his career in commerce working in a large trading firm there. According to Eduard's father, who wrote the foreword to his son's published

---

[3] Ibid., XIX, 368; Baptismal Register of the Evangelisch-Lutherischen Hofkirche in Weimar, 1798–1808, Jahrgang 1807, p. 534.

[4] "Document granting Knighthood in the Holy Roman Empire to Johann August Ludecus," July 6, 1792, translation in typescript, 6 pp. Courtesy of S. Stemmons, a descendant of Eduard Ludecus.

[5] Gitta Günther, et al. (eds.), *Weimar: Lexikon zur Stadtgeschichte* (Weimar: Verlag Hermann Böhlaus Nachfolger, 1998), 496.

[6] Ludecus, *Reise*, 195; see also Louis E. Brister, "Eduard Ludecus's Journey to the Texas Frontier: A Critical Account of Beales's Rio Grande Colony," *Southwestern Historical Quarterly*, 108 (January, 2005), 382–383.

[7] Ludecus, *Reise*, 296, 310.

[8] Marriage Register of the Evangelisch-Lutherischen Hofkirche in Weimar, 1801–1821, Jahrgang 1805, p. 48.

letters, Eduard wanted to work in business chiefly because he expected to earn enough money in a short period of time to be able to travel about in the world.[9] As Eduard describes himself in his sixteenth letter, he was evidently quite a dandy in Braunschweig. He frequently attended the theater and could become quite upset if he had forgotten to pull on his kid gloves before setting out for a stroll in the city.[10]

But, as time would tell, Eduard Ludecus was not suited to the sedentary life of working in the closed environment of a large import and export firm. After about five years, he began to suffer depression from the long hours spent sitting at a desk. His physician determined the cause of this condition to be sitting too long without activity and counseled him to change both his work and his place of residence. As Eduard considered this advice, he resolved to emigrate to America, a favorite destination at the time for many young Germans. To this end, he began preparations for his new life in the New World. He studied, among other books, Gottfried Duden's popular book about the prosperous settlements on the Missouri River, *Bericht über eine Reise nach den westlichen Staaten Nordamerikas am Missout in den Jahren 1824, 1825, 1826, 1827* (Elberfeld: S. Lucas, 1829). To prepare himself for the demanding life on the American frontier, Eduard sought training in horseback riding, swimming, marksmanship, and hunting.[11]

His first destination in the United States would be New York City, so before commencing that journey, he asked his employer, Herr Becker, for a letter of introduction to his (Becker's) relatives and business associates in New York.[12] According to the Braunschweig city directory for the year 1828, there were two merchants by the name of Becker in that city: an F. Becker, listed merely as a business man, and F. M. Becker, who operated a business selling various types of raw materials and spices.[13] Ludecus was very likely employed by the latter.

Eduard Ludecus sailed for New York well prepared for his new life as a settler on the western frontier of North America. As time would tell, his riding, swimming, and hunting skills would prove invaluable, and as a settler on the Rio Grande River instead of the Missouri River, his experience with foreign languages (especially Latin) would give him a great advantage over the other colonists. His letters indicate that he quickly learned enough

---

[9] Ludecus, *Reise*, iii.

[10] Ibid., 296.

[11] Ibid., iii–iv; "Reminiscences of Wilhelm Ludecus," dictated in July, 1849, (translation in typescript , 52 pp.), 49–50. Courtesy of S. Stemmons.

[12] Ludecus, *Reise*, 55, 62.

[13] *Braunschweigisches Adreß-Buch für das Jahr 1828* (Braunschweig: Verlag von Johann Heinrich Meyer, [1828]), 6.

Spanish to serve as translator or spokesman for the other colonists (both other Germans and English colonists). The narrative of his ship voyage, his sojourn in New York, his journey to Texas and the Rio Grande, and his life in the settlement of Villa de Dolores is best presented by Ludecus himself in his letters.

After leaving Dolores, Eduard traveled to Matamoros, and from the port of Matamoros he sailed aboard the schooner *Louisiana* for New Orleans on October 28, 1834. Because of frequent calms, however, the *Louisiana* did not sail into the mouth of the Mississippi River until eighteen days later, on November 15. On Monday, November 17, a towboat brought the schooner up to the port of New Orleans.[14]

According to genealogical records in the possession of one of his descendants, Eduard Ludecus met and befriended another German in New Orleans. Together they traveled to Little Rock, Arkansas, and in the vicinity of that city Eduard worked on one farm and then another in order to learn the methods for growing cotton. But as a result of the deprivation and hardships suffered on the journey from Dolores to New Orleans, he began having attacks of climatic fever. He sought treatment in Little Rock, but soon realized that these treatments would never cure him. Consequently, he headed north, up the Mississippi and Ohio Rivers to Cincinnati, where he sought additional treatment among the German community there. But after several months, he realized that the Cincinnati doctors were not helping much either. Thus, he continued on to Pennsylvania, first to Pittsburgh and then to Allentown, where he found a new homeopathic institute operated by Germans under the direction of Dr. Constantine Hering, a German native who had founded the institute in 1835. The North American Academy of Homeopathic Healing in Allentown was the first homeopathic medical school in the world—the first to teach this new method of therapy (pioneered by Samuel Christian Friedrich Hahnemann in 1796) based on the principle of stimulating the body's own healing powers to cure a patient's illness. At the Allentown Academy, as it was called, Ludecus was finally cured of the illness that had tormented him since leaving San Fernando to return to the United States.[15]

Eduard Ludecus is also reported to have met his future wife, Frederica Wiskemann, in Allentown. She convinced Eduard to leave Pennsylvania for New York City, where she opened a shop selling knitted and embroidered clothing that she imported from Germany for ladies. Her store was so suc-

[14] Ludecus, *Reise*, 352, 355; "Marine Journal," *The Bee* (New Orleans) November 17, 1834.

[15] "Descendants of Theodoricus Ludicus of Germany: Eduard Broeckmann Ludecus" (typescript, 2 pp.), 1. Courtesy of S. Stemmons; Ludecus, *Reise*, xv–xvi.

cessful that it prompted competitors to open similar businesses nearby. Consequently, Frederica and Eduard decided to leave New York and move south to Charleston, South Carolina, where they operated another business specializing in ladies' wear. After a short time they decided to move from Charleston to Georgia, where they wanted to buy a farm.[16]

The U. S. Census of 1840 lists Eduard Ludecus as a resident of the Sixth Ward of New York City. He is reported to be between thirty and forty years of age, married, and having in his household one male child under five years of age and two females (probably his wife and a servant) between twenty and thirty years of age. In 1850, he is residing in Chatham County, Georgia, near Savannah. He is listed in the census report as forty-five years of age and a farmer. He and the oldest female in the household, Frederica by name, are recorded as natives of Germany. His family includes two female children, Margaret (fourteen years old), and Wilhelmina (nine years old), born in Pennsylvania and New York respectively; and two male children, William (four years old), and Edward (one year old). Both males were born in South Carolina. In 1860, Eduard is reported to be living again in New York City. There is no mention of a family. In 1870, the Ludecus family is living in Montgomery, Alabama. Frederica is the head of the household. She is listed as being fifty-eight years of age and a milliner by profession. In her household are G. Werth, thirty-two years old and a shoemaker by profession, and Louisa Werth, twenty-nine years old and a housekeeper. They have one male child, three months old. W. A. Ludecus, probably William, is listed as a twenty-two year old male and a watchmaker by profession.[17]

Little is known about Eduard Ludecus's life in the United States. Evidently, he did not record his experiences and observations as he traveled through Arkansas, Ohio, Pennsylvania, New York, or South Carolina as he had in Texas and Mexico. If he wrote letters as colorfully descriptive and full of insight from the United States as those he had written from Mexico, they were evidently lost. He died on April 6, 1879 at the age of seventy-two. The cause of death was chronic dyspepsia, a disorder stemming possibly from the digestive illness that had caused him so much suffering in Mexico. He was interred in Montgomery, Alabama.[18]

[16] "Descendants of Theodoricus Ludicus..." 1.

[17] United States Sixth Census (1840), Population Schedules, New York City, Sixth Ward, microfilm, p. 560; United States Seventh Census (1850), Population Schedules, Georgia District 13, Chatham County, microfilm, p. 329; United States Eighth Census (1860), Population Schedules, New York District, Fourteenth Ward, microfilm, reel no. 384; United States Ninth Census (1870), Population Schedules, State of Alabama, County of Montgomery, microfilm, p. 311. (microfilm, Genealogical Division, Texas State Library, Austin).

[18] Eduard Ludecus, Record of Interments, City of Montgomery (Alabama Department of Archives and History).

JOHN CHARLES BEALES'S COLONIZATION CONTRACT

John Charles Beales was born on March 20, 1804, in Alburgh, Norfolk County, England. After earning a degree in medicine at the University of London, Dr. John Charles Beales went to Mexico in 1826 as company surgeon for the Tlalpujahua Company, one of the British silver mining associations there. In late 1828, after that company ceased operations, Beales entered private practice in Mexico City. In 1830, he married María Dolores Soto y Saldaña, a wealthy widow and the daughter of an aristocratic Mexican family. Her first husband had been Richard Exter, an English merchant in Mexico.[19] Before his death in 1829, Exter had obtained a large colonization grant in the region of Coahuila and Texas. Beales was persuaded to take the place of Richard Exter as the empresario who would execute the contract by promoting immigration to Texas, a land Beales would never have visited had circumstances not conspired to place him at the center of the rush to colonize the region.[20]

In the course of his efforts to capitalize on his role as empresario, John Charles Beales made three colonization contracts with the government of the State of Coahuila and Texas. The first and largest grant was with José Manuel Royuela, secured on March 14, 1832. This contract contained 45,000,000 acres in what is now the panhandle of Texas and part of New Mexico. After a few months Royuela withdrew from the project and assigned his interest to Beales. Alone, Beales failed to bring any colonists into the territory.[21]

Beales's second colonization grant was called the Beales and Mexican Company grant. That grant was located between the Colorado and Guadalupe rivers and contained only 2,000,000 acres of land. The contract was made on July 1, 1832 to settle 450 families on the land, but again Beales failed to introduce the required number of families into Texas.[22]

On October 9, 1832, Beales made a third contract, this time with Dr. James Grant, a Scot by birth and a naturalized Mexican citizen. The grant

[19] Raymond Estep, "Beales, John Charles," in Ron Tyler, et al. (eds.), *The New Handbook of Texas* (6 vols.; Austin: Texas State Historical Association, 1996), I, 434–435; Lucy Lee Dickson, "Speculations of John Charles Beales in Texas Lands" (M.A. thesis, University of Texas at Austin, 1941), 3.

[20] Dickson, "Speculations," 4.

[21] Ibid.; Carl Coke Rister, *Comanche Bondage: Dr. John Charles Beales's settlement of La Villa de Dolores on Las Moras Creek in Southern Texas in the 1830's* . . . (Lincoln: University of Nebraska Press, 1955), 23; Mary Virginia Henderson, "Minor Empresario Contracts for the Colonization of Texas, 1825–1834," *Southwestern Historical Quarterly*, 32 (July, 1928–April, 1929), 23–24.

[22] Dickson, "Speculations," 4; Henderson, "Minor Empresario Contracts," 24.

contained 8,000,000 acres of land between the Nueces and Rio Grande rivers. The boundaries of the grant were as follows: "Beginning on the line or reputed boundary line which separates the State of Coahuila and Texas from that of Temaulipas, running across the river Nueces and Bravo-del-Norte, and ascending on the left bank of the said river Bravo as far as the twenty-fourth meridian or degree of longitude west from Washington; from thence proceeding along the line of said twenty-fourth degree till it meets the twenty-ninth parallel or degree of longitude, from thence running on the said parallel as far as the aforesaid river Nueces whence a line is to be drawn downwards till it reaches the aforesaid boundary line at the place of beginning." Beales and Grant were required by the contract to settle eight hundred families on their new grant.[23]

It is important to remember that even though John Charles Beales had made three colonization grants with the government of Coahuila and Texas, he had never been to Texas. What he knew about the territory he had learned from hearsay, books, or maps. With his third contract, Beales seems to have been determined to settle the required number of families on his grant.

Beales and Grant were land-rich, but cash-poor, and there were considerable expenses attached to recruiting colonists, transporting them to the grant territory, and establishing them on the land. With Grant's permission, Beales traveled to New York and with the support of wealthy investors, he established the Rio Grande and Texas Land Company. In September 1834, Beales himself was appointed "empresario and general agent in Texas." Beales in turn sent William Henry Egerton and Thomas A. Power to Texas as his special deputies.[24]

While Beales was in New York organizing the Rio Grande and Texas Land Company and recruiting his first contingent of colonists for his grant, he met Eduard Ludecus. In his fifth letter, Ludecus recounts his meeting with Dr. Beales and the latter's plans for establishing a colony in Texas.[25] He (Ludecus) expresses interest in joining Beale's expedition and states his intention of gathering more information in order to make the decision to travel to Texas.

[23] Dickson. 4–5, 36 (quotation)–37; The original text of Beales's third grant contract can be examined in the Archives and Records Division of the Texas General Land Office. A typescript copy of the Rio Grande grant is also contained in the brief for the case, *John Charles Beales et al. v. The United States*. See "Grant from the Governor of Coahuila and Texas to John C. Beales with Grant to him in Fee Simple of Several Leagues" in the John Charles Beales Papers in the Private Manuscripts collection of the Texas State Archives and in the John Charles Beales Papers in the Center for American History at the University of Texas at Austin.

[24] Dickson, 36, 40–45; Rister, *Comanche Bondage*, 26, 27–28.

[25] Ludecus, *Reise*, 58–59.

JOHN CHARLES BEALES'S RIO GRANDE COLONY

TABLE OF CONTENTS

FIRST LETTER
Arrival in Bremen. Excursion to Hamburg. Bremerhaven.

Bremerhaven, August 7, 1833

Here I sit, in order to write you all here in my homeland for perhaps the last time. A favorable wind—and I leave this country for how long? One may ask only fate this question. In America the first goal of my journey is New York, and I have promised you all a brief but true account of the journey.

The assertion has been made that one should not leave one's homeland without being able to cite the most compelling reasons for doing so. In this connection I ought to relate here a long story. I ought to write my biography, if my character moved me to do so, or if my political views moved me, a history of my fatherland. Neither of them would hardly be read, for you all know the former as well as I, and to enrich the world with yet another jeremiad [about Germany] is as unnecessary as preaching reason to a dyed-in-the-wool aristocrat. Now, I know two other interesting reasons that could have brought me here. One would be an unhappy love affair, which would be good material for a novel. But I do not know how this novel will end. Since [Ernst August Friedrich] Klingemann's last tragedy, *Bianca di Sepolcro*, ends with seven corpses, as good taste currently requires of this genre, I will pass over this reason and name the second one: crime. This other reason would create a furor, especially if the novel was given a title by [August] Leibrock in Braunschweig. Scandals are and remain favored readings, and are not forbidden as are [Karl Theodor] Welcker's and [Karl Wenzeslaus Rodecker] von Rotteck's writings. These are terrible people who corrupt and stir up the people, incite them to become incendiaries, to lead revolts, and to overthrow princes. And with what? With a hundredweight of truth and an ounce of wit. The important thing about a book is the title. But now I cannot find one. Leibrock is not at hand, and the man who enriched the world with fine novels is to blame that my genius fails me now. I must ask all of you who are reading these letters to choose for yourself the reason compelling me to make a pilgrimage across the ocean that seems most interesting to you. With that I hope that I have satisfied you all and have skirted thereby a jagged reef. Now I have set all my sails and I am coming into the open water.[1]

---

[1] Ernst August Friedrich Klingemann (1771–1831) was a novelist, playwright, and theatre director in Braunschweig. Henry and Mary Garland (eds.), *The Oxford Companion to German Literature* (Oxford: Clarendon Press, 1976), 475.

Johann Ludwig August Leibrock (1782–1853) wrote many historical and suspense novels. He spent most of his life in Braunschweig, where he worked first as a teacher and then as a librarian. At the time of his death, Leibrock had published no fewer than fifty

From Bremen I wrote you the last time at length, but nothing about the city itself. What should one say about it? It is nothing more than a city of commerce, and boring, just as boring as "market price" and all his associates: the licensed German newspapers, and a free city in which the laws deny residence rights to Jewish Jews, because too many Christians live there. The market exchange becomes their place of assembly punctually at one o'clock. A few minutes before that one can see the traders come running like greyhounds, for anyone who comes after the chiming of the clock must pay a half *Thaler* admission. The social life in Bremen is said to be nothing less than pleasant, and a malicious caste system based on wealth is said to reign there. I can recommend "The City of Frankfurt" for overnight lodging. After lunch the three pretty daughters of the hostess in the inn serve complimentary coffee in the garden which is presided over by their mother.

As everyone knows, every city has its curiosities. Berlin has its Elysium, where *Weißbier* is served and where anyone who pays five silver *Groschen* can take along a half dozen *Houris* free of charge. Leipzig has its Rosenthal where no roses bloom. Vienna has its chamber maids, and Munich has its *Bock*. Frankfurt has its Herr von Rothschild, and Braunschweig its *Mumme*. Erfurt has its great Susanne, who to be sure banished the devil and the French, but not the Prussians, etc. Of course, there is no lack of curiosities in Bremen. In fact, there are several. The most notable one is the large Roland statue. The others, in order of importance, are the whale, which many long years ago was the object of a remarkable struggle between Sweden and Bremen. Then there is the wine cellar with the rose and the twelve apostles. In the large stomachs of the apostles some valuable relics are preserved, namely twelve spirits of the noble wine from the Rheingau. Then there is the *Bleikeller* and finally the museum.[2]

---

novels which, although not rich in literary value, are credited with having promoted literacy in Germany because of their popularity. *Allgemeine Deutsche Biographie*, LI, 623–624.

Karl Theodor Welcker (1790–1869) was at (different times) a professor of law at Gießen, Kiel, and Freiburg Universities. As a private citizen and later as an elected deputy to the German Confederation, this outspoken liberal representative pressed for freedom of the press in Germany. In 1832, the periodical, *Der Freisinnige* (*The Liberal*), which he had founded with Karl von Rotteck, was prohibited from publication. *Meyers Konversations-Lexikon: Eine Encyklopädie des allgemeinen Wissens*, 4th ed. (19 vols.; Leipzig: Verlag des Bibliographischen Instituts, 1889–1892), XVI, 517.

Karl Wenzeslaus Rodecker von Rotteck (1775–1840) was a professor of history and political science at the University of Freiburg. In 1819 and again in 1831, he was elected deputy to the German Confederation as a representative of the liberal opposition. Because of his outspoken political views, his writings were suppressed and in 1832 he was relieved of his post at the university. *Konversations-Lexikon*, XIII, 1003.

[2] No information about "Elysium" could be found. It may have been a garden, restaurant, or cafe.

Unfortunately, of all these splendid attractions, I saw only the first one and the last one, which the gentlemen of Bremen will kindly forgive me. I had had enough of the hulking giant [Roland statue] and of Madame Gottfried who attracted the attention of the public health authorities only after a dozen people had been poisoned. The fact that the whale had once been the cause of a prolonged dispute could not make it for me any more remarkable, for it is well known that wars have been fought over things much less

---

In Muslim belief, a "houri" is a beautiful maiden who lives with the blessed in paradise; or it may simply be a voluptuously beautiful young woman. *Merriam-Webster's Collegiate Dictionary*. (10th ed.; Springfield, M.A.: G. and C. Merriam Co., 1998), 562.

In Rosenthal, a ward in northwest Leipzig, there was a large forest park that was popular for weekend outings. *Meyers Konversations-Lexikon*, X, 662–663.

The reference to Vienna and its chambermaids is unclear; possibly it was a private joke among the family and friends of Ludecus.

In Munich (as elsewhere in Germany), Bock has long been a popular strong beer. See *Konversations-Lexikon*, II, 919.

Mayer Anselm Rothschild (1743–1812) founded the Rothschild bank in Frankfurt am Main. During the nineteenth century, it was the wealthiest and most renowned banking house in Germany. Soon after Rothschild's death in 1812, his children opened branches in Vienna, Paris, London, and Naples. *Konversations-Lexikon*, XIII, 999.

"Mumme" was a type of beer invented in Braunschweig by Christian Mumme in 1492, hence the name "Braunschweiger Mumme." It is a dark brown, nutritious beer. *Meyers Konversations-Lexikon*, III, 368.

The "große Susanne" (great or large Susanne) was a large bell whose inscription stated that its ringing would banish the devil. This bell was not in Erfurt, however, but in Halle an der Saale, 120 kilometers from Erfurt. The Severi church in Erfurt had a larger bell named "Osanna," but this bell bore no inscription. Perhaps because of their similar sounding names, Ludecus confused the two bells. He also credits the bell for having banished the French, who occupied Erfurt from 1806 to 1814. The Prussians were in Erfurt from 1814 to 1945. Harald Baum, Curator, Stadtmuseum Erfurt, e-mail message to author, Nov. 27, 2005.

The most famous monument in Bremen was (and remains today) the stone statue of the medieval warrior Roland, erected in 1404 on the market square to represent the jurisdictional rights of the city. The statue stands 9.6 meters tall. *Meyers Konversations-Lexikon*, III, 386.

No information about a dispute over a whale could be found.

The wine cellar with the rose and the twelve apostles was in the Ratsweinkeller under the Rathaus in Bremen. The rose represented the best wines available there (i.e., certain Rüdesheim and Mosel wines) and the apostles were certain Hochheim, Rüdesheim, and Johannisberg wines. Ibid., III, 387.

The "Bleikeller" refers to the crypt below the Bremen cathedral where the dry air and other natural influences caused the corpses entombed there to mummify. Ibid., III, 387.

No information about the museum Ludecus visited could be found.

important than a whale. I could have hoped also to see several whales, but living ones in the sea instead of mere representations. Generally speaking, this behemoth of the sea no longer stirs popular interest, since [Johann Friedrich] Blumenbach and [Heinrich Friedrich Wilhelm] Gesenius have demonstrated through exegesis that the whale which is said to have swallowed Jonah was really a tavern. Jonah had eaten his fill there and when he could not pay, he was held there and thrown out three days later.[3]

The rose would have interested me only if I had been permitted to take one of the apostles with me on board the ship. There it would have rendered excellent service in relieving the boredom associated with ocean voyages. But since the apostles are there only for sick people and royalty, and since I was not ill and was wearing only a jacket instead of a prince's cape, I moved on and went to the museum. In constructing the museum, the wise members of the Bremen senate knew how to combine the pleasant with the utilitarian. Whoever becomes faint at the sight of the head of the infamous Madame Gottfried preserved in alcohol on the upper floor has the opportunity to refresh himself in the rooms on the ground floor.

In order to fill the time I had until the scheduled departure of the ship, I made a detour to Hamburg, Germany's London. I left with the express mail coach at four o'clock and the following morning at ten o'clock I was standing in front of "The King of England," a second-class inn. The innkeeper there is known as an eccentric in Hamburg and beyond. Right away he paid me the compliment of calling me "old boy," and when he learned that I had no baggage, he gave me a room in the third or fourth floor. Fearing that my lack of baggage had given him an unfavorable opinion of me and in order to regain his good will, I remarked that my close friendship with his son, the actor in Braunschweig, had brought me to his establishment. The father considers his son to be the premiere genius of his time—an opinion also shared by the son. Immediately the ice was broken and the "old boy" was in the innkeeper's good graces again.

---

[3] Madame Gottfried could not be identified in Bremen's history.

Johann Friedrich Blumenbach (1752–1840) was a naturalist and professor of medicine at the University of Göttingen where he lectured on comparative anatomy, physiology, natural history, and the history of medicine. He was one of the first to elevate the study of zoology to a distinct scientific discipline in Germany. *Meyers Konversations-Lexikon*, III, 48.

Heinrich Friedrich Wilhelm Gesenius (1786–1842) was a professor of oriental languages and Old Testament exegesis at the University of Halle, where he lectured on church history, Oriental languages, paleography, Old Testament exegesis, and biblical archeology. His innovative work in Hebraic studies, especially his *Hebräische Grammatik* (1813), established his reputation as one of the foremost scholars in that field. *Allgemeine Deutsche Biographie*, IX, 89–93.

It was a wonderfully beautiful day and people were streaming in droves out through the city gates. I followed the crowd in the company of a young man whom I had met in the dining room of the inn out to several outdoor public gardens where small theatrical troupes were performing short comedies. Among all the trivial dialogue we heard several good, racy jokes, many of them with political allusions. These jokes were always received enthusiastically. The performance, however, was neither good enough nor bad enough to hold my interest for more than ten minutes. Consequently, I hurried across town to the "Hamburg Mountain." An immense crowd of people was assembled there and they were amusing themselves in a variety of ways.

Boredom drove me back to an outdoor public garden where another comedy was being performed. I sat down, already rather fatigued, and watched the end of the play: An ugly old fellow overcame through cunning the courtship of his rival, a very educated young man, and then he married the object of their adoration. With the exception of a few good, coarse jokes, the play was devoid of content. The beloved, who could not decide on either of her suitors, was so passive that I suspect she was a diplomatic "happy medium." However, far be it from me to find something spurious in the play. On the contrary, the plot is taken from life. The fact that the ugly old character and not the young handsome one was the victor, probably needs no explanation. The small theaters are no different from the larger ones—the directors like to choose for themselves the pleasant roles. I got enough of the comedies and decided not to go to the municipal theater, in the first place because I had heard that I would have to cross the Goose Market to get there. In the second place, I had read [on a poster] in the Old Pavilion that the Hamburg theater was the best one in Germany, and I did not want to complicate my life in the New World with memories of the old one.

I wandered around in the brightly lit public gardens at the Gate of Altona until late in the night trying to find someone that I knew. Earlier that day, in the morning, I had also looked for several people I knew, but I had had no luck then either. So, I returned to the hotel early enough to overhear some neat negotiations going on in the room next to mine. Unbeknownst to a young girl, she was being sold as cool as you please to a man. Here that is not uncommon and the person who conducts the negotiation is called a flesh broker.

The next morning I looked over the smelt catch of the day and viewed several parts of the city. Then I hired a man to row me around the harbor [in a rowboat]. I went aboard the *Süden*, a commercial frigate which had just come from the East Indies. It had thirty-six cannons and a crew supplied by fifteen different nations. A number of the crew had gone to London, and I saw only several Negroes and Malaysians who were sitting there naked forming rice into balls with their fingers and then devouring them. One of them spoke some English, but he was so taciturn that I could not get much out of him. He seemed to have a somewhat higher rank than the others. After this visit I paid another one to the water nymphs. I ordered my boatman to take me to a place where I could swim. When he asked me if I could swim well, my modesty compelled me to give him a modest answer, but swimming well means something different to sailors [than it does to most of us]. Consequently, I learned that water is sometimes not so soft. As usual, I dived headfirst into the water and hit something solid with such force that for several minutes I struggled to regain my senses. I hurled countless expletives at the boatman and then swam away from him. He apologized and said if he had known that I could swim so well, then he would not have brought me to such a shallow spot. In that moment I decided henceforth and in the future not to be so modest.

After lunch I called for the bill, which was not modest, and received from the innkeeper gratis a bottle of claret along with a couple of dozen of his business cards which he wanted me to pass along in New York, and then he dismissed me with a brotherly farewell kiss.

I had hardly gone aboard the ferry that was supposed to take me to Harburg when I had the pleasure of running into my friend Rischbieter. He had returned a few days earlier from Saint Thomas and he had brought with him a letter and an invitation from G. Meinecke in Puerto Cabello to come there. We had a lot to tell each other and made all sorts of arrangements to see each other again in America. In Harburg I told him goodbye, and now I am curious whether we will ever find each other again in that huge part of the world. The following morning I arrived back in Bremen without being really satisfied with my visit to Hamburg. However, the brevity of my visit there could possibly be to blame.

When one leaves a city where one has spent only a few days, it is inevitable that it becomes the chief subject of one's conversation, and that is the way it was on the trip back to Bremen. My fellow travelers in the express coach knew Hamburg fairly well and had lots to tell. It is common knowledge that the inhabitants of the free cities, like those of the imperial cities, are endowed with a great deal of ego. None of them allows to pass an opportunity to put its patriotic virtue into practice. Now it cannot be denied that in the free cities, and especially in Hamburg, there are not only a lot of institutions for the support of the poor and the sick, but these institutions are also actually sustained, for there are adequate funds available. Among these institutions one can count primarily the orphans' home and the beautiful, new, and perfectly equipped hospital. The people of Hamburg never miss an opportunity to show off these excellent aspects of their city. For example, every year a public display is made of the orphans which is called the *Waisengrün*. On a pretty day all the orphan children are led through the streets by a "captain of orphans" at the head of the procession. Dressed in pretty clothes and marching in pairs, they play instruments and sing as they march. They are given money, and in front of some houses refreshments. The procession ends at a public garden at the George-Gate, where they are fed. The position of "captain of orphans" belongs to the most well-mannered and diligent orphan boy. But it is said that the choice usually falls on the most handsome boy. However that may be, this much is certain: the captain of orphans, fitted out in keeping with his position, struts along very mindful of his dignified role. He is dressed in the most fashionable clothes, with his hat under his left arm, and in his right hand he carries instead of a commander's staff a cane. At some houses, where women and girls dressed in their best fill the windows, he is greeted, praised, caressed, and given gifts.

Several times it has been suggested that the girls should be led by a female captain. Since women and girls enjoy seeing the young male captain, then one can forgive this wish of the men. One should just imagine a pretty girl, dressed like the Maid of Orleans, wearing on her head a wreath of violet blue silk flowers on her head instead of a helmet. And instead of a sword she is carrying in her hand a shepherd's staff. And carrying a cute little basket on her arm for the collection of donations, she would lead the procession of girls. Some women and girls are said to have had misgivings about this idea, and so, things have remained just as they were before, which in the free cities, as we all know, is always the case. And perhaps for a good reason. On the one hand it is questionable when the very sensitive heart of a young girl would be made more susceptible to flattery by all the attention given her by the public. On the other hand experience has taught us something about the consequences of the rose festivals in Salency and other villages in the vicinity of Paris. The rakes of that Sodom and Gomorrah gather in droves for the crowning of the Rose Queen and leave with the desire that they could possess that fair flower.

Everyone will agree with me when I maintain that this begging parade is calculated solely to show off publicly the charity of the citizens of Hamburg.

When a businessman from Altona—which is very inconsistent with the nature of the citizens of this town—wanted to side with the city of Hamburg and maintained that among the free cities Hamburg deserves preeminence, a wine dealer from Frankfurt responded. He noted that Hamburg could not boast of having an academy of sciences as did Frankfurt am Main. For the Senckenberg Museum, he went on, was by its nature if not by its title an academy of sciences. The magnanimous defender of Hamburg, who was probably hearing the name of this institute for the first time, had not expected this response and could think of nothing better to do than beat a retreat. I decided to come to his aid, less out of a special predilection for

Hamburg than to diminish the wine apostle's joy in his victory. I replied that Hamburg as well as Frankfurt, Berlin, and Munich had an academy of sciences, and that it depended on one's definition of such a learned institution. The name was not important, but rather the institution itself. Accordingly, on the one hand Frankfurt could not claim an academy of sciences any more than Hamburg, but on the other hand it probably could. Everyone was listening attentively by now and seemed to be awaiting an explanation of my statement, which I felt duty bound to give them. Of course, Hamburg has an academy, I went on, namely the Alster Pavilion. It is only a matter of first defining the meaning of the word, then the rest follows in and of itself. An academy of sciences is an association of men from several different fields who come together every year on their founder's day, possibly several times a year, to eat and drink heartily, and incidentally also to read something to each other. In short, it is just about the way we have read in the newspapers about the meetings of scientists. These meetings are different from the first meetings I described only in that the members pose important questions from all the branches of the sciences which the learned members cannot answer for themselves, for example, what type of plow did Cecrops use when he sowed the dragon's teeth, or whether Socrates took poison made from arsenic or from prussic acid? These questions are posed for discussion.[4]

But now, anyone who has ever been in the Alster Pavilion must admit that in this famous institution all of the requirements for a learned institution are met. First of all, there is the eating and the drinking, and it does not take place only once a year. Anyone, invited or uninvited, can come any day and any time to a full table and choose from all the products of the earth, the air, and the sea. As soon as one's nutritional needs, the needs of the stomach, are met, and one feels the inclination for some intellectual nourishment, there are also foreign and domestic products printed in all languages spread

---

[4] The Senckenberg Foundation was established in 1763 in Frankfurt am Main by Johann Christian Senckenberg. In 1817, the foundation united with the new Senckenbergische Naturforschende Gesellschaft, which included a medical institute, a botanical garden, a library, and a museum. *Meyers Konversations-Lexikon*, XIV, 859.

No information about the Alster Pavilion (at the time Ludecus wrote) could be found.

Cecrops was a mythical king of Athens, in most accounts the first king. He is generally depicted as half-man and half-serpent, and a civilizing figure who established monogamous marriage, writing, and funeral rites. Simon Hornblower and Anthony Spawforth (eds.), *The Oxford Classical Dictionary*, 3rd ed. (Oxford: Oxford University Press, 1996), 305.

According to tradition, Socrates was poisoned neither by arsenic nor by prussic acid, but by poison hemlock (the herbaceous plant, *Conium maculatum*). *The New Encyclopedia Britannica*, 15th ed. (32 vols.; Chicago: Encyclopedia Britannica, Inc., 1974–2003), IX, 548.

out there. The Alster Pavilion even has merits over most learned societies. In those societies there is a certain clannishness. In Munich there are the Schelling adherents, in Berlin the Hegel adherents, etc. In the Alster Pavilion, where there are no children of Israel, there is in all respects tolerance for everyone. Periodicals from both political extremes lie there resting cozily beside and on top of each other—the *Journal des Debats*, the *Constitutionel*, and the *Courier*, the *Österreichischer Beobachter*, the *Politisches Wochenblatt* of Berlin, and the *Weimarische Zeitung*. Whoever wants to learn about fire insurance, livestock insurance, and life insurance, about annuities and assurance, about the price of wool and sugar, about the spread of mysticism in Berlin, Bremen, Breslau, Halle, and Königsberg, he will find here instruction, oral and written, about everything. One can take part in discussions about theatrical subjects, for example, whether [Sabine] Heinefetter or [Catherine] Kraus-Wranitzky sings better, or whether it is possible that someone can play Masaniello better than [Julius] Cornet, and whether a female dancer must be employed for Fenella, etc. Whoever wants to learn about the newest advances in medicine can read the *Allgemeiner Anzeiger der Deutschen*. There the discoveries of homeopathic therapy both in Germany and abroad are always presented for the use and benefit of the believers and the skeptics. Of course, there are always opposing views present in the Alster Pavilion and the place does not lack for critics, but all disputes end without the shedding of blood. One pretty female figure gliding by on the *Jungfernstieg* or another looking out from the Hotel de Rome is enough to calm the waves of rage.[5]

[5] Friedrich Wilhelm Joseph von Schelling (1775–1854) was, after Johann Gottlieb Fichte (1762–1814), the chief philosopher of the Romantic movement in Germany. With such works as *Erster Entwurf eines Systems der Naturphilosophie* (1799), *Philosophie und Religion* (1804), and *Philosophie der Kunst* (1809) he was a popular exponent of the synthesis of spirit, nature, religion, and art. From 1806 until 1841 he was General Secretary to the *Akademie der bildenden Künste* in Munich. Garland and Garland (eds.), *Oxford Companion*, 754.

Georg Wilhelm Friedrich Hegel (1770–1831) set out early in his academic career as a lecturer at the University of Jena to develop a system that would supercede the theories of relativity of Johann Gottfried Herder (1744–1803) and Immanuel Kant (1724–1804) as preparation for a new idealistic philosophy. In 1818 he was appointed professor of philosophy at the University of Berlin, where he remained until his death. Garland and Garland (eds.), *Oxford Companion*, 351.

Sabine Heinefetter (1809–1857) was an opera singer who, after studying in Paris, performed in Italy and later toured Germany. In Berlin particularly, she received exceptional acclaim for her performances. *Konversations-Lexikon*, VIII, 306–307.

Catherine Kraus-Wranitzky (1801–n.d.) was born Catherine Wranitzky, the daughter of Paul Wranitzky, the director of music at the two imperial court theaters in Vienna.

A fat butcher from Braunschweig who was traveling with us to make a hops transaction opined that everything had two sides, even eating and drinking. He knew that from experience. If the bone-cutters guild, [he ventured], did not have their usual feast at every quarterly meeting, no one would come. A young man [in our company], who was coming from Kiel and who called himself "Doctor"(Who is not a doctor or a professor these days?) took exception to our transition from an association of the sciences to a butcher's guild. He was just about to offer his arguments when fortunately another young man, who up to that moment had been a passive listener, asked me whether I had visited the beautiful Marianne. This question weighed heavily on my heart, for how was I supposed to answer? I had not seen the famous maker of coffees! My stay in Hamburg had been too short for me to be able to take a short trip to Eimsbüttel. The beautiful Marianne, whose grace, beauty, and conversation have already gained a reputation throughout Europe, will forgive me this terrible sin. (The duke of Lucca, in order to recover from the cares of government at home, traveled abroad for eleven months each year, from the shores of the Mediterranean Sea to the shores of the North Sea in order to have breakfast with the Aspasia of the north in "Marianneville.") I promise that it will be my first stop upon my return to Europe in order to offer her my homage.[6]

Catherine acquired a reputation in Austria and Germany as a star operatic performer. Following her marriage in 1831 to an official at the Vienna court, she performed under the name Kraus-Wranitzky. J. Fr. Michaud (ed.), *Biographie Universelle Ancienne et Moderne*, (45 vols.; 1854; reprint, Graz: Akademische Druck-und Verlagsanstalt, 1966–1970), XLV, 87

Tommaso Aniello Masaniello, a fisherman and merchant in Naples, led a popular insurrection against the viceroy, the Duke of Arcos, in 1647. Masaniello's rise to power and subsequent murder inspired Daniel François Esprit Auber to create the Italian opera, *Fenella o la Muta de Portici. Konversations-Lexikon*, XI, 305; Félix Clément and Pierre Larousse, *Dictionnaire des Opéras*, 2 vols. (1905; reprint, New York: Da Capo Press, 1969), I, 442.

Julius Cornet (1793–1860) was a tenor from Tirol who studied in Vienna under Antonio Salieri and performed in Italy and Germany. He earned rave reviews in Braunschweig and Hamburg and went on to Paris, where (under the direction of D. F. E. Auber) he studied the role of Masaniello in *Fenella o la Muta de Portici. Meyers Konversations-Lexikon*, IV, 281.

[6] Eimsbüttel is today an administrative district of Hamburg, north of Altona in the greater city of Hamburg. At the time Ludecus wrote it was a village, distinctly separate from Hamburg.

No historical record of Marianne could be found.

Aspasia, the mistress of Pericles, reportedly taught rhetoric and had discussions with Socrates. Ludecus assumes that Aspasia (like Marianne was beautiful; hence, his eagerness to pay homage. Hornblower and Spawforth (eds.), *Oxford Classical Dictionary*, 192.

Once I had arrived in my temporary lodgings, I met a Herr S., who introduced himself to me as a fellow traveler to New York. I got out of him some news about the land of my hopes. His news was very mixed. He had been living in New York for two years himself, but he did not want to praise it too highly. He said that the conditions for surviving there are so high that one has to struggle to get by. He seems to me malcontent, and if I am not mistaken, he is a Jew. The man has the appearance of one whom one should be wary of and I intend to do so. From my conversation with him I learned that he had spent some time in Riga, Warsaw, Frankfurt am Main, Berlin, Breslau, London, and Paris. I do not like people who with a wife and child travel all over the world. He is a businessman and he offered his services if I needed them. I accepted his help for the duration of the voyage where I will not need it.

On August 4, we finally received the order from the ship owners to get ready to go, since the *Louisa* and Captain Mehrtens were ready to sail. But the wind was still out of the northwest, and that is the most unfavorable wind that we could have here for putting out to sea. On Sunday, the sixth of August, I made an outing by boat down the Weser River with two acquaintances, Herr Zimmermann and Herr Hoffmann. Both of them are from Braunschweig and they made it their business to make my stay in Bremen as pleasant as possible. All my affairs had been in order the day before, and on Monday I climbed aboard the coach with Herr S., bade a fond farewell to Zimmermann and Hoffmann, and away I went past Bremen's boring gates, filled with anticipation to see the tarred hull of the *Louisa*. In an inn halfway to the harbor we met Captain Mehrtens and two young men from Bremen, one of them a salesman and the other a tanner, both of them cabin passengers on board the *Louisa*.

Captain Mehrtens could serve as a model for the image of Hercules. He is a handsome man, and he is described as a very pleasant person. I hope that it is so. By three o'clock we had traveled the seven or eight miles [to Bremerhaven], and it was raining. We went into an inferior inn (the good one was filled) and then we immediately visited our brig, [the *Louisa*], in order to choose our bunks. Unfortunately, out of the five bunks available, two had already been wrongfully taken over in Bremen by two men from there. The third one had been taken by a man from the area of Coburg who had arrived at the harbor the day before. S., who was more experienced in these things than I, chose his bunk immediately, and I had to take what the others did not want.

Although Bremerhaven was established just two or three years ago, there are already fifty buildings here, and it will certainly grow rapidly, even though Oldenburg, because its economy will suffer, obstructs Bremerhaven's growth as much as possible. This is the curse that rests on Germany.

Incidentally, the location is poor insofar as there is no fresh water there, which is a great deficiency for a port. The people are working to drill an artesian well, but they are getting along now with rainwater that they catch in cisterns and sell for four *Groschen* per hogshead. If there is no rainwater available, then it is brought from the little town of Bremeriche, which is thirty minutes away. A heavy artillery battery from Hanover has been set up opposite the sluice gates, where it overlooks the shipping lane.

Unfortunately, the wind is still blowing strongly from the northwest and it is keeping the boats carrying the provisions from approaching Bremen. For a few more days there is no prospect of leaving port. There are a lot of ships lying at anchor here. As soon as the wind changes, we will leave port and there will be a whole squadron of us when we leave. A number of ships have already tried to leave several times, but they were forced to turn back with damage. I am already feeling bored and irritable. I am yearning to get out to sea, although I am afraid of seasickness, for I know from experience that I will have a bad case of it.

August 9

That same old wind is still blowing with rain and fog. North Germany has such an ugly climate. I would not like to live here. I hope that I will be compensated for this weather in America. Yesterday, in order to dispel my boredom, I went aboard the ships lying in the harbor. One ship from Greenland was interesting to look over; it belongs to a company formed by farmers who bought the ship for a cheap price, outfitted it, and they are manning it. It has been a long time since there has been such a good catch as this one: ten whales and a thousand seals.

In the afternoon the weather cleared somewhat and we were hoping that the wind direction would change. I rowed out into the channel and went aboard the *Theodor Körner*, a three-master bound for New Orleans in order to see the Maid of Orleans. She was a young girl from a good family in the local area who was traveling all alone via New Orleans to her beloved, a failed school teacher who settled on the Missouri River and wrote to her to join him. Nothing has been able to prevent her from carrying out her decision. She is not devoid of education, and she speaks very calmly about her undertaking. She is leaving both her parents to pursue it. I hope to see her again in St. Louis. One would probably not find such love again very soon!

This morning a ship entered the port from Baltimore. A young man was standing on the deck who was immediately recognized by the local people. A few months ago he had sailed from this harbor to undertake something in America, but I do not know what. On the way over he became very homesick, and after a stay of only two whole days he shipped out again for Europe.

The German is a patient creature. Today a carpenter got into a dispute with a Spanish sailor. The latter drew his knife and thrust it into his adversary's body. The German, although superior to the sailor in every respect, did not retaliate and went home to bandage the wound which was not dangerous.

August 10
On board the Louisa *with Captain Mehrtens*

There is still no prospect for a change in the weather. I had no desire to continue spending my money in the tavern. So, yesterday afternoon I went on board. I would have to do it anyway sooner or later. I have the first night already behind me. And now a couple of words about the methods of the ship owners for the use and benefit of those who travel after me, of those travelers into whose hands these lines will perhaps fall. Since my decision had been made to exchange the United States for my fatherland, I was seeking information about that country from the people who I thought would know something about it. I inquired as well about the journey and what there was to see along the way in order to compare that with what I had read about the country. As for the ocean voyage, I had been given the advice to apply directly to the ship owners in order to be assured that these men, as owners of about fourteen or fifteen ships, would give me the best placement. I did as much, but my letter was indefinite about the time of departure, for I did not know yet for certain whether I would choose Bremen for my embarkation point or not. I received no answer. When my second letter demanded a definite explanation [for the delayed response], adding that I would be compelled to apply to another shipping company, I received by express mail all the information that I had sought. To my question as to what I had to pay for baggage and whether I should bring along some bedding, I received the following answer: For the former there was no charge, and the latter I could bring, if I wished, and if not, then the company would provide the bedding. How astonished I was, therefore, when I called for my bill and found a charge of fourteen *Thaler* for shipping and baggage, a charge which, according to other shipping companies, this company was not entitled to. The ship was also described to me as "a most praiseworthy and well-known vessel, equipped especially well for passengers' comfort." Now I am learning what one calls comfort in Bremen.

The bunk built into the side of the ship's wall is so short that my feet protrude six inches out over the end, and when I cannot endure this position any longer, I can pull my feet up over each other like a corkscrew. How nice it would be here in this situation if I could follow the advice of Dr. S. in B., who said to his daughters when they were complaining about their unusual height: "Girls, tie knots in your legs!" Furthermore, this bunk is set so low that one would not even think of sitting on it. And then, I am forced to lie in it backwards, that is, with my head toward the bowsprit and my feet toward the rear of the ship. The bunk, which formerly might have been only a wide cupboard bin, is at the back so narrow that I cannot even let my head rest there comfortably, much less my shoulders. The bottom of this bunk is just as confining and is deeper on one side, so that I had to put some padding in there in order to raise it enough so that I could lie on a level plane. But by doing that, the height is diminished so much that when I lie there my nose collides constantly and unpleasantly with the top of the bunk. There is not even a suggestion of a mattress here, not even a sack of straw, and in the town I could not find enough hay or straw to make one. My hard "mattress" consists of a piece of old sailcloth. Generally speaking, this cabin is the worst that I have ever seen; it is dirty, smelly, and small. On the other hand, one pleasant aspect about the ship is that on the deck there is a cabin in addition to the sleeping quarters for the captain and helmsmen. Whoever wants to take an ocean voyage and has the choice to make the voyage on a ship that has a cabin on the deck should express a preference for that one. It must be extremely pleasant.

After reading all of this, one can believe that I surely did not spend my first night here on a bed of roses. After a few hours, I had to get up—it was impossible to remain any longer in that cubbyhole. I hope that it will go better the second night.

Now I want to continue on to the other glorified comforts of the ship. Of course, there is a steward here for the cabin passengers, but he is constantly occupied in the service of the captain. He is just a cabin boy and he has at the same time duties to perform as a sailor. I am curious to see what duties he will perform for us.

There is only a single washbowl here and it serves simultaneously as a dishwashing basin, as a drinking bowl for the dogs, and will later have to serve as a spittoon, if we cannot keep down the consequences of seasickness. Chamber pots, hand towels, etc. are also not available. Later on there will be more on this subject when I have the opportunity to make some more observations.

Yesterday evening the captain told us over tea, which for economic reasons is drunk here on board without milk, that he had fifty-nine passengers die on one voyage from here to Rio de Janeiro. Cramming the ship too full was the reason that those poor emigrants found a celestial paradise instead of an earthly one. Such overbookings probably used to happen also when emigrants were being transported overseas to the United States, so that the government there found itself compelled to pass a law stating that each ship entering port there might have only a certain number of persons on board. The number of persons was determined by the tonnage of the ship. A heavy fine was levied for exceeding that limit.[7] Thus, the government on a faraway continent looks after the welfare of its distant cousins. Our own government would never have done as much. May the good Lord send us soon a good wind!

The wind is out of the west now—a little more to the south and we will be on our way! I have just come back to my writing. I spent all the European money I had with me buying fruit and zwieback, and I have gotten rid of all my cash down to three dollars that I got in exchange. The wind must change now for better or worse, for I have no more silver coins and must leave soon. Today at noon I came on board and heard screaming inside the ship. Curious to see who had such good lungs and who could make himself heard over the sailors' songs and the screaming and crying of the children, I stepped over to a porthole and saw a clergyman conducting a baptism. How indefatigable this good man was, screaming the poor child into Christianity! And that is called performing a sacred act! A half hour after the clergyman had finished his work I was playing billiards with him. He seems to be an altogether rational man and has become involved in an intense dispute with his colleague in Bremeriche who is a pietist.

Yesterday a young man arrived here with his alleged wife from Frankfurt am Main. Since there was no more cabin room available on board the *Minerva*, which is sailing to Baltimore, they have to travel in steerage. It fills me with pity to see that pretty blonde woman who seems to come from a good family crammed in there with rag-tag and bobtail types. But she has a lot of courage and is already comforting another tearful woman from Frankfurt in steerage who arrived here today with her husband.

This morning I climbed up on the mainmast, in order to watch a ship sail down the Weser. When I saw two sailors on either side of me coming up after me with ropes, I realized immediately what they had in mind and beat a retreat. The sailors, who did not know my knack for climbing, did not complete their mission and I escaped them easily. It is customary on board these ships, when passengers climb into the masts, to tie them to the mast and make them pay to be set free again. But if the passenger escapes, he is not pursued.

---

[7] Ludecus refers to "An Act regulating passenger ships and vessels," approved on March 2, 1819 by the Fifteenth Congress in Second Session. This act prohibited the master of any ship entering or leaving a U. S. port to transport more than two passengers for every five tons of the vessel. It also set a minimum standard for the types and amount of rations a ship must carry for its passengers. Richard Peters (ed.), *Public Statutes at Large of the United States of America* . . . (Boston: Charles C. Little and James Brown, 1850), III , 488–489.

August 15

Hurrah for the southwest wind! The ships that heretofore were lying at anchor on the channel have disappeared. One can barely see the tips of the masts of some of them. We are making preparations now to get out into the channel and then to get underway. There is a hustle and bustle in the harbor. Farewell, farewell to you all! These are the last lines to you from European soil.

Life Aboard Ship. Descent Down the Weser
[August] 15, the channel of Bremerhaven

Greetings to you all again, of course, not from European soil, but from European water! The wind is thumbing its nose at us. Already toward evening of the twelfth it began to turn back to the west again, and we watched the ships on the horizon that were the last to leave already dropping anchor. During the night of the same day a fire broke out on board. The timbers under the galley were burning. A man must have been quarreling with his wife until twelve o'clock at night and were keeping several jovial fellows awake. Unable to sleep right away, they had gone up on deck and noticed the smoke. The galley fire and the fire of the overheated couple were extinguished without my assistance, for I remained peacefully in my cubbyhole. At three [in the morning] a boat began towing our ship out into the channel, where at nine we dropped anchor. Then the wind began blowing out of the northwest again with full force, and by noon I was (God be praised!) already seasick or riversick. It is a terrible feeling. What will it be like when I do get out to sea? The captain cannot think of anything comforting to say to me. The weather was the same all day long and then the next one too, namely terrible. Now we cannot exchange the boredom on board ship for boredom on shore. Today it is finally calm and I feel considerably better. But an ill wind is still blowing.

[August] 21

I have a life like a cat. It has been two and a half weeks since I arrived in Bremerhaven and the boredom has not killed me yet! Whoever knows Bremerhaven, the surrounding area, and life on board ship knows also that of all the five thousand people who are waiting for a favorable wind to sail, not a one of them has died of boredom. They will give the lie to anyone who maintains that boredom can kill. Unfortunately, my indisposition on the water makes it impossible to busy myself with mental pursuits. I am not in any condition to read even a half hour without a break, and these few lines are the only product that my dizzy head can bring forth.

My hobby these days consists mainly of training a dog, a very smart animal, and doing so shall redound to my credit. He marches already like a Prussian soldier from the *Garde-Lehr-Bataillon*.[1] He dances to a tune like a state representative, and he barks like a minister at revolutionaries. He even allows himself to be whipped without grumbling like the good people of

---

[1] No record of the Garde-Lehr-Batallion could be found.

Germany. A second hobby, and a pleasant one, consists of studying the characters in my environment. Later I will bring you a brief account of my observations.

A third occupation of mine consists of trapping mice, and an abundant catch is the reward for my work. Their main highway from one of the supply cupboards to the bread bin runs straight through my bunk. I enjoy imitating a certain government [we know] and ordered the imposition of transit customs. But instead of paying the toll, they started to smuggle, and now I must be on guard all night long. My watchmen [constructed] of wire deliver to me three or four smugglers every morning, which I have executed without a judgement or a sentence from a higher authority. All of those people complaining about the policies of this government should spend one night lying in my bunk, and then I will ask them if it is not just to have these smugglers executed!

We continue to go ashore when the weather permits it at all. There we play billiards, read the village newspaper, or continue on to Bremeriche and eat *Kranat* there, a small pale red crustacean. Then I pay a visit possibly to the baker or his sister, a demure, thirty-five year old spinster. They are both very nice people who even gave S. and me a little coffee party. In return, we took our fine hosts to the carnival in Bremeriche. With the rapidly changing weather in this part of the country these amusements, if one can call them that, are often spoiled for us, especially when we miss the ebb tide. Several times, in spite of the sailors' best efforts, it was impossible to return to the ship, and we had to go ashore again. Another time we were saved only by a towline thrown to us by a pilot's cutter.

I was not wrong about S. He is a Jewish Jew, a sophisticated swindler full of dodges and tricks. Indeed, he is in general as corrupt a person as I have ever seen before. In order to give him a sense of security, I pretended not to notice his petty trickery or to treat it as a joke. But he had no chance to commit a serious swindle. This made him bold until he went too far and I confronted him several times none too gently. Yesterday I told him candidly what I thought of him and that I wanted him to keep his distance from me. With that he was taken aback and withdrew. Little U. is a good, innocent human being. He studied in Jena and failed his exams there. He makes no secret of it, however, and complains that in the jurisdiction of Coburg the middle-class students are flunked in order to be able to place the sons of the nobility. In general he may be right. As small a person as he is, he has dueled very bravely and he has a body covered with scars to prove it. During a lively conversation with him he makes gestures that are mostly defensive thrusts. For that reason it is dangerous to be standing too near him. He is on the same footing as I with S.

The captain is just as he was described to me—a thoroughly obliging man. Always friendly, and neither severe nor surly, he tries to make the passengers' stay on the ship as tolerable as possible. From a pecuniary standpoint his hands are very much tied by the ship's owners. The two cabin passengers from Bremen are still in their lodgings on land. Consequently, I have been unable to get to know them very well. Besides those two there are a hundred and eight steerage passengers on board, most of them from southern Germany. I wish you all could be here for a couple of hours and see the steerage compartment: heavens above, what a state of affairs! [There are also] two helmsmen, one cabin boy, and ten sailors, three dogs, one cat, and three dozen chickens. There is also a Polish man among us. The governments of all the German states have denied him a residence permit. Suffering from hunger in Frankfurt, he returned [to Bremen], and here he found some humanitarians who took him under their wing. They arranged with the municipal senate for a residence permit for him that was good for several days, and they started a public fundraiser that paid for his passage and they gave him some clothes. They are sending him with a letter of introduction to a distinguished Pole in the hospitable republic of the United States. He had served in the Romarino Corps[2] and had become an Austrian prisoner of war. He never talks about his two benefactors in Bremen without becoming deeply moved. His friend, a belt maker from Hessen, shares with him whatever he has. The friend was also in the Polish War and participated in the famous march to Wilna and in the even more famous retreat under General [Heinrich] Dembinsky.[3] He is an extremely skilled person. In the recent revolutionary uprisings in southern Germany he came under suspicion and fled one night when the authorities tried to arrest him.

I will not write anymore until we are about to put out to sea. I am tired of boring you and myself any longer with complaints about the wind and the weather.

August 29, in the North Atlantic

I am delighted that I can finally close this letter and report my departure to you. This morning the wind turned to the southwest and everything in the harbor was on the move. Every ship quickly took on some fresh provisions, fetched its passengers who were still living on shore, and about ten o'clock the fleet of about sixty sails (that many had accumulated in the meantime) set out downstream.

With great delight we saw that our ship was among the better sailing vessels. We passed several that were at the head of the group and only the

---

[2] No information about the Romarino Corps could be found.

[3] The information about Dembinsky could not be corroborated.

Neptune and the *Virginia* beat us. When the latter passed us she fired a full salvo as a salute to us, but from empty cannons of course. That same morning the ship had just left the harbor and her passengers had not yet become accustomed to the motion of the ship as we had. They were all standing on the lee side of the ship throwing up overboard. Every cannon shot was greeted from our ship with a hurrah. The strong movements [of the ship] caused by the swells have not yet had an effect on me. I am fine, whereas others are already suffering from seasickness. Perhaps I overcame it already while we were on the river. On the gray horizon I can barely still see a few narrow strips of land. To the east I see a flotilla of two hundred sails that have just departed Hamburg and Cuxhaven. It is a magnificent day and the sight of all this is delightful. I can hardly wait for that moment when the last strip of land will disappear. The pilot is leaving us now and I close with a cordial salutation and I wish you all good fortune in the fatherland. I am seeking my fortune in America.

It is said: Whoever goes aboard a ship for the first time and sees one's fatherland and everything else gradually disappear—friends, relatives, and customs—he will experience a weakness in his limbs and in his spirit which he cannot immediately overcome. However, I must confess that I was spared that condition. The more that I distanced myself from the land, the more my own past just seemed to recede also. Happily I was looking into the future.

THIRD LETTER
Storm. Church Service Aboard Ship. Ship's Rations. Shoals of
Newfoundland. Phosphorescence of the Sea.
Atlantic Ocean, September 8, 1833

Today we have a calm. I am using this opportunity to continue my correspondence. What a terrible time I have had. So terrible that these
hours will ruin sea travel for me forever. I shall hurry to report the details to
you.

The evening of August 29 was as beautiful as the day had been. The
moon was shining through white clouds and was reflecting in the dark
waves. The beacons of Helgoland and Wangeroog were shining on the horizon. The sight was as new to me as it was enchanting. I remained up on deck
until midnight to enjoy the view. But that all changed very quickly! The
next morning I was awakened by the intense rocking of the ship. I felt a little seasick and went up on deck. Heavens, what a change! The wind had
swung around to the southeast and it was raging with such force against our
poor *Louisa* that, in order to save her cloth garments, the crew had drawn
them all down and now, all naked and uncovered, she was running before
the wind with her rudder tied down. The force of this storm increased during the day and the inky dark sea resembled a monster that seemed to be
playing with us. [It was as if he was] not consuming his prey right away only
in order to prolong the enjoyment that much longer.

The majority of the passengers were lying in their beds seasick. Only a
few were able to drag themselves up on deck. The portholes were closed,
and wave after wave was crashing over the ship. The sickness came over me
with such a vengeance that even the captain had never seen it so bad. I had
enough control over myself to remain on deck, knowing that doing so
shortens the duration of the malady, but lying in bed diminishes the suffering. Until then I had been pretty much spared by the water. I found for
myself a place near a cannon where, wrapped in my dressing gown, I waited
for death and longed for it. But death would not come. Instead, a wave came
roaring up and washed over me and the entire rear portion of the ship. By
the afternoon my throat was so swollen that I could speak only a few sylla-
bles. The night was even more terrible than the day. The storm continued to
rage. The incessant roar and whistling of the wind, the cracking and groan-
ing of the timbers and planks, the pounding of the waves against the ship,
which is similar to the thump of a small cannon fired a short distance away,
and the trembling and rocking of the ship that follows makes the novice
traveler fearful that the ship is going to break apart any minute. My loath-
some bunk did not allow me much time for sleeping. With every rising and
falling motion of the ship there was a constant draft coming from the large

cracks in [the wall of] my bunk accompanied by an unbearable smell of tar. My feet were hurting me especially now because I repeatedly had leg cramps and was compelled to let first one foot and then the other hang out of my bunk.

On the thirty-first [of August] the crazy chase continued. The captain had already decided to sail to the north around Shetland, for the storm was driving the ship on a direct route toward the Shetland Islands, when the wind turned during the night to the east and the north. Then, if that is possible, it began blowing with even greater force and in as many hours it drove us back the hundred and twenty geographic miles that we had just covered. On September 2, the storm was blowing several times with the force of a hurricane. The violence of my seasickness had increased also to its peak. Then I began recovering to the point where I was able to bear the sight of the sea again without some aversion. The raging waves presented a grandiose sight. Often, when a wave that came rushing before the wind reached the ship and crashed stern first over it, enveloping it in clouds of white foaming water, I could not get enough of this beautiful drama as I stood under the roof of the passengers' cabin. However, it is dangerous to linger about on deck at that time. Such waves crash over the ship in a wink of the eye and they wash anything that is on deck into the sea. The captain told us about the following incident: A sailor was flung overboard by one wave and by the returning wave he was thrown back up on deck. Now I call that a stroke of luck.

During the entire time of the storm the portholes in steerage could not be opened and the poor passengers were closed up in there much like men confined not in a fiery furnace, but in a stinky one. Compassion had little place there. Only a few of the healthy passengers had enough compassion to care for the sick ones. My companion [Heinrich] Tallör had nothing to drink during the first three days but some water and on the fourth day a cup of tea. In addition, his part of the bunk is located directly against the wall of the ship, and as often as the ship rolled to one side, the four other fellows in that bunk fell over against him. And the ship's owners call this "a ship equipped primarily for the passengers' comfort." The situation would be easily remedied by the installation of boards that would separate the space of one passenger from the one next to him. But that costs a few *Thaler* more and how could the people who have fifteen ships at sea afford that?

On September 3 the wind was still blowing so fiercely that we could not risk entering the [English] Channel. We tacked about the whole day, during which time an English pilot's cutter approached us. It was frightening to watch how the small ship came swimming over the tall waves, disappearing and then reappearing again. I would never have thought that a vessel of this size, or rather, a vessel so small, could withstand those waves for even an hour, and yet these vessels are supposed to fare better in a storm than the larger ships. On the night of the fourth we got a strong northeasterly wind and we ran swiftly with it to the Channel. By three o'clock the next afternoon we were looking at the English coast and Dover. The French coast was too far away and visible only briefly from one of the ship's masts. We had good wind then for the next two days also, and we were able to cover about ten miles per watch (four hours) and we passed all the other ships that came into view.

These were extremely interesting hours [aboard ship]. The English coast, marked intermittently by high chalk cliffs and green fields, offers an impressive if not a beautiful sight. It is as if nature had erected a natural fortress. The tall lighthouses with their different beacons imparted a liveliness to the night. So, we sailed past Beachy Head, the Isle of Wight, and Start Point, one after the other, and on the evening of the seventh, we saw the beacon at Lizard, and with it we took leave of Europe. During the night we passed Land's End, the outermost point of England. Along the coast one can see the immeasurable fortifications which were constructed in 1805 against the [anticipated and] dreaded invasion by Napoleon.[1] What a horrific fear this great little man put into the proud people of England! Approximately in the middle of the English Channel there is a peak jutting up out of the sea. It is called Poor Fleet (*arme Flotte*). Some queen of England is said to have watched the destruction of one of her naval flotillas from this point and to have uttered that exclamation. Here we saw also the beautiful sea bird named for Johann von Gent.[2]

Today is Sunday and even nature is taking a day of rest. Not a breeze is stirring. The ocean resembles a boundless pond. Only the swells produce some movement [of the ship]. Otherwise the bluish-white surface is as smooth as glass. What a contrast in color to that of the days of the storm! A multitude of seagulls and sea swallows are swarming around the ship.

This morning church services were held. I have often seen people coming together either in a church or at a plaza in order, as they say, to perform divine services. The motives for their coming and going were then easy to perceive. The old grandmother came in order to sleep peacefully for an

---

[1] The fortifications Ludecus saw at Land's End had been built in 1804 in case of a French invasion of England. H. F. B. Wheeler and A. B. Broadly, *Napoleon and the Invasion of England: The Story of the Great Terror* (2 vols.; New York: John Love Company, 1908), I, 95; II, 145.

[2] No mention of the name Johann von Gent (or any variant thereof) could be found either in Christopher Perrins, *New Generation Guide to the Birds of Britain and Europe* (Austin: University of Texas Press, 1987) or in Roger Tory Peterson et al., *Collins Field Guide. Birds of Britain & Europe*, (5th rev. enl. ed.; London: Harper Collins, 1993).

hour; her married daughter in order to escape the cries of her small children. Her unmarried daughter was sitting there to show off her new hat and new skirt, while her son flirted with the object of his admiration. Even the young pastor in the pulpit had had his hair curled in order to insinuate his image with his divinely spiritual eyes into the secularly blessed purse of a rich merchant's daughter sitting directly in front of him. That was a church service on land. I will give you here a true, edifying picture of a church service at sea.

In the middle of the port side of the ship the clergyman, a schoolmaster from Württemberg, was standing, leaning on the railing of the ship and delivering a sermon. His former congregation, in order to get rid of him, for he was rarely sober, had collected enough money to pay his travel costs [to America]. The money was sent ahead in installments to the police officials in towns along his route where it was paid out to him. During our stay in Bremerhaven he was often the object of children's mockery. One evening I saw him drunk and with a painted face, bound to a ship's mast. The children and a number of fun-loving passengers were dancing around him.

To the right and left of the preacher a couple of the so-called devout [worshipers] were standing very near to him, in the belief perhaps that the nearer they were to the preacher, the nearer they were to heaven. Four paces away a mother was sitting on a beam with her child as her fingers pursued the numerous wildlife on the child's head. It was easy to see how plentiful the game was. Right behind her was the galley, and there one could see the dirty cook with the even dirtier Lotte, carrying on with their dirty jokes. As I am told, she is a rather engaging thirty-year old farm girl. A few paces away among other idle onlookers there was another mother on the hunt with her child. Some sailors were sitting on the capstan and training Neptune, my protégé. He had a piece of meat on his nose and was sitting there concentrating, as if he wanted to write later a severe review of the sermon. People were sitting all over the large lifeboat, the spare poles, and the spars, and talking with one another. The captain was standing beside the passenger cabin and, to set a good example, was looking very serious. Beside him stood Herr G., [who was] a cabin passenger and a pietist from Bremen. He was listening and looking into space, completely lost in thought. Beside him stood his friend A. who, it seemed to me, was pretending to be a pietist also.

One could read from U's face how very much the assembly interested him. In the space between the venerable clergyman and his devout listeners there was a small dog cavorting about. It was still suffering from the consequences of seasickness and was trying without success to relieve its constipated bowels. Before the end of the sermon I saw the cook slink into the pantry in order to partake illicitly of the brandy there. I was sitting on the large spar myself and was looking down on this entire spectacle with a great deal of admiration. Several times I was tempted to climb down and ring the ship's bell, which would have been the signal that brandy was about to be distributed. I am firmly convinced that our reverend can resist the devil, but brandy is no devil. At least there is nothing about it in his Bible. For sure, he would have been the first in line at the sound of the bell.

Our Hebrew passenger could not quite find the role that he wanted to play during the church services. I suppose he knew that we thought he was a Jew, no matter how much he tried to hide it. He was sitting near the cabin and pretending to be indifferent to everything. In spite of all of this our pietist was [nevertheless] very edified and was passing out little pamphlets among the passengers. I read one of those nonsensical things. It was an admonition not to curse, and following that there was a story about a sailor who had sworn and cursed a lot, and who suffered a broken neck and broken legs. It admonished us that much the same thing could happen to anyone, etc. Apart from that, these two [pietists] are very sensible and pleasant people, and they have given up trying to make converts of U. and me.

Around noon we had the pleasant spectacle of seeing a number of ships. From my perch on the tip of the bowsprit I counted eleven of them. Most of them were sailing toward the channel. An English ship signaled us but, lacking a signal book, we could not understand anything. We did communicate with another ship that was coming from Newfoundland with a load of fish.

The phenomenon of hunger, which we all feel, is striking. The preceding cleansing and the stimulating sea air may be the causes of our hunger. For example, today at noon I ate again as much for sure as any other human stomach on land can tolerate. The captain is afraid that, given my appetite on this long sea voyage, the ship's provisions will not last, but he is wrong. Not every day is Sunday, that is, we do not have every day a good bouillon soup, cake, and roasted chicken. That is the menu for Thursday and Sunday. On the other days we have only potatoes, beans, yellow peas in the hulls, salt meat (salted beef), and bacon (salted pork). Ham is kept unsalted. You all should see our cook who is a sailor. You would lose your appetite for sure, for he looks more like a smoked ham than a human being. But what can one do? Hunger is painful.

Our way of life is somewhat as follows: Early in the morning, if boredom has not already driven us from bed, the helmsman or the cabin boy comes and announces breakfast with approximately the following words: "*Schaffen unten und boben, unten und boben schaffen.*" (Eat, below and topside, below and topside, eat). Then we get up and find in the cabin on deck some strong coffee, and a half-hour later, some eggs, butter and cheese, ham, etc. are brought to us. Whoever wants some, drinks also a glass of gin. Then each one of us passes the time as well as he can with reading, or playing chess and cards. At twelve o'clock the captain makes his calculations with the helmsman. At one o'clock there is another call to table, where a few glasses of bad red wine are served. After that until coffee [time] many of us take a nap. At six o'clock we eat the evening meal. Tea, without milk or rum, of course, unless one has brought along the latter oneself, some potatoes, and meat make up the evening meal. Once a week, as a variation on this, we are given sago soup, rice with raisins, red wine with sugar, and boiled plums. The latter and the sago soup are recommended for indisposition. A major amusement consists of preparing for ourselves fine dishes: pastries, roasts, etc., and everything is prepared with the finest ingredients! The only bad thing about them is that they exist only in the imagination. But we do intend to eat all those fine things in reality in New York. Blow, wind! My mouth is really watering for those things.

September 24

I really do not like this shipboard life very much, although a sailor probably has the most carefree life in the world. It offers too little variety. However, there are probably sailors who are devoted to seafaring and who love it. But far be it from me not to make a few changes. I would use the first opportunity that presented itself to sail around the world, even though it would keep me at sea for years. Such a trip would always be connected with a great deal of variety. But I could not bear to travel year in and year out between Europe and America, and certainly not just between two or three ports.

During the night of the thirteenth a strong storm came up and persisted until noon the following day. One old sailor had the misfortune of being thrown from the brig spar, but he was rescued. A storm is followed by sunshine, and so it was here. The weather was pretty on the fourteenth with a temporary calm. This happens almost always in these regions when the wind inclines to the east. It begins to blow weakly and then gradually diminishes. More to the south the reverse is true. There the eastern trade winds prevail. A calm after a contrary storm is the most unpleasant thing for the sea voyager. With the contrary wind, he is driven back, and with the calm, he makes no progress forward. All other situations, even tacking, bring him nearer, albeit slowly, to his goal. "What kind of wind do we have?" is the passenger's first question when one of the crew comes into the cabin early in the morning. And the first thing he looks at when he goes on deck is the tip of the mast or the sails in order to look at the flag or at the fullness of the sails and to compare that with the compass. Whoever has never been to sea thinks that the wind blowing into the sails from directly behind the ship, called "running before the wind," is most advantageous for speedy progress. But that is a mistake. The wind that blows into the sails from a few compass points to the side propels the ship best, for it allows for more windbreak. If I want to sail to the west, and the wind is coming out of the east, then I can use only half of the sails on each mast. If I hoisted all the sails on the main-mast, then they would screen the sails on the foremast and the ship would not be in balance. But if the wind were coming three or four compass-points more to the north or south, then all the sails could be raised, which is called "running with the wind."

We spent the afternoon of the fourteenth, where I stopped [writing] last time, in pleasant pursuits. The sun was attracting mollusks and polyps from the depths of the sea, and we caught some of them with baskets. The weather was so pretty and the ocean so calm that the helmsman and I jumped overboard to go swimming. Doing this is always risky, however, and one should dare to do it only when precautions are taken to ward off any sharks that might approach. They like to linger about in the proximity of ships where they get food, but so far we have not seen any. Swimming in the open sea is by far not as pleasurable, for me at least, as swimming in a river. The highly repulsive taste of the sea water and the up and down motion caused by the swells, probably six to eight feet high even without waves, are unpleasant to me. Lastly, one is also much too aware of one's own impotence in the face of this powerful element.

As if the storm needed some convalescence also in order to catch its breath, it has been resting now for twenty-four hours. During the night of the fifteenth it started up again out of the southwest. The foremast was immediately taken down and the large spar, a supporting mast one and a half feet in diameter to which the foresail was fastened, broke apart like a reed. But the sixteenth brought us pretty weather again. In the course of that day several *Portuguese men of war* (Portuguese warships) were spotted. This is the derisive name that the British gave to the little mussel that floats on the sea with the aid of a bladder that is like a sail. The reason for this name is that Portugal did not formerly have a single warship that could hold its own at sea. Strangely enough, this little animal never sails "before" the wind, but always "with the wind." The seventeenth brought again a strong wind out the southwest which toward nightfall increased to storm velocity. During the night it played a dirty trick on us. We lost the brig sail, the only sail that had been left aloft so that we would not be driven back. It was replaced by a reserve sail which was torn to shreds like the first. On the twenty-first a North Caper (a kind of whale) came up to our ship; it was probably about half as long as our ship.

I probably do not need to assure you that we do not pass many pleasant hours during such [stormy] weather. We were suffering more or less from seasickness. The most unpleasant movement of the ship is not the rolling or the rocking from side to side, but instead the pounding, and it is most likely to cause seasickness. This pounding or jolting is caused by the ship struggling against high swells or against high waves under contrary winds. One wave falls and then it is raised up slowly by the next one. And this occurs frequently so that with strong winds this wave strikes against the falling ship, and as the wave breaks over the prow, the ship comes momentarily to a standstill. This is often accompanied by such a shock to the people in the ship that it literally jars the guts in their body.

On one of these stormy days we witnessed an amusing sight. In the distance, in the midst of tall waves, we saw a school of sixty to eighty *brown* fish approaching our ship. They resembled a troop of cavalry. The sight of them jumping out of one wave and disappearing into the next one was so comical that the entire crew laughed out loud at it. This fish belongs to the whale species, but it is small. One cannot weigh more probably than three to five hundred pounds. His head resembles that of a swine; for that reason it is called a "Meerschwein," and I am told that it can be found in all the oceans and seas.[3] I have seen also a number of flying fish, which like silver paper skimmed over the ocean and then disappeared into the water.

I am breaking off now, for the two Polish warriors are singing their national anthems on deck and I cannot possibly miss that.

October 15, 1833

Today is another day of rest. Truly, these equinoctial winds are keeping us thoroughly in check. I advise everyone not to choose this time [of the year] for a crossing to America. I had thought that I would be in the safe harbor of New York before they commenced. But man proposes and God disposes.

I allowed myself to be interrupted in my last report by the Polish songs. It was a splendid evening. The setting sun was magnificent. We were lying about like young sea cows on the roof of the passenger cabin, listening to the songs of the steerage passengers. After the evening meal this diversion was continued, and the evening was merrily concluded. I am now quite familiar with shipboard life, and the rocking, even during stormy weather, affects me very little. I often sit up for half the night on the tip of the bowsprit, about fifty feet ahead of the ship proper and out over the water singing my favorite songs. "Erlkönig" [*The Elf King*] is at the top of my list. This song, with its exquisite composition, used to put me into an odd mood each time I heard

---

[3] Ludecus was correct that the *Meerschwein* was (and still is) called a *Schweinswal* (swine whale) because of its swine-like appearance. The name porpoise derives from the Latin *porcus* and denotes any of the family *Rhocoenidae* of small, usually gregarious, toothed whales. It is not known why Ludecus calls them "Brown-Fische." See *Webster's New World Dictionary*, 1051.

it, and even now when I sing it, surrounded by the night, the fog, and the waves, I feel an urge to plunge into the sea.[4]

The third of October brought us finally a good southeast wind again. The plumb was thrown out, but it gave the lie to the captain who had calculated that we were at the shoals of Newfoundland. A hundred and twenty fathoms were measured and still there was no ground. However, on the fifth a few shorebirds that were off course came on board—a sign that we could not be too far from land.

The shoals of Newfoundland consist of a stony bottom which at several places juts out probably a thousand miles into the sea. Right in front of these shoals there is a smaller one, called a *jaquet*. Mariners try to avoid these shoals as much as possible. The voyage is much more dangerous now since the fog, which constantly prevails here, seldom lets the sun become visible. The ocean floor is covered with a lot of shellfish. There is also an astonishing number of fish of all kinds and of all sizes. The stockfish are so numerous that a large number of ships spend the greatest part of the year out here on account of the fish catch. There are said to be between two and three hundred ships occupied with fishing here without a decline in the fish population being noticeable. On the sixth we measured again a hundred and fifty fathoms without finding bottom. These last few days, just like the following ones, have been peaceful and beautiful. In the darkness we saw by the phosphorescence of the sea a lot of *brown* fish swarming around our ship. This phosphorescing of the sea, when it touches other objects, is a phenomenon that as far as I know has not yet been explained. It is not the same every day. At times the scintillation gleams as brightly as sparks from a fire can burn. I have often fished some of it out of the sea in a bucket and it continued to burn in my hand, and yet it left no residue in my hand after it ceased to glow. The faster the ship cuts through the waves, the greater is the amount of radiance, and at times the ship seems surrounded by millions of sparks. I do not remember having seen it in the North Atlantic. On the ninth we had a calm, during which time a shark paid us a visit.

On the eleventh a storm broke out and grew worse from hour to hour—the whole horizon was on fire. It was a very sad sight the following morning when we found the ship with a broken spar and torn sails. It stormed all day long, but nevertheless the spar was replaced by another one in the course of the day. Everyone helped as much as he could, and today, with a good north wind and full sails, we are in a position to move a good distance

---

[4] "Erlkönig" (Elfin King) is a ballad written by Johann Wolfgang von Goethe in 1782. It narrates a father's desperate ride through a foggy, windy night bearing his sick son. The boy is taken from him in death by the sinister elfin king. Franz Schubert set the poem to music in about 1814. Garland and Garland (eds.), *Oxford Companion*, 206, 781.

nearer to our goal. A dolphin has been accompanying us all day long. We tried unsuccessfully to harpoon it. This fish is a beautiful animal with a splendid iridescence. We had more luck with a shorebird. The coast must be very near, although the captain does not want to say so. But we know it is from the preparations: the anchors are being made ready, the cannons are being put in order, etc. My next report will be from New York.

BUSINESS REPLY MAIL

FIRST-CLASS MAIL PERMIT NO. 7418   AUSTIN TX

POSTAGE WILL BE PAID BY ADDRESSEE

TEXAS STATE HISTORICAL ASSOCIATION
PO BOX 28527
AUSTIN TX 78755-9804

NO POSTAGE
NECESSARY
IF MAILED
IN THE
UNITED STATES

WE hope you enjoy your recent purchase of a Texas State Historical Association publication. Please let us hear from you by completing this postage–paid card.

■ Check here if you would like us to send you a complete catalogue of all TSHA publications.

■ Check here if you would like information about membership in the Texas State Historical Association. Members receive a 20 percent discount on all TSHA publications.

Name _____

Address _____

City _____ State _____ Zip _____

www.TSHAonline.org

FOURTH LETTER
Arrival on the Hudson River. New York.
Life in Inns and Boarding Houses.

New York, October 26, 1833

So, after northwest and southwest, and again southwest and northwest [winds], we have finally arrived here. Forty-nine days at sea is to be sure not a long voyage, but such a forced run is always unpleasant and without a doubt I prefer a longer, calmer trip. The cause of this eternal fluctuation of the wind between these two [compass] points, on which one can seldom hold a course, has been explained or not explained by more knowledgeable people than I. But I am no wind expert and I do not know these people. Suffice it to say that in spite of the obstacles, we have arrived here.

What I want to say in addition about storms is that all descriptions of them that I have read before now are by far exaggerated. Towering waves, vast depths, and God knows what all some poor people have seen in their fear did not happen in my estimation as a calm observer of these things. What would become of the poor seafarers and the ships if waves several hundred feet high washed over them? In my estimation, they are forty to fifty feet high, and I believe this is quite high and will also do some damage. Whoever does not think that this is high enough should go to sea and try it for himself. To be sure, the water sometimes washes over the tips of the masts, but these are drops and not the waves themselves. The most unpleasant thing about these waves is the violent rocking of the ship. Once our ship lay [on its side] with a third of the deck in the water. It took a long time until the efforts of the sailors were successful in taking down the sails and thereby took from the wind its power over the ship and the ship righted itself again.

I have often noticed when I was lying in my bunk and my body was being constantly rolled from one side to the other how odd it looks when the sloping position of the ship causes a cupboard to fly open and the things that are in it do not fall out on the floor, but go flying across the cabin to the opposite wall, as if they had been thrown there. It happened frequently also that one had to stand with one foot on the floor and the other one on the wall in order to maintain one's balance. Eating soup then is an especially difficult business. The bowl has to be constantly balanced according to the motions of the ship. It has happened several times that everything gets tossed all around and we were cheated out of a meal. I am moving on now to the business of the day.

On the sixteenth we had a nice wind out of the south southwest and at thirty fathoms we found sandy ground. It was a beautiful day and everyone was filled with joy and hope that the voyage would soon be over. Several times during the day I climbed up on the mast in hopes of being the first who would discover land, but it was for naught. The captain's remarks caused us to surmise, however, that he thought he was very near to land. That night very little sail was raised in order to avoid the risk of running aground in the darkness. The seventeenth dawned and everyone was out on deck in order to be the first to sight land, but the horizon was shrouded in a thick fog. I climbed out on the tip of the bowsprit and held out there until ten o'clock when the fog thinned a bit and allowed us to catch sight of a small white point on the horizon. I climbed down to give the captain news of the sighting, and after examining it with his telescope, he declared it to be a lighthouse. In the meantime the fog had lifted more and more, and we saw a dark strip above the water with scattered white points on it. We soon recognized these to be attractive country houses. It is impossible to describe the feeling that overcomes a person when after such a long voyage he finally sees before him the land that he has longed for.

The ship ran swiftly in the direction of Neversink and, according to the captain's calculations, we were exactly at the position we were supposed to be, somewhat south of New York. Our course, toward the north now, brought us along the very beautiful coast which is covered with splendid green hills, forests, and magnificent country houses. How inviting and charming this land appears to the newcomer! Passing Sandy Hook, we soon found ourselves between Staaten [Island] and Long Island. Here a pilot's cutter reached us and the pilot himself, a fine young man, came on board and brought us the latest newspapers. By one o'clock we could see at a remote distance the forest of ships' masts at New York and the city itself. Here the anchors were dropped in order to await the quarantine physician. He came and inspected each of the passengers as they marched past him in a long line. In order to present themselves in the best light, the steerage passengers had been compelled to wash themselves and to dress in clean clothes. Everyone was pronounced healthy. While the anchors were being weighed then, the doctor was writing down the names of the cabin passengers. Even though we spelled our names for him and even wrote them down, the next day we found them most gravely mangled in the newspapers. A bottle of rum was the doctor's escort off the ship. Then we sailed past the powerful forts and batteries that guarded the harbor, some of them positioned on islands in the middle of the harbor. An enemy fleet would hardly be in a position to force its way through there.

The view of the harbor is magnificent. It swarms with ships and steamboats; we saw five of the latter in action at the same time! Schooners were sailing about in all directions and large ships were running in and out of the harbor. To honor our [German] flag, the men from Bremen had hoisted their flag also. We sailed then close by the battery, the outermost point of New York, and turned off to the right in order to drop anchor in the *East*

River (the eastern branch of the Hudson River which divides above the city into two streams and then the two branches reunite below the city so that New York forms an island). A schooner came directly toward us and with typical American audacity in sailing he tried to sail between our ship and another one. He came charging on through and received considerable damage. The remainder of the delicacies remaining on the ship were set out at noon and then the boat was lowered and we went ashore. Words cannot express the feelings that come over the newcomer here and what a pleasure it is, after so long at sea, to have the firm earth under one's feet again. However, I could not tell that it had affected my manner of walking.

We went through the busiest part of the city where most of the wholesale business is done. *Stores* (warehouses), one more attractive than the other, stand here in long rows. Four to five thousand wagons are busy carrying goods from and to the ships. Six to eight hundred of them are assembled all the time, for New York has attracted almost all the trade in the United States to itself. Its location on the ocean and its many connections with the interior of the country via good roads, canals, steamboats, banks of commerce, insurance companies, etc. give the city all the necessary advantages.

My first errand was to fetch some money. U.'s brother, whom we had found in the meantime, took us to the Atlantic Hotel where we wanted to get lodgings for the time being. After we had done this, we wandered around and looked up some acquaintances of the two men from Bremen. Then we walked quickly up Broadway (wide street) for about a half hour to Canal Street where U.'s sister-in-law set before us a splendid supper that featured a great number of oysters. On the way back we wandered again down the magnificent street Broadway all illuminated now by gaslight and were amazed at the glamour and opulence of the stores. Products from all over the world are displayed there in abundance. Every luxury that one can imagine can be found there.

When I returned to the hotel, I was assigned a small wretched room on the second floor furnished with a bed, a washstand, and a chair. I slept wonderfully and the next morning, when the bell rang, I ran to breakfast. This meal plays a greater role in the new world than in the old. A splendidly set table awaited us: Fish, chicken, duck, and other types of roasted meat, *sweet potatoes*, and other dishes and delicacies that were unfamiliar to me lay in heaps before us. Well versed in the local customs, we attacked the food like real Yankees. Each one of us, like a hamster, gathered together for himself a pile of the things that looked best to him. But then we returned to our former habits, and instead of being finished in ten minutes, we ate for at least a half hour, making up for all the deprivation we had suffered aboard ship. One guest after the other came and went, but we stuck to our guns and were regarded with curiosity by many of the other guests. At noon we found a table proportionate in every way to the one at breakfast. I must admit, the Americans know how to live! What abundance reigns at their tables! Only the wine is bad and expensive; it is usually mixed with alcohol and such. The usual drink of men is water with brandy, and Madeira is the women's drink. Herr M. from Bremen was kind enough to take me to his *boardinghouse* where I soon came to terms with the landlady, Mrs. Hossack, for a lodging there. I moved in the same day. There are many agreeable aspects to this kind of lodging and it deserves to be imitated in Germany. I am going to describe in brief the operation of such a house. The house of Mrs. Hossack is located on Broadway, the prettiest and liveliest street in the city. As small as the house is, she has to pay eighteen hundred dollars a year rent for it. The people who operate these houses are chiefly widows and those who have pretty daughters have a great deal of business. They never lack for guests. Our landlady, who has a pretty and talented daughter who speaks besides English, also Spanish and French, also dances, sings, plays, and flirts very nicely. I am told that one of her young relatives with the same charming attributes is not quite as successful.

These houses have usually in the lower floor two nice rooms that are connected by a kind of door in such a manner that one can push aside one part of the wall, and they are called a *parlour* (conversation room). In addition, there is a large dining room and several small rooms [on that floor]. The kitchen with several rooms for the landlady and the domestics are below ground level. The upper floors are furnished to be rented, each with a *parlour*, but without a kitchen. The rooms are quite small and poorly furnished; one bed, one chest of drawers, a washstand, and three chairs are all that I have. On the first upstairs floor it is somewhat better, but also more expensive. At seven in the morning a bell is rung as the signal that it is time to climb out of bed, and at eight o'clock again to come to breakfast.

Then we assemble, Germans, Columbians, Americans, Mexicans, French, Swedes, and Swiss (the first two nationalities frequent primarily this house), in the dining room where the landlady presides and pours the coffee or tea as one wishes. Otherwise, "everyone helps himself," as the English say. After breakfast everyone hurries off to his business, and at three o'clock, except on Sunday when it is at two o'clock, they show up for the noon meal, when again the bell gives the signal. Then most of the ladies sit together, unless one of them has an admirer who has probably been smuggled in. Five blacks or mulattoes (here the domestics are as a rule altogether blacks or coloreds) do the serving and are dressed in dirty, ragged coats. But the American is not disturbed by this. They serve also without a coat, in white shirt sleeves and a vest, which in any case looks better. At the end of the meal the ladies leave the table and the men rise from their seats as a sign of respect. Then they smoke and drink. About six o'clock, when business is done, the signal is given for tea and everyone gathers in the *parlour*, where several guests have probably also spent the afternoon. Tea and buttered bread is served, some business is conducted, some guests play whist or chess, or they play music and dance. It is rare that strangers, who are visiting someone, are not present; they enjoy the tea and buttered bread also and the persons being visited are not charged for it. On the other hand, at the noon meal a dollar is charged to a resident for each guest. After the evening meal, everyone assembles again in the *parlour*. Often small families live comfortably and cheaply in a *boardinghouse*; they have a *parlour* and one large bedroom. They do not need more, but light and wood [for heating] cost extra. The *parlours* are nicely furnished and the floors are covered with excellent carpets. The Americans cannot live without these. Service is bad, but always better than in the hotels where there is actually no service. In all, there are twenty-six of us at the table and one can hear four different languages there at the same time. I am experiencing what every foreigner experiences who has never had the opportunity to speak the English language with English people. At first I did not understand a word, but now it is going somewhat better. However, I must admit, the more I hear the language, the less I like it. How pretty, on the other hand, is the Spanish language, which is constantly in my ears as the antithesis of English.

I do not want to commit myself to a statistical description of New York; one can find this information in other works and in geographies, and it is boring to write about. I climbed up the Telegraph [Tower], which has been erected on top of the marble stock exchange in order to admire the large city, the harbor, and the rest of the charming surroundings. One finds many private houses of marble, or rather, the walls are faced with marble. Entire streets are [filled with houses] built with this material. House construction was and is one of the best speculative enterprises here. Entire streets of these houses are built by one man and then rented out. A German earned in this manner an immense fortune; he is said to own all of Broadway. He came as a beggar to this country and he is now the richest man in New York.[1]

In regard to its architecture, New York has little that is remarkable. The buildings are much too overloaded with columns and other ornamentation, and if several large buildings stand out for their stateliness, it is often due to the small houses and cottages [near them] that provide a certain contrast. Like the boulevards in Paris, Broadway is the pedestrian way of the inhabi-

---

[1] The wealthy German immigrant Ludecus alludes to was probably John Jacob Astor (1763–1848). The son of a butcher of modest means in Waldorf (a village near Heidelberg), Astor emigrated to London in 1777. From there he traveled (in 1783) to New York, where he made a fortune in the fur trade. *Allgemeine Deutsche Bibliothek*, I, 628–629.

tants. On both sides of the street are excellent *trottoirs* [sidewalks], which on hot days are shaded by linen curtains. Hundreds of the most elegant coaches stand there at the disposal of those who need them, and a number of omnibuses run constantly up and down the street. One signals the bus, the boy standing behind it rings the bell, and the bus stops. Then I quickly jump on the step, and in the same moment the bus drives on. Immediately, I climb into the bus and end up sitting perhaps beside a black woman in a beautiful blue silk dress. In true American fashion I lay my legs across the cushion and I do not move them for the passenger coming after me until he jabs me in the ribs, at which I take as little offense as he does. Things go on the water just as they do on the street. Steamboats leave every ten minutes to Brooklyn on Long Island, to Staaten Island, and to [New] Jersey. Every day others go also to Philadelphia and up the Hudson River. So, I was a little more than a bit astonished to hear someone say: "In two weeks I am sailing on a Tuesday at nine forty-five to Europe." It was as if he had control over the wind just as he had control over travel on land. To me, who recently had to spend four weeks lying at anchor in a harbor due to an unfavorable wind, the qualifier, "if wind and weather permit," was understandable. But I was mistaken, for here no one pays much attention to such things. In the harbor the clock strikes nine forty-five, and the passengers must by then be assembled on the steamboat. It pulls aways punctually at the stroke of the clock and brings them to the ship. Whoever comes late can watch the others depart. If the wind is unfavorable for departure, then the ship is made fast to the steamboat, and off they go to the channel, and then, with or without tacking, if the wind permits, the ship sails to Europe.

These packet boats resemble floating hotels. What luxury they offer inside—cleanliness, service, and an abundance of the most select foodstuffs! It must be a pleasure to travel on them, compared to a ship from Bremen! The difference in price is significant to be sure: a hundred and forty dollars, I believe, to Le Havre. However, I advise everyone to give preference to such a travel opportunity if he possibly can.

But now I am going to return from the ocean back to Broadway. About eleven o'clock the genteel world begins to show up there. The ladies in their best finery ride and stroll from *store* to *store*. The rich make purchases, while the poorer people look everything over, find fault with it, and go on, just as in Germany. The young gentlemen and the old ones travel and ride up and down the street, and it is really no small pleasure to see how a genuine American rides a horse here. In one hand he holds the reins and an umbrella, and in the other he holds a large apple, and chewing half of it between his teeth, he trots along at a billy goat's gait.

On the same street is the City Hotel. A stranger goes by and is quite astonished to see instead of peoples' heads protruding out of the hotel windows, the peoples' feet. The American is very easy going and likes to rest his feet. If he is standing at a window and there is nothing to see on the street below that arouses his attention, he drops down onto the chair standing behind him and props his feet up on the window frame. Nor is he any more self-conscious in a room with strangers. A gentlemen often comes who wants to speak with one of us [in the boardinghouse], and he comes into the *parlour* without greeting anyone or taking off his hat. He calls for the desired person, speaks with that person off to one side or after going into another room, and then this gentleman leaves just as he had come. However, this occurs only when the person these gentlemen are looking for is unknown to them. If a gentleman has been previously introduced to the person or if he desires to be [formally] introduced to the person, he does not behave as such a boor. By the same coin, one would not receive an answer from a young lady if one presumed to address her before being introduced to her. But as soon as this is done, one stands on the most informal footing with her. I would then have the right to visit her and to ask one of the servants very boldly, not if the mistress (the mother) is at home, but if Miss X. (the daughter) is at home. I have made the acquaintance here of a young man from Guadalupe, who is engaged to be married. But he visits a female friend, Miss W., once or twice a week and his fiancée is not jealous of her.

The North Americans—they are a beautiful nation. Of course, at this moment I can only know the New Yorkers as such, for I have not yet seen any others. The beautiful black-brown hair, the dark eyes, the white complexion, and the healthy appearance are their dominant features, which are complemented by the usually elegant, always clean suit (an exception here are at times the blacks; some forty thousand are here). It is a pleasure to see the workers, even the blacksmiths, working in radiantly white shirts and black vests. All of this testifies to prosperity and merit. One sees the ladies in the street dressed in the most elegant apparel. They all wear silk. Even the servant girls, who stroll along Broadway every day like their employers, are often seen wearing silk stockings. The fashions here are the newest things from Paris and London, and I have to add that everything produced here is prettier than what is said to be manufactured even in those two capital cities. It is not surprising, therefore, when one hears what prices are being paid here. A worker who receives ten dollars and more for a pair of boots can produce somewhat better ones, to be sure, than the worker who can ask only four or five dollars. And that is the way it is with everything, especially as regards luxury articles. I have seen a ladies saddle that cost four hundred and fifty dollars, etc. Therefore, whoever visits this country should bring everything in abundance with him. There is no import duty on items intended for one's own use, but firearms are excluded. Customs inspections are not strict, but depend more or less on the customs official who, when he finds something subject to duty in one's trunks (for example, unfinished textiles, linens, etc.), sends the trunks back to the custom house where a careful inspection is undertaken. But here too the officials are not too strict, as I know from personal experience. The smuggling trade is carried on with ease. H.S. provided a living example of this. But one should not attempt to smuggle by bribing the customs officials, for this rich republic pays its officials so well that they are not likely to put themselves at risk by letting themselves be exposed.

I have paid all my social calls. I found Herr S., the Prussian Consul, to be a very courteous man and he was helpful enough to provide me with all the information he had about everything I wanted to know. It was another thing with Herr Zimmermann, the Consul of the Netherlands, to whom I had a letter of recommendation from His Highness, Duke Bernhard of Weimar.[2] This man had had the misfortune of going bankrupt and he works now as a clerk in another bank branch. I looked him up there and presented my letter to him. He was busy and seemed embarrassed. For that reason I proposed visiting him at his house. Instead, he promised to come to my house and asked for my address. I gave it to him, but I have not seen him since. I do not know the reason for his behavior. Even if he did not owe me the courtesy of a visit, it is nevertheless a sure lack of respect toward the noble writer of the letter. However, my third acquaintance made up for this slight more than twice over. Herr Becker in Braunschweig had been kind enough to write a few lines introducing me to his relative Herr Wilmerding.[3] Twice I walked for about an hour down Hudson Street to his house, and when I did not find him at home, I left my address. That same afternoon I had the pleasure of seeing him at my *boardinghouse* and I found him to be a very amiable man. I did not fail to accept his invitation to tea the next day. He showed me his house, his garden, and his greenhouse. Everything was done in the finest taste. His

---

[2] Bernhard, Duke of Saxony-Weimar (1792–1862), was the second son of the ruling duke of Saxony-Weimar, Karl August (1757–1828). He had a brilliant military career in the Napoleonic Wars, serving first in the army of Saxony and later in the army of the Netherlands. He probably knew Eduard Ludecus through his father, Wilhelm, who was a court official in Weimar. *Allgemeine Deutsche Biographie*, II, 450-453.

[3] From the remarks Ludecus makes in his letters and from the editor's comments in the foreword, it is clear that before emigrating to North America, Eduard Ludecus worked for some years at a large trading firm in Braunschweig. His employer there directed the young man to a business associate and friend in New York, probably F. M. Becker, whose firm dealt in raw stores and spices. Also in Braunschweig was a J. G. Wilmerding and a Heinrich Wilmerding and Co., which manufactured and sold fabrics. No doubt these businessmen were instrumental in directing young Ludecus to a useful contact in New York. Ludecus, *Reise*, III, 5; *Braunschweigisches Adreß-Buch für das Jahr 1828* (Braunschweig: Johann Heinrich Meyer, [1828]), 6, 45.

wife, a few of her lady friends, and her mother were also present. She is an extremely charming old lady; she speaks German, and very well for having spent only two short years in Germany twenty years ago. Her home is in the state of Ohio where she owns an attractive farm. When the *races* (horse races) on Long Island are over, she will go home again. Her son-in-law's black mare, "Black Maria," which won in the races last year, will run again this year. Someone offered him eight thousand dollars for her. [I wonder] why the foolish man does not sell her? If she is beaten, then no one would want to offer him eight hundred dollars for her.

I have solicited the opinions of a number of gentlemen concerning my plan to settle on the Missouri River, but I have learned little. The people living on the coast are not familiar enough with the interior of the country, and consequently, all of their opinions are different. The more people I ask, the more opinions I have to listen to and I am not sure which one I should believe. The information I have heard about the route I should take to St. Louis is just as confusing. Should I go via Pittsburgh or Albany? The first route [to Pittsburgh], although that city is nearer, is described as the more expensive one due to the longer overland trip it would entail, but it would take me through Philadelphia, the prettiest city in the United States. The other route goes up the beautiful Hudson River, close by Niagara Falls, which I can view by taking a twenty-four hour long detour. Herr Wilmerding has promised to get information for me at the post office. I must hurry, for the [winter] season is approaching, and if I chose the northerly route, ice might eventually block my way.

FIFTH LETTER
Proposal for a Trip to Mexico. Colonization Plan in Texas.
New York, November 4, 1833

The doubts that I had about which route I should take to St. Louis seem about to be resolved in a very simple way; that is, I will probably give up that project and instead visit Texas in order to choose a homestead there if I like it. In Germany people were already beginning to pay attention to this province, and [Stephen F.] Austin's colony is described as being in a prosperous condition. This province is now the object of interest among North American land speculators, and many inhabitants of the western states are leaving their homes in order to seek new ones in Texas.[1] The conditions there are as follows:

---

[1] This remark suggests that Ludecus had some knowledge about Texas before he arrived in New York, but the source of his knowledge is unknown. By the time he left Germany, writers such as J.Valentin Hecke and Johann von Racknitz had already aroused popular interest in Texas with their stirring praise of the province as an attractive land for German colonization. Hecke had traveled through North America in 1818 and 1819, and in 1821 published an account of his observations in which he praised Texas as a region perfectly suited for the resettlement of large numbers of Germans. J.Valentin Hecke, *Reise durch die Vereinigten Staaten von Nord-Amerika in den Jahren 1818 und 1819 . . .* (2 vols.; Berlin: H. Ph. Petri, 1820–1821), I, 196–202; II, 170–178. In 1832, the year before Ludecus left Germany, Racknitz had published a booklet describing his negotiations to establish a colony of Germans on the Colorado River in Texas, and in December of that same year he published a lengthy descriptive notice in the weekly supplement to the newspaper, *Frankfurter Journal*, soliciting emigrants for his proposed colony. Johann von Racknitz, *Vorläufer für Auswanderer nach dem Staate Texas, an dem Flusse S. Marco, oder der Colorade, auch de la Cannes im Gebiete Neu-Mexico in Nordamerika* (Meersburg: n. p., 1832); *Beilage zum Frankfurter Journal*, Dec. 14, 1832. See also Louis E. Brister, "Johann von Racknitz, German Empresario and Soldier of Fortune in Texas and Mexico, 1832–1848," *Southwestern Historical Quarterly*, 99 (July, 1995), 48–79.

During his brief stay in New York, Ludecus likely obtained a copy of Mary Austin Holley's new book about Texas, which he took with him on the journey to Texas. In the latter part of the eighth letter, written in La Bahía, he retells an anecdote about Stephen F. Austin from Holley's book. See Ludecus, *Reise*, 105–107; Mary Austin Holley, *Texas: Observations, Historical, Geographical and Descriptive in a Series of Letters, . . .* (Baltimore: Armstrong & Plaskitt, 1833), 90–94. Ludecus most likely is referring here also to Holley's published letters, in which she recounts her investigative visit to Stephen F. Austin's "flourishing colony of North Americans on the Brazos and Colorado rivers." Ibid., 10. However, Holley has little to say specifically about the interest in Texas among North American land speculators. She remarks only that "thousands of industrious farmers and mechanics, with their families have already located themselves" in Texas. Ibid., 10.

There was likely considerable interest in Texas among North American land specula-

The Mexican government, realizing finally that the nation could improve itself only by increasing the numbers of its industrious and respectable citizens, began promoting the immigration of foreign individuals. It took as a model the United States which has very rapidly increased its population and has soared economically. Due to a lack of money, one used to compensate men in the [Mexican] military with land grants, which the officers took possession of with their soldiers. Texas and Coahuila, which are almost uninhabited, provided abundant land for this purpose. Later, Mexicans who immigrated to these provinces were granted free of charge one *legua* of land, about forty-four hundred acres, but the foreigner was given only one *labor*, about a hundred and seventy-seven acres, and they were allowed to choose the location of the land. However, the foreigner would have his *labor* increased to a *legua* if he could demonstrate that he owned a hundred head of cattle.[2] In hopes that it could gain money from the sale of land grants, the [Mexican] government later changed the law and grouped these grants into larger sections, each of them containing eleven *leguas*. It then offered them up for sale and stipulated that one person could not own more than one of these land districts. However, this change must have been without success. Then the Mexican government accepted the proposition of a few men to entrust to them a tract of land for colonization. The government awarded them an extensive tract of land which the men were supposed to populate within a certain number of years with a certain number of families in proportion to the size of the tract. If they were not able to fulfill the contract within the stipulated time, then the land they had received went back to the government, but the settlers retained the property they had acquired. Further, every immigrating family was permitted to import duty-

---

tors, but the source of Ludecus's information is unknown. The history of attempts at colonization has been thoroughly investigated and documented by Mary Virginia Henderson in her excellent article, "Minor Empresario Contracts for the Colonization of Texas, 1825–1834," *Southwestern Historical Quarterly*, 31 (July, 1927-April, 1928), 295–324; 32 (July, 1928–April, 1929), 1–28. The extent of early speculative interest in Texas is illuminated also by Mattie Austin Hatcher, *The Opening of Texas to Foreign Settlement 1801–1821. University of Texas Bulletin*, No. 2714 (Austin: University of Texas, 1927).

[2] The source of Ludecus's information about Mexico's colonization law of 1824 is unknown. Mary Austin Holley cites only the 1825 colonization law of Coahuila and Texas, which granted "one league of land to families, and a quarter of a league to single men. A Mexican league," she explains, "is 5,000 Mexican *varas* square; equal to 4,428 acres English measure." Holley, *Texas*, 134. It seems very likely that Ludecus had, in early November, 1833, obtained additional information about the Mexican colonization law and the abundance of available land in Texas from sources other than Holly's new book, possibly from Dr. John Charles Beales himself, who was living in the same boardinghouse as Ludecus.

free two thousand dollars worth of tools and equipment. Thus, Colonel Austin's grant, which extended from the Gulf of Mexico to the road from [San Antonio de] Bexar to Natchitoches, and includes within its boundaries the two large rivers, the Brazos and the Colorado, was most rapidly settled. Every immigrating family received forty-four hundred acres, a single man eleven hundred acres, and he was free to choose the location of the land. Ten to twelve thousand people are said to be living there now and the land is reported to be selling for a more or less expensive price. Many have found good fortune there and even now, multitudes of North Americans are constantly leaving the states of Missouri, Arkansas, and Louisiana in order to settle in the northern and northwestern grants, which are not yet fully settled.

I have now made the acquaintance of an Irishman, Dr. J. C. Beales, a very amiable man who is a physician and who for a long time practiced medicine in Mexico. He married there the widow of a Mexican from a good family. This man had been the owner of such land grants, but had not been able to fulfill the conditions of the contract. Through his own and his wife's connections, Mister Beales received a grant with an area of about seven million acres, located partly in Texas and partly in Coahuila. With his twofold prize he traveled to New York. Here an association of wealthy people was formed, to whom he assigned his grant for fifty thousand dollars, whereby he retained, however, a one-third share for himself as a member of the association. But he had to accept the duty of leading at his own expense and in person the first expedition to the colony. Furthermore, Dr. Beales can select seventeen thousand acres for the establishment of a farm for himself at the location he chooses as long as it is three English miles from the town that is to be built on the Rio Grande. That strip of land is to be reserved for the first settlers, each of whom will receive a hundred and seventy-seven acres and a house site in the town.

The remaining land will then be sold for two dollars per acre. A steamboat is supposed to inaugurate communication from there with Matamoros and thence by schooner to New Orleans. Immediately after our arrival, steps will be taken to investigate the river. One has little doubt that it is navigable, even if not during the entire year.

Mr. Beales is living in the same *boardinghouse* with me and day before yesterday I had a conversation with him to learn about the details of his enterprise. To be sure, he has never seen this part of Mexico himself, but one of his friends has traveled over the grant on his behalf and has given him a favorable report about it. The schooner he has leased is lying at anchor in the harbor ready to sail.

I must decide quickly, therefore, and I am now busy making inquiries about the country and about Dr. B[eales]. Consul D. knows the latter and knows only the best things to say about him. He is advising me to give Texas a try. The trip will not be too costly, even if, contrary to all expectations, it should go wrong. I will pay thirty dollars for myself and twelve dollars for Tallör (who has decided to go there with me) for passage on the schooner. If I decide to take [all] my baggage with me right now, I will buy a wagon. Besides, Dr. B[eales] is bearing the cost of meals. Should I decide to return, then I can travel on the boat that will be built to investigate the river as far as Matamoros, and from there I can make the trip to New Orleans in four or five days. All the people I know here are very exited about this plan, but I cannot make up my mind definitely just yet, and I am still trying to gather more information.

Sixth Letter
Decision and Preparations for the Trip to Mexico. A Ball.

New York, November 6

After I had finished my last letter to you day before yesterday, I hurried to Herr Wilmerding's house. He was quite astonished at my plan. He advised me against going, but he gave no reasons and had to admit that he had not yet heard anything negative about the province [of Texas]. On the contrary, he knows that Colonel Austin's colonies there are experiencing the greatest prosperity. The one questionable aspect [of the venture] is the instability of the Mexican government, and he may be right about that. The truth of the matter seems to be that Herr Wilmerding is an American and nothing that is foreign and that is not in or from the United States can find favor in such a person's eyes. Further inquiries yielded responses in favor of the project, and so yesterday morning I agreed to go. Dr. Beales's character, his experience, his activities, his knowledge, and the fact that he has invested considerable expenses in the venture give me assurance that he is not undertaking the impossible. I have been hurrying to put everything in order, and yesterday I was on the move all day long trying to buy a farm wagon, but without success. There were no new ones available and the old ones were too bad. I came home thoroughly exhausted about eight o'clock in the evening. This morning I hurried off to Brooklyn, the capital of Long Island. Two steamboats leave here every ten minutes for Long Island, which is covered with leased farms and Brooklyn is inhabited by the mechanics who serve the needs of these farms. Without finding what I was looking for and still in a rush, for today everything had to be on board, I was finally approaching every farmer who drove by with a wagon calling upon him to sell it to me. This approach finally brought a good result: for fifty-five dollars I got a good, almost new chassis. Only the body was in poor condition. The farmer unhitched the horses and I paid him the money. Unfortunately, I noticed just then that he had removed the singletrees, and as I claimed them, he responded: "These don't belong to the wagon and have to be paid for separately." Nothing I said could change the rascal's mind. Then I proposed letting a wagon maker in the neighborhood decide the issue. But his judgment went against me, hoping probably to get an order to make two new singletrees. Such things happen frequently, and foreigners are the victims. I went down Broadway to buy a saddle, and soon found what I was looking for, but fifteen dollars for a saddle of inferior quality was too much for me. In an out-of-the-way street I bought one of equal quality for half the price. The price of the first one might have been so high because it was on Broadway and I was a foreigner.

But now I must close so that I can attend to my toilet. Mr. Beales is giving a big party today, as they call "socials" here. There will be tea, dancing, and dinner. I am very curious how it will go.

November 9

We go on board this evening at ten o'clock in order to set sail early tomorrow morning. I have just completed making my farewell calls, and I received from Herr W[ilmerding] several letters of introduction to [people in] Matamoros, New Orleans, and St. Louis. He was firmly convinced that I will not like it in Texas. I was not happy to take leave of this gentleman to whom I will always be indebted, much as I was to Herr Becker, through whose kindness I met Herr Wilmerding. I paid another visit on the mother of young Thomas Addicks. This young man is going with us in the capacity of private secretary to Dr. Beales. His mother speaks some German and is an intelligent woman, but too eccentric. She operates a school for young women, in which French, Spanish, and also Greek is taught. The last language is taught probably in order [for the students] to learn how Lycurgus cooked his Spartan soup. I paid a third visit on Mr. Plunkuet, a fellow traveler who is related to Dr. Beales; his family will come later with the family of the latter.[1]

You will probably all be curious [to know] how the party on the sixth went. Truly, this type of fête has a thoroughly different character than in Germany. I arrived rather late, about eight thirty, and I found that most of the guests were already gathered there. Both *parlours* were open, so that with the width of the door's opening, it was possible to dance through. The musicians, a white man, a mulatto, and a black, were sitting in a corner. The music in New York is generally bad. To be a good host at a party here is really no small task. The host has to arrange everything; the hostess concerns herself

---

[1] See Note 3 to the fourth letter.

Thomas H. O'Sullivan Addicks, personal secretary to John Charles Beales between 1833 and 1834, apparently did not remain long in Texas after the abandonment of the Dolores settlement. It is unlikely that he participated in the Texas Revolution, for his name appears nowhere in John H. Jenkins (ed.), *Papers of the Texas Revolution 1835–1836* (Austin: Presidial Press, 1973). However, in 1839 Addicks gave a deposition in Philadelphia about the colony and declared himself a citizen of the Republic of Texas. "Deposition by Thomas H. O'Sullivan Addicks" (Philadelphia, 1839), 12 pp. Dr. John Charles Beales Papers, 1832–1855, Center for American History, University of Texas at Austin.

Lycurgus was an Athenian statesman who lived from about 390 to 325 BC. The reference Ludecus makes to his recipe for Spartan soup is unclear. Hornblower and Spawforth (eds.), *Oxford Classical Dictionary*, 897–898.

Thomas James Plunkett, brother-in-law of Edward Little, likely left Texas soon after the abandonment of Dolores, for neither the name Plunkett nor any variant thereof appears in Jenkins (ed.), *Papers of the Texas Revolution*.

with nothing. Only the invitations are made in her name. One never says, "I was at a party at Mr. So-and-so's house," but rather, "I was at a party at *Mistress* So-and-so's house." The host asks the young men who can dance whether they want to dance, and then introduces them to the ladies with whom they wish to dance, if the young people do not know each other yet. Then they pair up to dance. A young man runs the risk of being refused, [if he asks a lady to dance] before being introduced. If a new dance begins, the host calls out, "Ladies and gentlemen, give us a waltz," etc. At this signal, everyone engages his partner for the dance. After several dances there is an intermission, and there is music then too. The ladies do not stand on ceremony as they do in Germany, but go to the *fortepiano* without feigning modesty or bashfulness. One young lady was an accomplished player on the instrument and another sang very beautifully. A musician from Bremen played Paganini's concertos incredibly badly, and yet he won the admiration of the company that evening and in public concerts in New York. Herr S., a gentleman from Vienna, displayed a great deal of taste and skill on the guitar. In addition, several games of *whist* had been organized. There was no wagering going on, which is usually the custom in America. But one should not believe that the Americans play with less enthusiasm than we do, for that would be a big mistake. On the contrary, they are extraordinarily involved in the game, and before it begins, none of the players fails to challenge his opponents, and after the game the winner mocks his vanquished adversary and loudly announces his good fortune to the others. This mania to be considered a good player is common here and sometimes infects the Germans too. For example, the following incident happened to me and involved a compatriot, a Viennese by birth who is employed in Boston as a professor of mathematics. He has been living here for some time. I did not ask his name.

Mrs. Hossack's *boardinghouse* has been known for a long time as a place where good chess players can be found. When I was challenged to a game [recently], I beat my weak opponent in such a manner that it caused a sensation. People told me a lot about another chess player and suggested that I ought to play him. I thought nothing more about it, for I had not traveled to America for a game of chess. One evening I was sitting with the ladies, another German gentleman, and several Americans in the *parlour*, when a gentleman came storming through the door, uttering a torrent of words and gesturing energetically. Soon he turned to me and challenged me to play chess with him. Without waiting for my answer, he fetched the chessboard, placed the chess pieces on it, and with the most fluent tongue in the world he assailed me with a barrage of questions. Annoyed at the man's behavior, I said [in German] to the Germans in the room: "This fellow thinks that I speak English as well as he does." I then explained, as I turned to the pettifogger, that I was German and had just arrived in the country and did not speak English fluently. I was very astonished then when I heard this chatter-box continue talking, but instead of English, he spoke in equally fluent Vien-nese German. Taking into account the other aspects of the gentleman's behavior, I did not think it necessary to apologize for calling him a *Kerl* [fel-low]. He ignored the word, and with furious haste, played an opening *gam-bit* on me. After five or six moves, he was finding fault with everything about my game, and he was boasting about it all to the people in the room in rapid-fire English. Really, the behavior of this man made me so confused that I lost the first two games. He was showing off like a turkey gobbler, and he lost the third game. Then he won the fourth game and lost the fifth and sixth one. At this point, when he became too insufferable, I broke off the match. The ringing of the bell for dinner presented a favorable opportunity to do so. When I went back [to the parlor], I was quite surprised to find him waiting for me there in order to continue the match. I noticed, however, that he was as unappealing to the others as he was to me, and I turned him down.

The next day he was there again challenging me, but he did not get what he wanted. Then he played whist, but he behaved in such a way that one of the players stood up and left the table. The third day he appeared again and when he saw that I was going to decline to play any more games with him, he could not restrain himself and exclaimed: "Like him, I considered myself to be the greatest chess player in New York. He considered himself superior to me as I considered myself superior to him, and therefore I am afraid to play with him." At that, I answered him succinctly that for his part he could be arrogant if he wanted to, but for my part, I rejected it, and I would give him in writing a statement that he was the greatest chess player in the world, if he would pledge in return not to come back since no one desired his company. Without saying anything in reply, he turned to the other Germans, cursed about the Americans present in the most vulgar manner and left, without ever coming back. It was very unpleasant for us Germans to have to call this uncouth chess buddy our compatriot. Now, back to the party.

About twelve o'clock an extraordinarily magnificent dinner was await-ing us. The meal was inaugurated with drinks, with champagne and port wine. Everyone tried to excel with a clever *toast*, and we drank more than was necessary, which attracted, however, no undue attention. After dinner the dancing continued and concluded finally at three in the morning.

All of my business is finished here and I am leaving New York and the United States and taking with me a high opinion of them both. To all appearances, at least, everyone here lives in good circumstances. And if many have lived here for years without getting ahead, they nevertheless have as much income as they need to clothe themselves and to feed themselves well. During the whole time of my stay in New York I saw only one beggar.

Perhaps I am wrong, but the one thing that I could not become accustomed to is the situation of the military. I do not expect it to be maintained in the European manner, but to someone accustomed to the European system, the American military system seems to be a game. Several times I had the opportunity to be present during the drills of the militia. Everyone was doing what he pleased, stepping on the heels of the man in front of him as a joke, and executing a right or left face movement when ordered to execute an about face movement, and not just about face once, but three times, and so on. It might be different with the regular army whose members are paid a salary. It consists of twelve thousand men and that is adequate for this enormous country. The United States does not need a large standing army of regular soldiers. If they should ever become involved in a land war, they have two million national guard troops who are determined to die for freedom and fatherland. Who would dare attack this giant nation?

The situation at sea is somewhat different. Every nation will find the republic in this respect well armed. I visited the Navy Yards on Long Island and admired the beauty, the durability, and the clean-cut qualities of the ships. Four of the line were lying at anchor on the East River. Two other beautiful ships have been standing for ten years now in a covered shed in dry-dock and can be ready to sail in two months. As dry as the wood is, they must be extraordinarily watertight. What caught my attention was the small caliber of the cannons; they must not be larger than thirty-six pounders.

So, I am ready now to entrust myself to the waves once again. How quickly we forget the suffering we have endured! If anyone had said to me during the first two weeks of my ocean voyage that after spending four weeks in New York I would voluntarily go aboard ship again, I would have laughed him to scorn. I hope we will have more luck with the weather than I did on the trip from Europe. And so I bid you a last farewell from the North American continent! Wherever my destiny may take me, I will continue to write my reports and send them to you whenever I possibly can.

Farewells. Digressions. A Party of Travelers. Bahama Islands. Piracy. The Gulf Stream.

On Board the Amos Wright, Captain Monroe, November 25

So, once again I am surrounded by nothing more than sky and water, but this time under very different circumstances. The *Amos Wright* is a beautiful, new, and clean-cut schooner. I have a very comfortable cabin and the people are as nice as anyone could wish for. We are setting out on an extremely interesting journey and we are equipped with the best of everything we need. We have even some pâté de foie gras on board. Unfortunately, a woman is traveling with us also who does not want to let her husband travel alone. She is living in our cabin with her daughter, but she seems to know nothing about a sea voyage. She wanted to bring even her table, sofa, and chairs along. Well, she has a lot to learn! There are several women in steerage. I am afraid that we will experience some unpleasantness on the ship because of the lack of space. But I am going to return now to the narrative of events in chronological order.

On November 9, just as I was closing my letter to you, I was called to Dr. Beales's room. I found there his family and Mr. Plunkett's family gathered together. Mistress Beales sat crying on the carpeted floor, resting her head in her husband's lap. The two cute little girls, his stepchildren, were standing at his side. I would like to see this grouping in a painting, for he is one of the most handsome men I have ever encountered. Soon the hour struck for departure. Mistress Beales arose, bade us farewell, and went into the adjoining room with her husband and children. A minute passed, and the difficult moment was over. He came out, completely in control of his feelings, and behind him came his servant Marzelino, a brown-skinned Mexican, who bade a tearful farewell to the two girls. Accompanied by all the male house servants, we set out on our march to the harbor. There we bade a heartfelt farewell to them all, jumped into the boat, and even after we were far out among the waves, we could still hear their wishes called out to us for a successful voyage.

On board ship we found all the other passengers already present, among them were Mr. Beales, Mr. [Thomas A.] Power, the commissioner of the company, and Mr. [Edward] Little, formerly a ship's captain, and the brother-in-law of the latter, Mr. [Thomas James] Plunkuet. [Also present were] Mr. Paulsen, a German who will probably travel later at company expense to Germany to recruit emigrants for the colony, Mr. [Thomas H. O'Sullivan] Addicks, and myself. There are three German families in steerage by the name of Dippelhofer, Wetter, and Schwartz, all from Oberelsbach in the region of Fulda. Elizabeth Corbé, the fiancée of young Dippelhofer, is traveling with them. There are also three English families and twenty-seven men representing all the trades. Among them are two men who are especially remarkable. One of them, Mr. [Victor] Pepin, a Frenchman, is a small man in elegant, black garb. By profession a pyrotechnist, he traveled in his youth throughout Europe with a company of circus riders. He became the director of such a group in New York, made a great deal of money, and then lost it again. His destiny led him to Mexico and to the islands of the West Indies, then to the western states of North America, and God knows where else. He is going with us to the colony now as a kind of equerry for Dr. Beales.[1]

[1] Beales recorded in his journal, which he delivered to the directors of the Rio Grande and Texas Land Company in New York, that there were fifty-nine colonists in the first expedition to the grant. William Kennedy, *The Rise, Progress, and Prospects of the Republic of Texas* (1841; reprint, Fort Worth: The Molyneaux Craftsmen, Inc., 1925), 391.

Throughout his letters, in one context or another, Ludecus mentions a total of forty persons in the first expedition to Dolores: these included Marzelino (the Mexican servant of Beales), the others in Beales's retinue, and additional colonists.

Among the three German families in steerage (whom Ludecus mentions in various letters) were twelve or thirteen individuals: Herr and Frau Schwartz; Herr and Frau Wetter and their sons (one of them five years old); Herr and Frau Dippelhofer, their son, Elizabeth Corbé (their son's fiancé), and Herr Dippelhofer's two sisters. Including Beales's associate (Herr Paulsen), Tallör, and Beales himself, there would have been fifteen or sixteen Germans in the expedition. Ludecus, *Reise*, 68, 135, 194–195, 226, 274. However, in his eighth letter Ludecus reports that there were sixteen Germans in the expedition and this number probably did not include Herr Paulsen. Ludecus, Ibid., 92.

Among the three English families in steerage there were at least six individuals: Mr. and Mrs. Horn, Mr. and Mrs. Harris, and Mr. and Mrs. Migrain. Ludecus, *Reise*, 193–194. Ludecus never mentions the Harris couple by name, but they are known as members of the colony, chiefly through Mrs. Horn's account of her Comanche captivity. Carl Coke Rister, *Comanche Bondage: Dr. John Charles Beales's settlement of La Villa de Dolores . . .* (Lincoln: University of Nebraska Press, 1989), 12.

Ludecus also mentions by name (albeit rather unflatteringly) a single Irish woman, Miss Emeline, who served briefly as a cook in the colony. However, in the eighth letter, Ludecus reports that eight members of the expedition were Irish. Ludecus, *Reise*, 92, 249.

In his journal, Beales mentions a couple named Page with a six-month old girl. Kennedy, *Texas*, 418. Possibly, it was this Page family whom Ludecus identified as a Scotsman, his wife, and child, who (with Ludecus and the Negro Henry) left San Fernando for Matamoros. Ludecus, *Reise*, 274.

Of the twenty-seven tradesmen in the expedition, Ludecus mentions eight by name (not including Jack Clops and Victor Pepin), all of them either American or British: Mr. Hartman (a master carpenter and builder) and his brother, Mr. Patterson, who left the expedition in La Bahía; Mr. Rasbon (a construction worker); Mr. Wykop; Mr. Magnani (a gardener); Mr. Allen (a carpenter); Mr. Wilson; and Mr. Swansen (a cartwright). Ludecus also writes that an American shoemaker accompanied him on the journey from San Fernando to Matamorus. Ludecus, *Reise*, 108, 212, 238, 240, 246–248, 274.

The other man, by the name of Jack Clops, is the perfect likeness of a pickpocket. About nineteen or twenty years old, he has a body as thin as a pencil and the kind of eyes that, if I had to defend him as his lawyer in a court of law against a charge of theft, I would demand his accuser to prove that he had eyes. This would be difficult if not impossible. But he can see out of his eyes as well as Argus himself. A snub nose, a mouth that speaks nothing but insolence, a small forehead, and two very long ears are the other parts of this jailbird-face. His clothing consists of an old black felt hat without a lid, a tattered black dress coat, the tails of which hang all the way down to his knees, white linen trousers which also come down no further, and under the ends of these peek the remnants of another pair of brown cloth. The ensemble is completed by a pair of shabby shoes, one of which fell overboard today. This character is a joker or the ship's clown. No one can get a sensible answer out of him, and I must admit that two-thirds of everything he says is witty. If Walter Scott had seen him, he certainly would have portrayed him in one of his novels.

On the morning of the tenth we were waiting in vain for the pilot to arrive, and since he did not come, we called another one on board. But the sails had hardly been set on the pilot's orders, when the original pilot appeared, and although he saw his place taken, he came aboard anyway. The two pilots were from different companies which were always competing to outdo the other one. The second one to come aboard demanded his place at the helm, but the captain refused to comply, and the dispute became heated, when the pilot called the captain a liar. At this, the helmsman, a hot-tempered man himself, grabbed the pilot and only our intervention prevented him from throwing the insulting fellow overboard. He boxed the pilot around until the fellow beat a retreat to his boat.

The wind was contrary, so we tacked, and we were able to enjoy the view of the harbor and the channel that much longer. At Sandy Hook we dropped anchor and some [of those aboard ship] climbed into the boat in order to fish in the nearby shoals. The next day we had a more favorable wind, and on the fourteenth we found ourselves at the latitude of Cape Hatteras.[2] Under a strong wind, as it usually is in that area, we crossed the Straits of Florida and were driven about forty-five geographic miles to the east. A packet boat, a beautiful three-master sailing from Boston to New Orleans,

---

[2] It is evident from the landmarks Ludecus cites that the *Amos Wright* sailed along a route closely parallel to the coastline of the eastern U.S., then across the Straits of Florida, and into the Caribbean Sea past the northern coast of Cuba. See Arch C. Gerlach, et al. (eds.), *The National Atlas of the United States of America* (Washington, D.C.: United States Department of the Interior Geological Survey, 1970), 9–11, 13; *The Times Atlas of the World*, 10th comprehensive ed. (New York: Times Books, Random House, 1999), 112.

caught up to us. It had a chronometer on board and corrected our degrees of longitude. But the captain [of our ship] was following his own uncertain calculations in his log, and it so happened that we had to sail for two days to the west before we sighted the Great Abaco Island to the north, and on the island the place called "Hole in the Wall." It is an opening in a high cliff through which the sea flows. Several whales, which we used as targets for our rifles, accompanied the ship these last few days. It did not appear that we had harmed them any. We were approaching then the shoals of the Grand Bahamas and the Berry Islands, notorious on account of the privateers there outfitted mostly by the merchants of Havana to the shame of the Spanish government and on account of the frequent shipwrecks, which are almost unavoidable in bad weather among these small islands and cliffs. It is difficult to believe that in this century such nefarious deeds can still be committed.

The English government refuses to erect lighthouses on the Berry Islands, which are British possessions, in order to prevent the shipwrecks experienced here every year by vessels belonging to the United States. The latter's proposal to build lighthouses here at their expense and to maintain them has been rejected [by the British]. Another disgrace is the despicable business carried on by merchants in Havana with these pirates. The former equip the latter with ships who then hide out among the small Bahama or Lucay Islands, and then they attack by night the small ships which drop anchor there. They murder the crew and bring the ship's cargo to certain secret places on the island of Cuba and divide the plunder with their [Cuban] ships' owners. It is difficult or almost impossible to seek out or to pursue these pirates. They retreat immediately into the shallows of these small islands where no ship would dare go in pursuit. Two or three years ago a United States ship succeeded in taking prisoner with his gang the boldest of these pirates who for a long time had been the terror of these waters. But all of the Americans' attempts to force a confession from them about the identity of their accomplices in Havana were in vain. Even the offer to exempt them from the death penalty could not persuade them. They were all executed.

Interesting stories are told about the audacity, the nerve, and the cleverness of this extraordinary man. He customarily sailed in and out of Havana harbor in plain view and the courts could not or did not want to do anything to him, even though his business was well known. Captain Little saw him once sailing out of this harbor, his large frame wrapped in a large red coat, leaning against one of his masts, and casting scornful glances at the other ships lying at anchor there. Just the day before, he had been acquitted of the charge of piracy. We were too well armed [on our ship] and we had a crew large enough that we did not fear an attack. But we had the pleasure once of chasing after another schooner, which because of the large number

of people on our deck probably did not consider ours to be the most rep-
utable ship at sea and tried to avoid us. We were sailing faster than he was,
but when he saw us in pursuit, he held a course closely to the wind and,
because of our heavy load of cargo, we could not keep up with him. We
passed the Berry Islands under the most beautiful weather and wind. On the
first island there is a small house where the British raise their flag.

Soon we saw a small dark speck between two of the smaller islands and
recognized it to be a boat. A half hour later a black man and a mulatto pulled
up alongside, offering to sell us some magnificent fish with the most beautiful colors and the strangest shapes. We bought all that they had, and then
they suddenly rowed away again.

Yesterday we saw the Orange Cay and today we sailed along the coast of
the island of Cuba. So now I am below the latitude of the tropics and I am
in the tropical zone. Really, it must be quite warm here in the summer, for
now, around midday, it is so hot in the sun that without available shade one
does not know how to protect oneself. And yet the sea breeze is still cool-
ing. But the nights are wonderful and I usually sleep on deck. The ceremony
of baptism to mark our crossing the tropical latitude was not carried out, for
there were too many of us neophytes on board. For the rest, we are living
wonderfully well and happily. Our table is set every day with the most delicious foods and we have wine in abundance. I fear, however, that our provisions are being squandered and that we will have to fast later perhaps for
having done so.

My fine compatriots on board are often quite a nuisance. They complain
almost every day about being slighted in the distribution of food and they
may not be completely wrong. The man who distributes the food is a num-
skull who is completely under the thumb of his wife. She is a real dragon.
The Germans are traveling at Dr. Beales's expense. He is supposed to deliver
them free of charge to the colony and give each family a hundred acres of
land, and in return they must work for him for six months. A number of the
workers are going to the colony under the same arrangement; the others, a
larger number of them, are traveling at their own expense, but now, I believe,
they are already eating Dr. Beales's provisions. Every day there are signs that
some of these provisions are being shamelessly stolen. The Germans and the
distributor of rations and his family members are living now in open hostility, and whatever injustice there may be going on, one party blames it on the
other. Dr. Beales is trying with all the patience possible to alleviate the ani-
mosity, but he cannot eliminate it completely.

On pretty days gymnastic exercises are practiced on board, and I must
admit, the Americans and the Irish are good at them. There is also an astonishing amount of competition at play here. Everyone tries to outdo the others: "Who can beat this?" And then one hears from all sides: "I can!" Every-

one is also keenly interested in the competitions. Our pastimes are chess, checkers, backgammon, and *whist*. There are plans being developed also for houses and farms, and a lot of castles in the air are being built right now. Last week we had one beautiful, calm day and everyone was busy climbing and jumping, when someone suggested a swim. Immediately we stripped off our clothes and, after we had been warned about the danger from sharks and whales that are often sighted in the vicinity of ships, Captain Little jumped overboard, exclaiming "No danger for me!" We all jumped after him and in a second the ship was surrounded by swimmers. So, we pass the time very pleasantly. Our course is set now to the north again, in order to cross the Gulf [Stream] once more, which will no doubt make a few seasick faces on board. Then we will approach land again, and sail along the coast in order to look for Aransas Bay. I will write more from there.

Arrival. Landing in Aransas Bay. Mexican Customs. Preparations for
an Overland Trip to Texas. The Mission. Discontent of the German
Settlers. A Wild Indian Tribe. A Difficult Passage through the Lagoons.
La Bahía. A Festive Ball.

Aransas Bay, December 24, 1833

Praise God! Once again I have solid ground under my feet, and I can go
to the right or left, forward or backward, as I wish, without encountering after a few steps a wet boundary. We have experienced extremely interesting but dangerous hours, and I will hurry now to describe them.

As we had expected, the Gulf Stream caused us to have a few days of
mild illness, but we got through it quickly. We sighted after a while some
large tree trunks in the sea and assumed that we were in the proximity of the
Mississippi River. On the morning of the thirty-first [*sic*] we saw land and
so, we sailed in to inspect the Mexican coast. It was an extremely low coastline covered with small trees, and behind the trees there was a stream. The
sea had been covered with heavy fog for several days and the sun was not
visible for a single minute that would have allowed us to measure our latitude. These were boring days: the sun, the moon, the sky, and the earth, even
the sea was enveloped in heavy fog, and in it I had a glimpse of chaos, for
even my mind was for a long time forced into inactivity. Due to the fog, the
captain had no clear idea about our location. The ship hardly moved forward, because the depth of the water had to be checked with the sounding
line in order to know with certainty its depth and not run aground. We
could learn nothing from the profile of the coast itself, for it looked almost
the same everywhere. The charts are also too inaccurate [to offer much
help]. We set our course toward the southwest, for this much was certain—
we were too far north. Before long a schooner coming from Matamoros
gave us some information [about our position] and we continued on our
previous course.

On December 1, we had a calm at sea. We went swimming and caught
young sharks on large hooks. Someone cooked a piece of the smallest one
and I tried it, but it had an unpleasant taste. Toward evening Captain Little
harpooned a porpoise (brown fish), which was brought on board only with
considerable effort, for it must have weighed three or four hundred pounds.
Its flesh has a taste resembling that of beef. On the fourth we sighted land
again and assumed we were in the vicinity of Galveston Bay. The cloudy
weather still did not permit us to measure our latitude. On the other hand,
the night was illuminated by the burning prairies on land.

Finally, on the third [of December], as we were sailing to the southwest
and sailing past Matagorda Bay, we were rescued from uncertainty, and at

two o'clock our ark reached its destination, Aransas Bay. The captain, who had already visited this coast once before, declared the bay before us to be Aransas Bay.[1] The difficulty of landing on the Mexican coast is known worldwide. The lagoons and sandbanks make it difficult even for small ships to drop anchor there. Even the harbor at Veracruz is not accessible to larger ships; they have to remain at anchor in the vicinity of the fortress San Juan de Ulua.*

* Many writers maintain that in the Gulf of Mexico as well as in the Baltic Sea there is neither low nor high tide, and they try to explain it by saying that the volume of water that is delivered to the Gulf of Mexico by the Mississippi River, the Rio Grande, and other rivers prevents the advance of high tide, and by the reverse effect, the diminution of the sea's volume, or low tide, cannot occur either. But this is wrong, for we have seen the waters of the gulf rise considerably on the Mexican coast during high tide, and seen the water flood the shoreline, although I must admit that the level of high tide was not the same each time.

The sea moves constantly from east to west, which one notices less at sea than on the coastline, and on the shore of the Atlantic Ocean there is rarely a discernible difference [between tide levels]. This movement of the water [at sea], the swells, is very much heeded, however, by the sailors on their voyages, especially to America.

The movement from east to west is caused by the daily rotation of the earth on its axis from west to east, that is, in a retrograde motion.

[*Author's Note*—Eduard Ludecus]

The entrance was narrow, enclosed by a strong ring of breakers, which made passage seem almost impossible. A long "war council' was held, but no decision could be reached. Then the captain climbed up the mast again in order to reconnoiter the terrain, and when he came back down, he declared that this spot was indeed the correct entrance and he wanted to try to get through. A description of the coast here mentions a shallow cut across the bar that is about seven or eight feet deep. Our ship drew seven feet. Hence, if that was so, we could attempt passage without danger. We turned the ship somewhat to the south and approached the breakers, and then we dropped anchor. Captain Little climbed into the boat with several men in order to go looking for the channel. A narrow where there were no breakers showing on the water's surface was considered to be the likely passageway. A white flag was to be the sign for the ship to follow.

With keen attention, we followed the little boat's progress until we could not see it clearly even with the aid of a telescope. With nervous anticipation

[1] Beales also recorded that on December 3 in Matagorda Bay, land was sighted. On the fourth, he wrote, "at 9 o'clock a.m. land was made, 30 miles north of Aransaso inlet . . ." Kennedy, *Texas*, 391 (quotation).

we saw it go through the line of breakers and disappear. For a long time we were uncertain about the fate of our fellow voyagers, and then all at once, we saw a dark speck appear this side of the line of spray and foam. After an apprehensive half hour Captain Little climbed back on board and brought the depressing news that he had not found a passage with more than six feet of water. The war council assembled again and everyone expressed the wish to go on land, that the attempt to go through should be made, even if there was only some probability of success. The conclusion was that the waves could carry the ship safely over the bar and in case of an accident, the land was near enough that the lives of the passengers would be saved. However, one could not apply to the insurance company for restitution of the goods that would be lost, for the company would not have to replace anything lost in such a hazardous undertaking.

It was decided that the attempt would be made, and immediately everyone went to work. The sailors were at their posts, reinforced by some of the passengers, in order to handle the sails more quickly and to have the anchor ready to drop if it should become necessary. All the other passengers were ordered to remain on the forward portion of the ship in order to increase the weight there. Captain Little was standing on the extreme tip of the bowsprit calling out to Captain Monroe, who was standing at the helm, the direction the ship should take. Mr. Power, who also used to be a sailor, was standing by Captain Monroe's side, and Mr. Beales was among the passengers on the bow. I was hanging in the rigging of the forward mast to observe the interesting scene below.

Below me the helmsman was calling out every minute in a monotonous voice the number of feet which the sounding line indicated. Otherwise, there was not a sound to be heard on the ship. A deep silence of apprehension settled over the schooner. Slowly at first it began to move, then faster. Nearer and nearer we came to the crest of white foam created by the waves as they broke over the invisible sandbank below. The dull roar of these frightening waters stirred in the breast of each of us an apprehension that I probably did not feel so keenly because I was distracted from the danger by my interest in the events playing out below me. Every moment the silence grew more profound. Not a breath could be heard and in everyone's face I could see the different degrees of anxiety that each felt. Only Captain Little's firm voice issuing orders and Captain Monroe's tense figure bore witness to their unbending composure. The latter was watching steadfastly over the length of the ship toward the breakers that were drawing nearer and nearer, when suddenly he said something to Mr. Power and immediately the call, "Mr. Beales!" rang out. Beales ran quickly to the stern of the ship, exchanged a few words with the captain, and then the ears of the anxious passengers heard the captain's calm order, "Tack shift!" In an instant the maneuver had been executed: the schooner turned to one side before the breakers like a cavalry regiment before a cannon battery, and sped away.

The attempt [to cross the bar] was abandoned for the day as too dangerous. We removed ourselves a considerable distance from the coast in order not to run into the danger of a storm throwing us up into the shallows. The evening was passed in lively debate about the possibility or impossibility of passage, about the true location of the passage, and about what we should do if we could not find it. These were the topics of our conversation. The next morning, with the return of high tide, the crew set the sails, and we approached the north end of the sandbank where the day before someone had noticed another opening. Again, Captain Little climbed into the boat and again he was watched with the same interest as the first time. The telescopes were fixed on him steadfastly until someone shouted with delight, "The flag is waving!" As soon as the captain was assured of this fact, the ship got underway and ran swiftly in a straight line toward the sign of the boat waiting on the other side of the breakers. We followed the same procedure as the day before, and again there was the same breathless silence on board and I had again taken up my old position too. After a little while we saw the breakers right before us. The sounding line was still showing fifteen feet, when it suddenly dropped to thirteen, and then nine feet. This rapid drop in depth was the cause for many pale faces on board. Everyone was extremely tense for a few minutes more. Then we found ourselves surrounded by nothing but the foaming sea. The helmsman called out "Seven feet!," and we were expecting any minute for the ship to run aground with a jolt. Then we heard the helmsman's song, a sign that we had found deeper water and that the danger was past.[2] Everyone breathed a sigh of relief. Soon we caught up to the boat and Captain Little again. We dropped anchor near a narrow island which runs along the coast, and a boat went ashore to catch some fish. Everyone was very cheerful as we ate the noon meal and when it was over, the ship was towed further along in the channel by her anchor chains.

After this work had been done, we went ashore in order to shoot [enough game] for a good dinner from the multitude of pelicans, flamingos, geese, ducks, woodcocks, and snipes. Everyone rushed to get into the boats and go ashore. What energy! We were living scenes from [James Fenimore] Cooper's novels. Of course, Cooper describes the hazardous scenes at sea very beautifully, but what is that against reality![3] In a short time we had

---

[2] At one o'clock on December 6, the schooner crossed the bar in nine feet of water. Ibid.

[3] Ludecus was probably referring to Cooper's novels *The Pilot: A Tale of the Sea* (1823) and *The Red Rover: A Tale* (1827). Both contain numerous vivid descriptions of stormy and calm seas and of the life of sailors aboard ship, descriptions that were drawn, no

caught three hundred fish, large and small, and had shot a lot of feathered game. In the lagoons one can see at one glance a thousand birds, geese, ducks, cranes, ospreys, cormorants, pelicans, swans, flamingos, herons, etc. Woodcocks, snipes, oysters, fish, and magnificent crabs are our daily fare here.

When darkness fell, everyone returned to the ship with an abundant harvest of game, while the fishermen among us brought several hundred pounds of beautiful fish. So, this first day on the Mexican coast we went to bed extremely content. The next morning the hunt continued, and now some went searching also for mussels. I ventured a little further ashore and saw that the coast forms a vast sandy plain as far as the eye can see, partially covered by water and countless oyster beds. It is easy to see how this land was gradually formed by the retreat of the sea and even now it must be flooded at times during storms.

On one of the islands we found fresh horse tracks—a sign that either the island is inhabited further to the south or that the *mustangs* (wild horses) have come down this far. At night we heard the howling of the prairie wolf.[4] The water on the coast is so shallow that in a boat one can come only within forty or a hundred paces of the shore and then one must wade through the water. As I was walking with Addicks along the island that forms the bay, we noticed a fire a considerable distance away. We assumed some Indians were there and decided to investigate it. Tallör, who was with me, thought the plan too dangerous and remained behind, but instead of Indians, we found our own people who had ventured so far away from the ship. Again the hunting and fishing yielded a rich bounty, but our wishes were not granted for a favorable wind the next day so that we could sail further into the bay. I was going to be tormented even in Mexico by fog, rain, and a northwest wind.

Weary of waiting, we began towing the ship up the channel. When we came to a bend, we set the sails and before very long we had run up on the sand. The impact was not very severe, however, and after an hour the ship was free again. The efforts of the whole crew could not move us further than an hour's distance of travel, no matter how hard they tried to move the ship

---

doubt, from Cooper's own experiences in the U.S. Navy from 1806 to 1811. James D. Hart (ed.), *The Oxford Companion to American Literature*, 5th ed. (New York: Oxford University Press, 1983), 164–165.

[4] Early nineteenth century Germans on the Texas frontier typically called the coyote a "prairie wolf" because its appearance and nocturnal cry reminded them of the European wolf. Herman Ehrenberg, for example, called them "Präriehunde" (prairie dogs). Herman Ehrenberg, *Der Freiheitskampf in Texas im Jahre 1836* (Leipzig: Otto Wigand, 1844), 40, 99.

faster. The evening was foggy and rainy, but in spite of that four of us tried with the approaching darkness to increase our supplies of game by shooting some geese. We had heard their cries from the island on our right and we hoped to approach them easily in the darkness. But it grew dark too quickly and the fog became heavier and heavier, so that after wandering around for a long time in the water, we were soaked to the skin and happy to find the ship again. The next day it was raining and a strong wind was blowing out of the northwest. We remained at anchor until noon when the weather improved somewhat. Right away I went ashore to go hunting. I wandered far inland in pursuit of several *gallos* [prairie chickens] until the approaching darkness reminded me to return to the ship. But the position of the ship that had turned about during my absence pointed me in the wrong direction. I went too far to the north and could not find the boat again. A few signaling shots showed me its position and I tried to get there by walking along the shore, but my way was blocked by lagoons cutting deeply into the shore. I walked around the first one, but the second and third one forced me to swim through them with my rifle on my back. Then I fired my rifle and heard an answering shot, whereupon I found the boat even after nightfall. Wet and bleeding from falling into cactus and agave plants, I came on board where I was refreshed by a glass of punch.

On December 10, we took up the work of towing the ship again. In a short while the changing wind saved us this work and brought us slowly into the bay, where we dropped anchor at a point of land, *Live Oak Point*. An attempt to go ashore that same evening was not successful. We were not able to go until the following morning. The vegetation was beginning to be taller, and the shore was covered by a lot of live oak trees. They remain green in the winter and supply a wood well known for its hardness.[5]

Hoping to get a shot at some deer, I wandered more deeply into the woods, but I found nothing more than a castoff snake skin. The yield from hunting and fishing was poor. The fruit of the *nopal* has a pleasant taste and resembles in its shape a fig or a pear, for which reason it is called in English *prickly pear*. (This is the cactus on which the *cochinilla* is cultivated, I am told,

---

[5] Beales wrote in his journal that the men aboard the *Amos Wright* began warping the schooner up the bay on the morning of December 8. On the ninth, a strong gale from the north temporarily halted further progress, and on the tenth they began warping the vessel up the channel. Kennedy, *Texas*, 392.

Live Oak Point was at the entrance to Copano Bay from Aransas Bay. The Spaniards and Mexicans had once maintained a fort there called "Aranzazu," from which they guarded the entrance to Copano Bay. The *Amos Wright* was following the principal approach of the period from the gulf to the coastal region that is today Refugio County. Hobart Huson, *Refugio: A Comprehensive History of Refugio County from Aboriginal Times to 1953*. (2 vols.; Woodsboro, Texas: The Rooke Foundation, Inc., 1953–1955), I, 4, 9–10.

but I doubt that this one is the correct species because I have not noticed, at least in Texas, that *cochinillas* are harvested here. Just as there are several types of *cochinilla*, the cultivated type and the wilderness type, there are also several types of *nopal*, for example, the *cactus opuntia*, the *cactus tuna*, and the *cactus ficus-indica*.).[6]

As far as the eye can see, this countryside consists solely of prairies, which in places are covered by water. I am afraid that we will have a very difficult march. This country is also almost completely uninhabited. One man will march with a bell at the point of our procession so that no one will get lost. Many in the procession will also be wearing a compass around their necks. However, I am afraid that there will be a lot of trouble caused by the laziness and uselessness of the Irish who are the most numerous group in our expedition. At night they cannot be roused from bed even though they have to stand watch for only four hours every other day. They cannot do anything if one does not give them an example to follow.

After an hour of sailing [into the bay], we were quite surprised to see at the end of the bay a kind of house [on the shore], and before our eyes there was also a small schooner. Our assumption that the building might be a customs house soon proved to be true. A short distance from land we dropped anchor, and the captain hurried ashore. He soon came back in the company of a Mexican officer and three soldiers and a young Irishman. The latter is the son of a settler, one of four or five families that have settled about thirty miles from here. The officer was a small courteous man about forty years old. The three enlisted men had the faces of the most genuine scoundrels that only a [painter like] Salvator Rosa could select. The officer was urged to have dinner with us, and everyone was regaled with cognac, which made such an impression on [the officer] Don Miguel that after a half hour he no longer knew what he was saying. Moreover, the cognac had an effect contrary to what it was supposed to achieve. Instead of making Don Miguel agreeable in business matters, as he became more intoxicated, he became

---

[6] Ludecus appears to have been well informed about the landscape into which he was traveling. He correctly associated the "prickly pear" with the nopal cactus (any of the genus *Nopalea*), including the prickly pear, *Nopalea cochinellifera*.

Opuntia is the largest cactus genus of the family *Cactaceae*, which is native to the new world. The prickly pear cactus (a flat-stemmed, spiney cactus) is a sub-group of the genus *Opuntia*. The *Opuntia ficus-indica* (or Indian Fig) is noted for its dark, ripened, fig-shaped fruit ("prickly pear"). Found in cultivation (at the time Ludecus wrote as well as today), the *Opuntia ficus-indica* was the species most commonly used in raising cochineal insects. *The New Encyclopedia Britannica*, 12 vols. (15th ed.; Chicago: Encyclopedia Britannica, Inc., 2003), VIII, 973; IX, 694; R. A. Donkin, *Spanish Red: An Ethnogeographical Study of Cochineal and the Opuntia Cactus, Transactions of the American Philosophical Society . . .*, vol. 67 (Philadelphia: The American Philosophical Society, 1977), 11–12.

more difficult, until finally, as he was going through the [customs] papers, which he was holding upside down, he declared that they were not in order and refused to send them to the customs authorities at La Bahía. He and Dr. Beales got into a violent argument then, and the three soldiers came into the cabin. I thought that we were going to have a serious situation on our hands, but then the turmoil calmed down a bit. One of the soldiers let us know that the next day, when Don Miguel's drunkenness had passed, one would find in him a most agreeable man. [7]

This incident could have had for us undesirable consequences. Some imports are, of course, duty-free, but this exception applies only to goods intended for one's personal use. We were carrying with us a quantity of merchandise, including the two kegs of gunpowder, which absolutely counts as *contraband*. To be sure, this officer was not actually a customs official, but was the commander of the coastal guard here, which was established because of the lively smuggling trade. But he could easily exercise a negative influence. We were extremely happy, therefore, when we saw him rowing out to the ship the next morning. He asked for the papers which he immediately sent to La Bahía. The weather that day was bitterly cold, and so the preparations for disembarking were put off until the following day. We could find no place to set up our camp other than a spot thirty or forty paces from the water's edge on ground scattered with mussel shells and near a small pond

---

[7] The Irish families mentioned by Ludecus were indeed natives of Ireland, but they had been recruited to the San Patricio colony by the empresarios John McMullen and Patrick McGloin in the vicinity of New York City. After arriving in Texas between 1829 and 1833, the Irish colonists camped for months at the Refugio Mission. Huson, *Refugio*, I, 122–123.

In February 1834, some months after Ludecus had stopped in San Patricio, another traveler to Texas, Benjamin Lundy, arrived there from Montclova. Lundy learned there that "Dr. Beales has brought to Aransas Bay, Texas, some thirty families . . . and gone with them up the country to occupy the land of which he has a grant. My informant thinks that they will all leave him." Thomas Earle, *Life, Travels and Opinions of Benjamin Lundy* (1847; reprint, New York: Arno Press, 1969), 102 (quotation).

Salvator Rosa (1615–1673) was noted for his rustic landscapes, seascapes, and realistic depictions of historic battle scenes. During his lifetime, especially in his later years, his paintings were very much in demand and commanded a high price. Emmanuel Bénézit (ed.), *Dictionnaire critique et documentaire des Peintres, Sculpteurs, Dessinateurs et Graveurs, . . .* Nouvelle Edition, (10 vols.; Paris: Librairie Gründ, 1976), IX, 84–85.

Beales made no mention of the young Irishman described by Ludecus, recording only that "the master of the schooner . . . went ashore, and brought off the captain of the Mexican coast-guard and all his force, consisting of a corporal and two soldiers, noting that he had at supper the pleasure of the officer's company who went ashore at 7 o'clock completely intoxicated." Kennedy, *Texas*, 392 (quotation). Kennedy, *Texas*, 392.

filled with hot water. We cleared the ground for the tents, and while we were doing that we had to shoot one of Dr. Beales's dogs, a Newfoundland breed, that was displaying symptoms of rabies. Right after that one of the hunters brought in a rattlesnake. I skinned it and dried the hide. The rattle had seven rings, a sign that the snake was seven years old. This snake is very common here and every day several of them are killed. But this animal is not as dangerous as many people say, for it bites only when it is provoked or injured, and when one approaches it, it rattles as it is retreating. The sound of the rattles closely resembles the sound of a baby's rattle. It is said that the Mexicans know remedies for the snake's bite. This snake here is different in size and color from the one found in North America (*crotalus horridus*). All of them that I have found here have a skin covered with silver-gray scales, and the rattle consists of small white rings, which one can hear rattling only in the snake's nearest proximity.[8]

I spent the night ashore with my company of five men with two other officers and the men in their companies. Here I must mention something that I forgot to note in my earlier letters. I do not like doing it, for it sheds an unfavorable light on a man to whom I feel drawn in every respect and to whom I cannot deny my testimony to his great righteousness in every other action he has undertaken. The matter I allude to is the following: One afternoon, just as we had entered the Gulf of Mexico, I believe, all the passengers were called together and orders for posting a guard were read aloud to us. These orders would be in effect after disembarking in order to protect ourselves against attacks by Indians. Everyone was amazed at this news. To me it seemed more of a fanciful measure, which was completely consistent with Dr. Beales's character. Nothing had been said to anyone before about this, or if something had been said, it had not been presented in such a way that anyone would have thought that there was a danger to us personally. But now, even before we reached land, orders were issued for establishing a guard. The cabin passengers, six of us, became the officers and five men were assigned to each one of them. Each watch was to be three to four hours long, from six o'clock in the evening until six o'clock in the morning. I drew the number, "one," and I therefore had the first watch.

---

[8] Beales's decription of the work to unload the party's effects from the schooner and to set up camp at Live Oak Point supplements well the account of Ludecus.

The information Ludecus provides here about rattlesnakes appears to have been largely hearsay. However, it is worth noting that rattlesnakes are divided into two genera, *Sistrurus* and *Crotalus*, and the genus *Crotalus* is the larger of the two. Ludecus correctly identifies the timber rattlesnake of North America as *Crotalus horridus*, but the description of the rattlesnakes he found at Live Oak Point provides few clues regarding their species. See Manny Rubio, *Rattlesnake: Portrait of a Predator* (Washington: Smithsonian Institution Press, 1998), xvi, 3.

Many [of the colonists], perhaps most of them, would not have joined the expedition if before embarkation someone had revealed to them in general the kind of dangers they would be exposed to on the trip overland through the wilderness, and especially that they could be attacked by wild Indian tribes. The next day we began unloading the ship and everyone lent a hand in order to speed up the work. At high tide everything that could stand to get wet was thrown overboard and the water carried it ashore. The rest was put into a boat and brought as near to the shore as the shallow water would permit. Then it was carried to shore by the members of the expedition. We worked at this until the seventeenth [of December]. On the last day of this work the customs officer came from La Bahía with his wife and a female friend. All three of them were squat and fat, and the latter of the three was very brown. We did everything we could to make their stay with us as pleasant as possible. We showed them the ship and greeted them on their return [to the shore] with a salute of rifle shots. They set up their residence in the barrack of the customs guard, where they slept on the bare ground or on a cowhide, wrapped up in their *frazada*, which is a type of rug impervious to water. They were accompanied by a soldier and a small, eight-year old Indian boy who went about completely naked. They had come down the San Antonio River in a small boat. The women were clothed in white muslin dresses, which hung on them very loosely, a *mantilla*, and a cotton or silk shawl that they wore over their head, leaving the face uncovered.[9]

An old Indian is also walking about in our camp. He is naked except for the customary loincloth, common among the savages. When I have had more opportunity to observe the natives, I will report about them in more detail. Two days after their arrival, our guests left us, but they were found by one of our people under a bush, about an hour's walk distant from our camp, where they had taken refuge from the freezing rain.

How soft have the inhabitants of the cold climate become in comparison to the inhabitants of the warm zone! Would a German woman be able to survive if she had to spend a night in the wind, rain, and freezing temperatures huddled under a bush and clothed only in a muslin dress and wrapped

---

[9] Beales wrote that the collector of customs, Don José María Cosio, made his appearance on December 15. He recounts that Cosio, his wife, and their female friend were invited to dinner aboard ship, but makes no mention of a soldier or a small Indian boy. Kennedy, *Texas*, 393–394.

A *frazada* is defined as a "manta peluda que se echa sobre la cama," a shaggy or furry blanket, large shawl, or poncho used to cover a bed or couch. *Diccionario de la lengua española*, 21st ed. (Madrid: Real Academia Española, 1992), 702.

A *mantilla* is a cloth head-covering worn by women. It is made of silk, wool, or other fabric and trimmed with lace or fine netting of silk or other fabric used for veils and scarves. Ibid., 931.

in a rug? On such nights we have a lot of trouble getting our troops to move out on post. Several Englishmen and Americans have already declined to go out. I have in my command the Germans and only one Scotsman, and I can complain only about the latter. If we should remain here long, sickness will break out among us. Already a few people are complaining of a fever. This should not surprise us, however, for the weather is at times terrible. A few days ago we had a terrible storm with rain and freezing temperatures. In an instant the tents were ripped down, the water rose high up on the shore, and both boats were torn from their moorings and driven toward the shore. We had given them up for lost when the wind calmed a bit and we succeeded in mooring them again. The wind was so violent that as I was coming back from the beach, where I had retrieved something from the water that had been washed away by the rushing tide, I was blown back several times, no matter how hard I tried to stand my ground. As soon as the storm was over, birds gathered in large numbers along the shore. Within an hour Captain Little and I had killed sixty-four snipes to bring home.

The surrounding countryside is a sad sight. I went out hunting, but I did not find any deer. The meager forests consist of live oaks that are no larger than cherry trees. The lower portion of this country consists of savannas (prairies under standing water). Wood for construction is nowhere to be found. One small species of partridge and another species about the size of a guinea-fowl are numerous here and provide, especially the latter species, a particularly tasty dish.[10] Waterfowl are available here in countless numbers, so that one member of the expedition killed ten woodcock and snipe yesterday with one shot. I enjoy very much watching the pelicans as they catch fish.

My chief occupation now is to get my wagon in order. Several parts of it were burned [for firewood] due to the prevailing disorder on board ship and the firewood shortages. I bought more thick planks and boards from the captain, and now I am working with Tallör to restore it to good condition. I hope it will be possible for Tallör and me to sleep in the wagon. During this time Mr. Beales has been in La Bahía, also called Goliad. He set out on a very bad road when he left the first time and when he found that the lagoons were too deep [to cross], he had to come back. He reached the town by another road, put everything in order with the customs authorities there, and bought some oxen that we must use instead of horses which we were expecting. Horses are used here only for riding and rarely as pack animals, but never to pull wagons. As soon as the oxen arrive, we will begin our trip

[10] Ludecus was probably describing the Greater Prairie Chicken (*tympanuchus cupido*), which was a large hen-like bird found in Texas on the coastal prairie from Chambers and Jefferson counties to Aransas and Refugio counties. Roger Tory Peterson, *A Field Guide to the Birds of Texas and Adjacent States* (Boston: Houghton Mifflin Co., 1963), 74, 129.

overland. Dr. Beales gave us a strange description of the town of La Bahía, but I will see it myself and report to you about it.

Our trip overland has been delayed in a most unpleasant way, and everything that we hear about the road does not give us confidence that on it we will be able later to expedite the journey. The fever affecting many of us makes it very urgent that we leave this marshy shore as quickly as possible. Otherwise, a number of us might soon be completely unable to follow along in the caravan. Personally, I have not been affected by it. My next letter will come from La Bahía.

Letter from La Bahía

La Bahía, January 20, 1834

A belated happy New Year! I am a bit late with these wishes, at least in writing. Orally, I called them out to you on January 1 from the spit of land that extends a hundred paces out into the bay from our camp. If you did not hear them, it is not my fault, but two thousand German miles is a considerable distance even for a good set of lungs. I must admit that on that day I really longed to transport myself magically for a few hours into your company. But unfortunately, I did not inherit Faust's [magic] cloak and that day it was too cold here for Mephistopheles to venture forth from behind the stove. It is also possible that he did not understand the incantation, but no one could translate it into Spanish for me. I had to summon him in German.[11]

In order to satisfy my curiosity, I went out into the prairie to find my oxen. They had arrived the day before and on New Year's day they were supposed to receive the mark of their new master—an arbitrary mark burned with an iron onto each animal's back. If they go astray, then one can reclaim them by that mark. They cost sixteen dollars apiece. They are larger and

[11] Ludecus refers to Dr. Faust's magic cloak, which was given to the legendary sorcerer by Satan and enabled him to fly swiftly to any place in the world. In Goethe's [Johann Wolfgang von Goethe] version of the popular legend, the owner of the cloak is Mephistopheles, the servant of Satan who was sent to tempt Faust and to serve as the scholar's consort. *Goethes Werke*, ed. Erich Trunz (14 vols.; Hamburg: Christian Wegner Verlag, 1962–1963), III, 67; R.-M. S. Heffner, Helmut Rehder, W. F. Twaddell (eds.), *Goethe's Faust: Introduction, Part I Text and Notes* (Boston: D. C. Heath & Co., 1954), 376.

Ludecus's mention of Mephistopheles venturing forth from behind the stove refers to the first "Study" scene in the first part of Goethe's *Faust*. In that scene, Faust has just returned from a stroll outside the city. He has been followed home by a dog, which enters the study and finds a resting place behind the stove. As Faust begins translating from the Bible (the book of Genesis), the dog begins to howl, which causes Faust to suspect that the dog's form conceals a demonic spirit (i.e., Mephistopheles). He recites several incantations to try to force the demon to reveal itself. Trunz, *Goethes Werke*, III, 42–46.

stronger than any oxen I have ever seen before, although at the moment they have lost some weight for lack of feed. On Christmas Eve a strong punch was brewed up and distributed to the whole party, the men, women, and the children.

The waste that has been going on since the first day [of the expedition] is showing now the most disastrous results. We are lacking many of the most necessary things, but in spite of that nothing is being done to stop the waste. Every day I am forced to watch costly food supplies being trampled in the mud. My job as translator for the [other] Germans is the source of many hours of unpleasantness for me because, with or without the knowledge of Dr. Beales, they are being neglected over the others, even if it is not to the degree they imagine. Unfortunately, I must now tell you that the information gathered by Mr. Beales about this country is very incomplete and his preparations and calculations have been very superficial. One of the things he promised is already beyond discussion: he had promised to give the Germans a tent and to allow the German women, children, and old Herr Wetter, who has a crippled foot, to ride [on the overland journey]. But the whole time we were camped on the bay, the tents were occupied by us [cabin passengers], our baggage, and the other passengers. The Germans were given some laths and boards for the construction of huts, and then, when these materials were needed, someone tore down the Germans' huts while they were away. By the same token, half of the Germans will have to walk, for it is impossible for all the women and children to ride in the one wagon set aside for them. All of this has happened, however, without the knowledge or intent of Beales, for he has done everything in his power to improve their lot.[12]

The day of January 2 dawned and it was even colder than the first. The small pond behind our camp was covered with ice. Who would have expected this below the twenty-eighth degree of latitude?[13] We felt the effects of the cold all the more since we were not at all prepared for it. The wagons were loaded, but it soon became obvious that even though our eight wagons and the ten carts we had rented were full, a portion of our baggage

[12] The letters of Ludecus provide a valuable, almost daily account of the oversights, missed opportunities, and irresponsible lack of attention to the welfare of the colonists on the part of Beales and his lieutenants. This notation is the first of several in which Ludecus writes about the causes of the colony's failure. See Louis E. Brister, "Eduard Ludecus's Journey to the Texas Frontier: A Critical Account of Beales's Rio Grande Colony," *Southwestern Historical Quarterly*, 108 (January, 2005), 368–385.

[13] La Bahía, now called Goliad, is located precisely at 28° 38" northern latitude. Deanna Schexnayder, Lois G. Shrout, and Sylvia Cook (comps. and eds.), *The Climates of Texas Counties* (Austin: University of Texas at Austin, 1987), 198.

had to remain behind. The wagons and carts were being drawn by fifty-eight oxen and ten mules. Mexican carts resemble ours very little. There is not a single piece of iron to be found on the Mexican cart. The wheels are cut from a large tree trunk, cut thin on the edge and thick in the middle, through which a hole has been bored for the axle. Each shaft of the cart is usually made from a single [small] tree, and the rest is made by fitting together beams and stakes. The oxen are driven by long poles that are sharpened on one end. They are yoked together in pairs, with each pair under a single yoke and a driver rides along beside them.

So, as the third of January dawned, the oxen were yoked up with a great deal of trouble in this manner that was unfamiliar to us. I set out about twelve o'clock following the Mexican carts, I on one side [of the oxen] and Tallör on the other, constantly busy trying to keep the skittish animals under control. After a short while the procession came to a standstill: here a trace was broken, there a chain, or a shaft. After a half hour break everyone finally moved forward again. Then the road led into a marshy prairie and in places it was very bad. However, I got through safely with my load, which was not very heavy for four oxen. Only the shaft suffered some damage which required a repair. [Then], bad news that came in from the rear guard persuaded us to call a halt in a dry area and make camp. No less than two carts and one wagon were broken down, although we had not covered more than one hour's travel.

That evening it began to grow freezing cold. Everyone crowded around the fires, trying to make themselves as comfortable as possible. The German families had received one small tent for the sixteen people in their group while the Irish, eight of them, were occupying the large tent. But they [the Irish] were embittered also because the English women were being given preference in riding on the wagons over them [the Irish women].[14] The day of January 4 dawned with even colder temperatures. Everyone was busy, some of us repairing the vehicles and some of us bringing up the baggage from the damaged ones. This business was finished in the course of the day and it was decided that the undamaged wagons should go on the next day to the lagoons and wait there for the others to catch up.

Dr. Beales went hunting with Addicks and Captain Little. We waited in vain for their return until darkness had fallen, when we became concerned. Bright fires were built and firebrands were thrown up into the air. We fired our rifles and rang bells, but nothing worked! Fearing that they may have

---

[14] As indicated in Note 1 to the seventh letter, Ludecus mentions (not including himself, Tallör, and Herr Paulsen) twelve to thirteen Germans in the expedition. The sixteen individuals cited here probably included some children not named specifically in the letters. Ludecus, *Reise*, 92; see also the seventh letter, Note 1.

fallen into the hands of Indians, we sent out Marzelino and a few Mexicans on horseback. Beales came in about midnight on Marzelino's horse, but we watched for Marzelino and the others in vain. The next morning, at dawn, I set out on horseback to look for them. The horse could hardly walk in the breaking ice, and soon I did not know anymore in which direction I should be going. After wandering around a long time, I fortunately found the lagoons, rode around the edge of them, and came upon our camp and the missing members of our expedition who had returned during my absence. On my ride I came across a *mustang* (wild horse), a beautiful, glossy, brown stallion.

After the noon meal I set out with the majority of the wagons and carts. At first the road was not bad, but soon we came to water, ice, and mud. We had to beat the oxen to keep them moving. Some teams even got stuck, including the wagon with the women. My wagon kept up with the best, but soon we came to such a bad spot that the Mexican carts, each pulled by a team of six oxen, were able to get through only after a lengthy struggle. At this point I made the mistake of leaving the road. We went off into the savanna and soon the oxen did not want to go on and could not go on any further on the ice breaking under their hooves. So, standing in water up to our hips, we had to wait until the oxen had rested. Tallör had recently caught a cold and he was complaining even before we came to this icy wet spot. I had a sore foot too and was [consequently] wearing shoes. You all can imagine, therefore, that this outing could not have been good for our health. With frequent stops and starts, whereby we had to go [ahead of the oxen] breaking through the ice with our feet for a short distance, we moved forward only a quarter hour's distance. Then the route became better and better until about two o'clock we arrived at the campsite chosen by the head cart. But we had traveled altogether not more than the distance of a normal hour's travel. We waited in vain for the women's wagon. Unable to go ourselves to help them and hoping that someone in the main camp would send help to them, we huddled around the fires to dry out and to warm ourselves. After darkness had fallen, the Germans arrived on foot, for in spite of the help that had been sent, they had not been able to get their wagon loose. Their tent had been kept in the main camp and so, they had to camp under the stars. Fortunately, they had brought their beds with them on their backs and they were able therefore to warm themselves under their [feather] beds, although they had waded through water up to their hips.

The next morning the report came that the wagon that had been stuck was free again. With that news, everyone got underway. In the expectation that we would not move on that same morning, I had made no preparations to leave. I was able to find my oxen only after a long search and as I was returning, I saw my wagon surrounded by fire. One of the German boys had thrown a burning object onto the prairie and the fire was spreading rapidly. With his usual meticulousness, Tallör had wanted to tie everything [in the wagon] down first and yoke up both pairs of oxen to the wagon. But this time I had to take control, for before I could have made it clear to him that by delaying too long our belongings would burn up, they would have already been burned. That is how obstinate he is in defending his opinion every time we disagree. I yoked up one pair of oxen and drove the wagon away even as he was working on it.

This impractical propensity of Tallör's often goes too far. What trouble I had with him when we were getting the wagon in shape! He cannot accommodate himself at all to the circumstances at hand. I was prepared any minute to hear him suggest that we order a joiner's bench from Europe just so we could plane a board for the wagon.

We traveled the two hours to the lagoons without any further difficulties. Toward evening the women's wagon came along and with it Mr. Power's carriage drawn by six mules. Camp was made on the slope of a hill near the lagoons. These lagoons are made up of a series of small lakes and marshes that extend inland as an arm of the bay; they are mucky and therefore difficult to cross. Accompanied by another man, Mr. Pepin rode through the lagoons in order to hurry ahead to Bahía and get a few carts there. When the other man saw Mr. Pepin, who was ahead of him, get into deep water, he turned off to the right where the firm ground seemed nearer. But the shorter way is not always the best way. His horse got stuck in the deepest mud and got out only with a great deal of effort. This scene made us very concerned for our wagons.

The next morning Mr. Power and I went hunting and took the route back toward the bay in order to meet any wagons still on the road there. Here we came across large coveys of partridges and some beautiful, rich land that needs hardly more than a strong harrow to make the soil arable. After an hour we met the rest of the caravan and Mr. Beales. As a sort of welcome his horse kicked and struck me on the thigh. However, the injury from his unshod hoof was not serious, and I could limp happily back to camp. On the way back we came upon a sleeping rattlesnake of extraordinary size. Captain Little shot a ball through the snake's body in two places, so that the parts were being held together only by individual sinews. But as one of the Mexicans was about to chop it through with a hatchet, it raised straight up on its body stump and struck at him. It fell short, however, and it was killed. It was seven feet long.

Passage through the lagoons was planned for the following day. Tallör was lying sick in the wagon. A bad cold had settled in his chest, and this was now even more inconvenient for me, since I needed his help the next day more [than usually]. The morning of the next day dawned and brought somewhat milder weather so that the ice at the edge of the lagoons was melting. Everyone was hurrying to round up his oxen, and all but one of them was found. The lack of food for the animals caused them to wander too far away in spite of the fact that their front legs were fettered. This is called *to hobble*. The vanguard was formed by the Mexicans who know this route. The load [of each wagon] was lightened and the number of oxen pulling it was doubled. They went in a straight line out to the center of the lake, drove the oxen to the quagmire, and successfully reached the bank on the other side. Only one cart got stuck as it was going up the bank and every effort to pull it out failed. They had to simply unyoke the oxen and leave that cart behind for the day. So, this route was abandoned, and the next wagons drove straight through and they came out okay. Now it was time for the large Ohio wagon to go through. Built in the state of Ohio, it was one of the rented vehicles. Because of its size, it required three yoke of oxen and three auxiliary yokes were added.[15] The oxen were driven by three men on horseback and on foot. The wagon got into [deeper] water and unfortunately, there was only one driver on that side and he was not able to move through the water fast enough. The driver on the other side could not control his horse, and Marzelino came along too late to bring the oxen onto the right path. The oxen were by now in such deep water that only their heads were above water and, although trying with all their might, they could not move the wagon. Then several men were sent in to help, but their efforts were just as futile. During this time the two pair of oxen for my wagon were brought back. Mr. Power's light carriage was hooked to my wagon, which was supposed to follow one of Mr. Beales's wagons that was being driven by Mexicans. The mules [pulling his wagon] were supposed to be driven right on through the water. But earlier attempts to get them through had met with no success since they had sunk so deeply into the mud that they could not get out again pulling their load. While we were also trying without success to drive them into the water, the wagon ahead of them drove ahead. Against my advice the oxen that had been brought back for me had been yoked up in front of mine. Those oxen knew already the difficult passage [that lay ahead of them] and refused to move. Nothing worked, even turning in a different direction did not help. Then I yoked a pair of my oxen in front. In the meantime, the wagon in front of me had already reached the bank on the other side, and with it my hopes that my oxen without a driver would follow the other wagon. Captain Little and I decided to take over this business ourselves. I hired two Mexicans for pay and at first everything went well. We were joking and happy, and were already foreseeing our wagons on the other bank.

---

[15] The term "Ohio wagon" could not be identified. It likely referred to a sturdy farm wagon and was possibly manufactured in Ohio.

But then the tide turned. Having reached the middle [of the water], the drivers on the left side turned the oxen to the right toward the route first taken by the Mexicans. I called out to them to keep going straight ahead, but no one obeyed my directions. Then I rushed forward as swiftly as my sore foot and the water would allow, drove the oxen back onto the correct route, but I had no sooner gone back [to the wagon], than the drivers again turned off to the right. Before I could alert Captain Little to this, it was too late. The rear oxen fell in the marsh and the wagon was stuck. Three hours of indescribable hard labor achieved nothing more than getting it stuck even deeper in the muck. Often we had to pull the animals themselves out of the muck, and as we did so, first one animal and then another one became stuck so deeply, that each animal had to be helped out by the others. Exhausted and bleeding from the jabs and blows, the oxen were finally unyoked and driven to the bank. The same thing was done to the oxen pulling the Ohio wagon.

Almost frozen stiff from several hours in the water, I struggled to get to the bank as quickly as possible and I rushed to the campfire. But I was pulled away by the Mexicans and wrapped in their *frazadas*, and only later was I permitted to draw gradually closer to the fire. Marzelino and several others were in the same situation. The Germans gave me some dry clothes and soon I was warmed up and as good as new. After several hours there was a renewed attempt to pull my wagon out. A fresh crew brought down six pair of oxen and my wagon was fastened to a long towline which the oxen pulled on at some distance where they could stand on firmer ground. But this did not work either. The towline broke and the effort had to be abandoned. It was necessary to leave Tallör in the wagon overnight. I made my bed under a bush and after my exertions I slept fine.

The next morning the bell awakened us at dawn to a new day's work. All the oxen were rounded up in order to use their combined strength to pull out the Ohio wagon. All the towlines were twisted together and one end was attached to the wagon and the other end brought to the bank. On this end twenty-four oxen, in combination with fifteen to twenty men, worked for three hours to pull the wagon onto dry land. During this time I hurried down with a Scotsman and a horse to bring Tallör to land any way I could. It was a difficult chore to carry him through the water and the muck to the horse, which would go only to within thirty or forty paces of the wagon, without me, him, and the horse sinking into the mire. But I succeeded. Then I fetched his blanket, some clothes, and many of the most essential things for myself. To do this I was forced to make two trips to the wagon. After a short rest, we went back down to the water again to wrestle Mr. Power's wagon and my wagon out of the mire. We changed our strategy, and unhitched his wagon from mine. Then we hitched several oxen behind his wagon and pulled it backwards out into the water and onto a better spot on the bank. This successful effort gave me hope that my wagon could be quickly pulled out in the same manner. But I was very disappointed, for neither two, nor three, nor four pairs of oxen, which were brought one after another, were able to move it.

After several hours of work, we gave up on that strategy and began digging the wagon out of the muck. We took hold of the wheels, and nine men were able to do what eight oxen had tried in vain to accomplish. We pulled the wagon a few paces backward. Then the oxen were hitched up in front of the wagon and they finally brought it out. I watched them do it from the hill where our camp had been set up, because I had not been able to remain any longer in the water and had withdrawn a half hour earlier. The whole time Mr. Beales had on horseback directed the work and encouraged the men. The task had really needed his talent and the influence which he exerts on the men for them to be able to make such a supreme effort. His servant Marzelino and Captain Little were the heroes of the day. From morning until evening they were in the water. Without the former's help all the work would have probably been futile, for he alone was able by cunning and force to get the oxen into the water. I have never seen a man who in such difficult circumstances would have been able to work as indefatigably as he. I have never seen a servant who could have been more loyal and untiring! His physiognomy and his color show clearly, however, that he is no descendant of the Spaniards, but is rather an Indian. The Mexicans had early that morning already transferred the load from their carts that were stuck to other carts and then driven these carts to the bank. Since their shameless demands [for payment] had been rejected for the help they offered, they acted as if they thought we could not get along without their assistance. Consequently, they had not traveled on ahead. They played cards and watched us out of the corner of their eyes as we brought out the last of the mired wagons without their help. I have faithfully described here this troubled expedition in order to show what unpleasant situations one can encounter and the difficulties and dangers emigrants must risk in coming here.[16]

Mr. Power, who had crossed the lagoons on the first day, had failed to bring some dry clothes along and on the distant bank he was forced to dry his wet clothes on his body. Because of this he got a chill in his abdomen. He became seriously ill during the night of the following day. None of the remedies tried had any effect. Bleeding him did not help either. He was suffering the most intense pain. The next afternoon Mr. Beales was persuaded to operate on him, and the catheter rewarded Mr. Beales's efforts finally with a successful recovery. By evening, Mr. Power's life was out of danger. All of

---

[16] At this point, the letters take on a more cautionary tone and pragmatic purpose.

this caused a delay of twenty-four hours that I used to round up my oxen, which in the confusion of the day before had been unhitched and allowed to run loose. One pair was found the next day, but the other pair and a pair of Mr. Power's oxen remained missing. I rode all around in the area without any success in finding them. The search for them the following morning was also futile. Mr. Beales lent me a pair of his oxen and at noon I left camp with over half of the other wagons and after several hours I successfully reached the mission. Along the way five rattlesnakes were killed. One of them bit our best hunting dog on the neck when, unaware of the danger, he had attacked the snake. In a half hour the wound swelled up so terribly that we gave up the dog for lost, but some Mexicans advised us to make a few punctures in the swollen area. The dog was definitely saved by those punctures. It was done in the mission and after a quantity of water had drained out [of the swollen area], the dog recovered in a few days.

The mission is an old church or monastery that was erected by the Spaniards with the help of the Indians, and later it was destroyed by the latter. Now it serves as a type of storehouse and as the home of one of the four Irish families that have settled here. They live in huts constructed of small tree trunks set up side by side in a row [to form the walls] and covered with reeds. This is the same kind of dwelling that Prudentia has, the *chief* or leader of the *Carancowasos* or *Carancouas* [Karankawas]. Some of them live here, and others in La Bahía and the surrounding area. Although they have been forced to live among the Mexicans for about ten years, they are still completely wild and are under strict surveillance. During this time their numbers have diminished considerably. When Colonel Austin's grant was *settled*, they invaded there and killed anyone they found. This prompted the *empresario* (the name for the owner of a grant) to send out an expedition of sixty to eighty men against the Karankawas and they succeeded in exterminating half of the tribe. The remainder fled to the district of La Bahía where they promised to live peacefully, but they did not keep their promise. The Mexicans found themselves compelled to kill half of the survivors in the tribe. Since then they have apparently been living peacefully, but still individuals here are occasionally murdered by them, but no one has been able to implicate them.[17]

[17] For a complete account of the establishment of the mission Nuestra Señora de la Bahía del Espiritu Santo de Zuñiga, its subsequent moves, and near destruction, see Craig H. Roell, "La Bahía," *The New Handbook of Texas*, III, 1179; Kathryn Stoner O'Conner, *The Presidio La Bahía del Espiritu Santo de Zuñiga, 1721–1846* (Austin; von Boeckmann-Jones, 1966), 10, 24–26, 32–33.

The Irish colonists mentioned here were families in the colony of John McMullen and Patrick McGloin. They were natives of Ireland who had been recruited in and

They [the Karankawas] are tall, with a powerful build, well over six feet tall, reddish brown skin, with a conspicuously hooked nose, a narrow forehead, and prominent cheekbones. Their long, black hair hangs down over their shoulders, and they wear in the hair over their forehead a small white feather from a predatory bird. Their movements, especially their manner of walking, are hasty. With their upper body bent forward, they lunge ahead some distance, so to speak, and then they stop suddenly, stand motionless for a moment, and then begin the process again, whereby the first steps are as swift as the last ones. They are tattooed with a stripe on the forehead, over the nose, the mouth, and chin, and with small rings on the cheekbones. Their clothing consists only of an apron around their loins, and their weapons are a long knife, a bow, and arrows. They are said to have a distinct tendency to steal, and we had, of course, an opportunity to convince ourselves of this. One of them stole a bottle of brandy from one of the settlers' huts and ran away with it. When he saw that he had been discovered and was being pursued, he put the bottle down on the ground and ran away. Someone remarked that this incident will not prevent him from coming back in a short while. The *settlers* complain a great deal about the trouble that these Indians cause them, but they cannot do anything about it and have to try to remain on a friendly footing with them.[18]

We were happy to get some milk, butter, and eggs here, but they are all so scarce! The cows are rarely milked. The herds, which are the *settler's* greatest asset, run around unutilized on the prairie. That evening and the following day we had splendid weather, and the horizon on the east, the north, and the west was marked by a burning prairie. It created an extraordinarily beautiful effect. The people here set the dried grass on fire in order to make room for the new grass which sprouts immediately.

Today the rest of the caravan of wagons arrived. Prudentia, who speaks

---

around New York City. Huson, *Refugio; A Comprehensive History*, I, 123. They lived in huts called *jacales*, which were typical for Texas as well as Mexico and much of the Southwest at the time. The *jacales* could be built quickly from materials at hand—small tree trunks set side-by-side on the ground to form common walls, which were smeared with clay and fitted with roofs of reeds and straw.

Ludecus got his information about the recent Karankawan wars (against the settlers in Stephen F. Austin's colony and the local Mexicans) from Holley, *Texas*, 95–97.

[18] Ludecus provides here a remarkable amount of information on the Karankawas and one of their chieftains—information that is not based on hearsay but on personal observation and interaction with these natives. His description of their physical build, dress, and weapons agrees with those found in studies of the Indians of Texas. See W. W. Newcomb, Jr., *The Indians of Texas; From Prehistoric to Modern Times* (Austin: University of Texas Press, 1961), 63–65; *Encyclopedia of Texas Indians*. (2 vols.; St. Clair Shores, Michigan: Somerset Publishers, 1999), I, 205–206.

Spanish rather well, paid Dr. Beales a visit. He wears a white cotton cloth tied around his head as a mark of distinction. He told the following story with the brevity and assertiveness typical of the Indian's manner of talking (not a word too many or too little) which Mr. Beales translated word for word into English. It was about the rescue of an American (which everyone here is called who does not speak Spanish) from the hands of the *Tawakanoer* [Tawakonis]. They, the *Leperes*, and the Karankawas were out on a raid together when they took an American captive. The Tawakonis were just about to kill him when Prudentia voiced his opposition and got into a fierce argument with the chief of that tribe. In order to avoid physical violence, their arms were taken from them, as is the custom of the Indians. Nevertheless, the Tawakonis quickly began tying their victim to a tree, when Prudentia stepped forward to stop them and was struck in the face by the chief of the Tawakonis. Greatly angered by this, Prudentia seized a knife that he had concealed and killed his opponent on the spot. In the confusion his wife hurried to the tree and cut through the thongs with which the captive had been tied, and he escaped unharmed.[19]

Prudentia is a famous warrior. He showed us eight marks that had been burned onto his shoulder as a sign that he had killed eight enemies with his own hands. Mr. Beales suggested to him that he should go with us and settle with his tribe in the colony. He seemed to want to accept the offer, and he has come with us this far in order to discuss it with his people. However, I hear that they are not pleased with the idea. If they were loyal to us, they could be of great value in defending against the Comanches, who are their mortal enemies. The Comanche tribe is the most numerous and belligerent of all the Indians in Mexico. They fight on horseback with lances, rifles, arrows, and tomahawks, and they always have with them a great number of horses. They do not have houses and usually take their *squaws* (women) with them. Two of the women ride at the point of the column and like buglers they lead the movements of the column with their shrill voices. When these Indians catch sight of a prey for attack, they race more swiftly than lightning in a column towards that prey, but at a certain distance they split into two columns and surround their prey. They live mostly from the hunt, chiefly from buffalos and wild horses. They call the Americans their friends, but they kill them when they can do so with advantage and secretly. It is said that when the chief learns that one of his tribe has taken an American captive

---

[19] Beales, who according to Ludecus carried on a brief conversation in Spanish with the chieftain, did not record the encounter.

The Tawakonis (Tahuacano) were a Caddoan tribe of the Wichita group. Newcomb, Jr., *The Indians of Texas*, 250–251; *Encyclopedia of Texas Indians*, I, 332–336. No information could be found about the so-called "Leperes."

and has killed him without putting him on trial, then that Indian is put to death. It is another matter with the Mexicans; between them and the Comanches a war of extermination is being fought. A native [Mexican] never says, I can kill a buck at a hundred paces, but [I can kill] a Comanche [at a hundred paces]. These Indians, which were called Comanches by the Spaniards, used to be called "Snake-Indians." They live to themselves in bands west of the Mississippi and Arkansas rivers, but they extend their raids out into the boundless plains which lie between Mexico and the United States, and as far [south] as the left bank of the Rio Grande. They own a great many horses and mules, and are true nomads. Of all the Indian tribes they are the most formidable. On their swift horses they traverse the plains here and there interrupted by mountain ranges which offer them the opportunity to lie in ambush to attack travelers, rob them, and kill them if they offer resistance.[20]

The Comanches force their neighbors into the position of always having to carry arms or to travel in caravans. They remember the cruelty with which the Spaniards conducted a war of extermination against them and literally hunted them like wild animals. They still assert their claim to their traditional hunting grounds and centuries may pass before they abandon their nomadic life. Since the withdrawal of the Spaniards, the present government finds itself in a very problematic situation and for the inhabitants the state of affairs in Texas is very unfavorable, for they are now on their own and can do nothing for their defense. I think the following anecdote that Mrs. Mary Austin Holley narrates in her book about Texas will interest you. It concerns one of her relatives, Colonel [Stephen F.] Austin, and delineates very well the character of the Comanche.

On his way to the capital of Mexico in 1822 he arrived in Bexar accompanied by two other people. He was told there how dangerous it was to continue on without a large escort because several people had been murdered by the Comanches on the highway the day before and that with all his baggage he would be a real prize for them. Not expecting to find a larger escort and pressed by the urgency of his business, he continued on his journey and the first day he was not molested at all. The next morning he felt indisposed and decided to make himself some coffee. His companions warned him that if Indians were in the vicinity, he would betray his presence by the smoke. But he flattered himself that by choosing a sheltered spot and by making a small fire, he would not be discovered.

[20] Ludecus got most of his information about the Comanches from Holly, *Texas*, 88–90.

He explained that with his headache he must have some coffee in spite of the danger.

They were on an open plain and for several miles around there was besides themselves not a living person to be seen. His companions had gone to look for their horses, the coffee was done, and he was about to drink it when he heard suddenly the sound of many horses approaching. As he looked up, he saw a short distance away about fifty Comanches on horseback racing swiftly toward him. As the column approached him, it divided into two half circles and in no time he was surrounded. Instinctively he went for his rifle, but in the same second he realized that resisting this large number [of Indians] would be futile and so he gave up his defensive attitude. The plundering began. Everything in the small camp was taken, but he did not lose his presence of mind. Showing as much composure as possible, he went directly to the chief, addressed him in Spanish and with the few Indian words he knew. He identified himself as an American and asked whether his nation was at war with the Comanches. The chief answered, "No." "Do you like Americans?" "Yes, they are our friends." "Where do you get your lances, your blankets, etc.?" "We get them from our friends, the Americans." "Very well, do you believe that if you traveled through our land, that you would be robbed as you are robbing me?" The chief thought for a while and answered, "No, that would not be right." Then he ordered his men to give everything back. Every item was returned with the same haste as it had been taken, except the saddlebags which contained the money. No one admitted to knowing anything about them. Austin was almost in despair, for the money was absolutely necessary to him for the continuation of his trip. Then he saw in a thicket a *squaw* whipping and kicking her horse to spur it into motion, but the animal did not want to leave the others. Immediately, the colonel went after the female robber and found his property. Then the entire band raced away at a gallop.[21]

I have had ample opportunity here to ask the local settlers about the land in general, for I am on the point of settling here myself. However, they could tell me little or nothing about the area of the Rio Grande. They praised the land where they are living, but as on the coasts of all warm countries, people here are too susceptible to the fever and some of them have been suffering from it for a long time. Others have died from it.

One also does not find much timber here. We used some to equip our

---

[21] This anecdote is cited in German translation directly from Holley, *Texas*, 91–94.

wagons with new tongues, etc., for they had received only temporary repairs earlier. Several ponds in the vicinity are covered by countless wild ducks. One of the species looks altogether similar to our domestic German ducks. In general I have noticed that this country produces many of the animals we have [in Germany]. I have seen summer birds flying around here especially on a warm day in the middle of January. I had caught that species often in Germany. I have not yet seen any unknown species, but they will probably not appear until summer.

Tallör has been gradually recovering. It was chiefly the buttermilk that seemed to agree well with him. So, on the fourteenth [of January] we set out again. The day before, Marzelino had found all of the oxen that had been lost. But I had been able to find only one of mine that I had been looking for to hitch up to my wagon. I had ridden all around in the vicinity but without success. On my way back I turned off the road into a small thicket where I found a couple of them calmly grazing, and while I was driving these two back to camp, I saw the third one lying behind an isolated bush in the prairie. I was very happy as I drove them back to the mission. I cannot describe the immense difficulties I have had with those beasts. Hobbled or not, they run off at night sometimes a mile away. And with the number of cattle that run around loose on the prairie here, it is very difficult and time-consuming to find them again. The great lack of feed for them may in all likelihood be to blame. They roam all around to find something to eat, and accordingly, mine must have the largest appetites of them all because they are always found furthermost from camp.

Mr. Patterson left us the same day. Differences seemed to have come up between him and Mr. Beales, or he let himself be persuaded to leave us by the information he had gotten about the other colonies. Everything was tried to convince him to remain with the expedition. There was some concern that his return to New York would create a bad impression. However, one did not want to meet his demands. In New York he had performed the duties of Mr. Beales's agent in charge of recruiting settlers. He remained behind in La Bahía to sell his wagon and oxen, and then return home by way of Matamoros.

The next day the trip from the mission to the first watering hole was certainly very short and was completed without further incident. The area there was for the most part marshy. Prudentia, who may be between fifty-five and sixty years old, hiked along behind a cart on which he had placed his small son. As the Indians are wont to do, he walked along silently, looking neither to the right nor to the left. He had left his wife and other children behind in the mission. On the fifteenth we set out early in the morning and I found myself compelled to travel on with only one pair of oxen, for all of my searching for the pair I had just recovered [the day before] was fruitless. As far as one could see on the open prairie there was not a sign of them, and since the horses could not go any further in the marsh, I had to give up the search. The day was rainy and we were not able to reach La Bahía. I arrived in camp a half hour later than the others. The night was cold and it was raining constantly, which made standing watch very uncomfortable. This [standing watch] has fostered more and more discontent and already at the mission there had been some talk that several individuals were going to remain behind in La Bahía. The next day, as the morning was approaching, the weather cleared up some. Everyone was up and about very early, curious to see La Bahía, also called Goliad. Due to the lack of an adequate team, I arrived in La Bahía an hour later than the others.

For a long time I did not know what to make of the scattered white specks, which in their form resembled bricks standing on their ends. However, as I came nearer [to La Bahía], it turned out that the specks were houses. They are constructed for the most part of thin tree trunks, oblong [in shape], with a flat roof and plastered all around on the outside with white clay. La Bahía is located on the right bank of the Rio San Antonio on a slope so that it is difficult to travel on the road even with oxen. The number of inhabitants must be about fifteen hundred.[22]

I caught up with our caravan at the foot of the hill where they had stopped at the edge of the river. The plan was to cross the river immediately and set up camp on the other side. It was being done partly to provide better grazing for the oxen and partly to avoid the obtrusiveness of the town's inhabitants. The commandant [of the garrison], a young fellow about eighteen or twenty years old, was standing on the riverbank in full uniform in order to watch us cross. He was wearing a brown felt hat with a very broad brim, over which a golden braid was fastened with its long tassels dangling far over the edge of the brim. He had on a yellow Spanish overcoat with a blue lining and blue lapels. His uniform was blue with red and silver epaulets and embroidery. His trousers were the same color. Before we began to cross the river four or five people declared their intention of leaving the expedition and, of course, all of the carpenters were among them, for they had heard that the Rio Grande as well as the surrounding area were completely barren of construction timber and that there would be no work for them there. After much discussion back and forth, Mr. Beales finally persuaded them to continue on. Then the river was crossed without great difficulty and camp was set up on the opposite hill.

The view from here is extremely unique: the town is built in a series of

---

[22] While Ludecus was struck by the mirage-like appearance of the houses in Goliad, Beales dismissed the settlement as "a wretched village" of about eight hundred souls on the right bank of the San Antonio River. Kennedy, *Texas*. 395 (quotation).

terraces on the steep bank of the river, [revealing] the white, peculiar clusters of houses, and the prevailing barrenness of the landscape on that side of the river, for there is not a single tree to be seen there. This alien race of people and their clothing, etc. is providing me with material for hours of entertainment. I regret very much that I did not equip myself better with drawing materials in order to be able to use the opportunity to sketch this town.[23] In the middle of the town, on a small prominence, one can see three Indian huts. Earlier there were eight, but five of them have been torn down. Behind us, about a quarter hour distant, one can see the ruins of a mission. It was once, I am sure, a very significant structure, but the Indians destroyed it and now not a single inscription or anything else remains that could provide reliable information about the building's origin.

The first night here passed rather noisily. I had the first watch from nine until twelve o'clock, and during that time there was an infernal noise going on in the town. Combined with the cry of a number of human voices, which one could hardly distinguish as such, there was the howling of a thousand dogs. Not being familiar with the customs and the character of these people, in whose midst we found ourselves, the strangest notions came to my mind. Finally, I thought that people were making the noise merely as a distraction in order to cross the river unnoticed and launch an attack on our camp. It was a pitch-black night and the noise was coming from the side where Karankawas had their camp. In order to investigate the disturbance, I took two men with me and we reconnoitered both banks of the river, but we could find nothing. Upon my return, I found everyone awakened from their sleep, but gradually the noise diminished and soon it stopped altogether. The next morning shed some light on the situation: we saw only two Indian huts still standing. During the night the third one had been torn down, because the owner had died in his hut and he was being mourned with all the clamor.

A number of male inhabitants of the town came over on horseback to offer some horses for sale, but the price was too high and I postponed my purchases until later. That afternoon I went to town with Mr. Beales to buy a number of different things. An American is keeping a *store* over there, but he complains that he is able to sell very little, and I believe him, for the people here need nothing the way they live.

Out of curiosity I visited the Indian huts there. They are round and are constructed of small branches. In the middle of the hut is the fireplace and at the top the huts have little covering in order to let the smoke out. I

[23] It is regrettable that Ludecus and other early visitors did not sketch the landmarks in the Texas landscape. Searches of the archives yielded no contemporary images of La Bahía, Béxar, and the farming settlements.

stepped into the first one and right away I thought I had been transported into the tale of "A Thousand and One Nights." In the middle of the hut a fire was burning. Immediately to my right lay an old woman with a child wrapped in an [animal] hide. The man of the house was sitting behind her. He was a man between forty and forty-five years old and with a Herculean build. His physiognomy was more handsome and more stately, but also more savage and warlike than that of other Indians that I have seen up to now. His face was strong and covered by coarse, black hair. His *squaw* was sitting beside him, a woman who was his equal in every way and as large as I have ever seen, but with a beautiful build and over her forehead she was wearing in her black hair a silver ornament that resembled a moon. To my left a young Indian male and a female about eighteen or twenty years old were reclining, one and then the other, around the fire. Awe-struck by the beauty of their physical build as well as by their type of facial structure, my eyes lingered on them. Never have I seen a more beautiful anatomy, neither in art nor in nature. When I saw [Antonio] Canova's statue of Hebe in the Berlin Museum, I thought that nature could never produce anything like her. Now I am persuaded that it can. A more or less faithful copy of the scene [that I witnessed] would make an artist immortal.[24]

I bought a nice rope made of [horse] hair from the older male Indian for four *reales*. I was told that this [purchase] would cost a horse his life that same day in order for another rope to be made from its mane. These Indians love alcoholic beverages very much and will give anything to get some. In fact, many of them are said to have died from excessive consumption. In several other huts that I visited I found mostly ugly faces and no more perfect bodies.

Earlier I wrote about the few needs of the Mexicans. I want to elaborate on that. The interior of the Mexican's house has usually only one section where there is a fireplace for cooking. However, the poorer classes do not have even that much. Many people living in the huts do not live better than the Indians. The rich Mexicans have sometimes several rooms, but in none of them is there a wooden floor. Instead, the firmly packed earth must fulfill that function. The walls [of the house], if they are built of stone, are very thick, but there are few houses like this. The flat roofs are rarely water tight,

---

[24] Ludecus did not identify the tribe of this Indian family, but they were probably Karankawas.

The statue of Hebe, Greek goddess of youth and cupbearer to the gods, was created by the Neoclassical Italian sculptor Antonio Canova (1757–1822), considered by many to be the greatest sculptor of his time. The statue of Hebe is still in Berlin today, in the Dahlem Museum. Christopher M. S. Johns, *Antonio Canova and the Politics of Patronage in Revolutionary and Napoleonic Europe* (Berkeley: University of California Press, 1998), 73.

and during a heavy rain only the bed usually remains dry. The bed, one or more trunks, a table, and a bench or chair are the only pieces of furniture [in the room]. The size of the bed depends on the number of people in the family who lie there together. It is made of a woolen mattress and over that a white sheet of *shirting* material is spread, and a *frazada* is used as the cover.[25] Their food consists of the following: The woman cooks maize in an iron pot, often the only cooking utensil in the whole household. (Everyone plants as much maize as he needs for himself.) Then she grinds the maize to a pulp on a flat stone, as she kneels before it, with another stone that is sufficiently round [for this purpose]. She kneads the mass together, takes a piece of it, and tosses it from one hand to the other until it is formed [into a cake] with the appropriate thinness. These women possess a remarkable skill in tossing this cake to achieve an extreme thinness. These cakes are as large as a medium-sized omelette. When it is ready for baking, it is placed on a metal sheet over hot coals and in a few seconds it is done. They are called *tortillas* and the women who make them to sell for money are called *tortilleras*. I find their taste to be rather unsavory and very different from the bread made from cornmeal. It would not surprise me if the flavor that they have does not come from the sweat of the hands that prepare them. But many other people consider them a delicacy. Beans, by the way, are the only vegetable. Beef is [eaten] fresh and dried in the sun. Everything is heavily seasoned with the red pepper that grows here, so much so that I am not able to eat any of it. They do not make butter or cheese, and even milk is not always available, and then only in small amounts.

Among the poor people, the clothing [of the men] consists of a shirt made of *shirting* material that is always clean and white. (But many men do not have this.) They wear also a jerkin and trousers made of deerskin, which are slit halfway up the calf, and under those they wear undertrousers of white muslin that show below the trouser legs. They wear shoes or sandals that they make themselves and fasten to their feet with straps. The wealthy wear trousers and a jacket of white linen or of [some other] cloth. I have seen the women of the wealthy class dressed in muslin, cotton, and even in silk clothing; on special occasions they wear also the *mantilla*. Moreover, they wear better shoes than the men, although one occasionally sees the most elegant women [going about] barefoot. The lower class people wear clothes of inferior fabrics.

The chief necessities of the Mexican [man] are a horse with a saddle and bridle, a *frazada*, a firearm, and a knife. He travels on foot very little and even

---

[25] A *frazada* is described as a blanket-size covering of heavy woolen fabric; it often has an opening at the center so it can be passed over the head and worn as a poncho. See Note Nine to this letter.

from childhood on, he is accustomed to ride a horse at every opportunity. If several of them are together and there are not enough horses available, two or three of them will ride on one horse together. They have an abundance of horses, and these are not counted as anything special. Their saddles and bridles may be the same type as those once brought into the country by [Hernan] Cortez. The seat of the saddle resembles that of our cavalry, with the exception that the front and the back of the seat are higher. Otherwise, it is a kind of leather armor such as the knights in former times placed on their horses. The bridle, or rather, the bit is extraordinarily sharp and with it the rider exercises great control over the horse. The most striking things are their spurs which are so frightfully large that I could not get enough of admiring them. I have seen some with wheels that were three and a half inches in diameter and were shaped with long spikes on them. If the points were sharpened, it would not be difficult to kill a horse with them. They are fastened to the [rider's] leg with a chain, and they hang loose there, more under the heel than behind it which makes walking with them extremely difficult.

When the Mexican does not need his *frazada*, it hangs over the saddle, or when he walks, it hangs over his shoulder. It has a hole in the middle through which one sticks one's head, and thus resembles a choir robe. Brightly colored ones are most popular, and a great deal of extravagance is invested in them. Some of our drivers had such that had cost twenty-five to thirty pesos. They are, by the way, manufactured here in the country by women. The third thing, the firearm, is the Mexican's constant companion. As soon as he is a few hundred paces out of a town, he places his shotgun on his shoulder. He is in constant danger from Indians who will massacre people, especially unarmed people. A shotgun will often turn back an entire band [of Indians], and that makes this weapon necessary and customary. The saber and lance form also part of the Mexican's weaponry.

The Mexicans are born riders, but they ruin their horses by riding them at a constant gallop. On the other hand, they never ride at a lively trot since it is too uncomfortable for them. They are furthermore the most passionate gamblers in the world, for they use every idle moment to play dice and they rarely stop until everything has been won or lost. Several times I have seen our drivers place five or six pesos on [the speed of] a cart, and often thirty or forty pesos were lost by one of them in one night. After driving oxen all day, they customarily spend the night, even in the cold weather we have had, lying all night on the cowhides, which are used by day as covers for the carts, and gambling. A *frazada* serves as the gambling table and the campfire provides the light. A few hours sleep are sufficient for their recovery. And at times, when we stopped in order to let the oxen rest a bit, the gambling table was immediately set up again. When they have no more money, then they gamble with their horse, their saddle, and their last item of property. The lack of opportunity to put their money to better use, their ignorance of business, and their idleness occupying whole days easily explain their inclination to gamble. They do not know what they should do with the large amounts of money earned so quickly in transporting freight. The Mexicans are keenly aware of class distinctions. The humble man is more subservient and more polite to those above him than his counterparts in the United States.

The facial structure of the men can generally be considered handsome. They are, however, too thin and often very brown, so that they resemble Indians. But they have especially beautiful black eyes and fine features. It is another situation with the female gender. Of those that I have seen up to now, I cannot call a single one pretty, let alone beautiful. Their mostly coarse and heavy features, their fat, flabby figures, and their wrinkled, yellow or brown skin deny them any distinction as the fair sex. Nor have I yet seen a girl with some bloom of youth; either the girls were still children or had already matured beyond the bloom of youth. Small children of both sexes, even those of the upper classes, crawl and run around up to a certain age completely naked. This is quite offensive to the eyes of a foreigner, especially since the children of the lower classes look more like little pigs than people and are rarely or never washed.

These are the preliminary observations that I have made about these people. If I should find something more that is noteworthy about them, I will not fail to make a supplementary entry.

Upon my return to camp, I found once again several horses that had been brought there for sale. One young brown stallion appealed to me. It was three years old and had beautiful conformation. I negotiated for it and purchased it for only six pesos. The reason for this bargain price, I am told, is that the horse had been stolen and the seller was afraid that he would have to return it. It comes from one of the best stud farms in Alabama (United States).

Yesterday was Sunday and with it we were granted the gift of a beautiful day. I believe it was only the third or fourth time in about five or six weeks that the sun has condescended to warm us with its rays. However, we have become unaccustomed to the sun, and soon we thought it was too warm. During my absence (I had gone to investigate the ruins of the mission.), we had a visit from a number of young ladies from the town. They had been ferried over the river in boats and I returned just in time to see them getting back into the boats and going back. A number of them were wearing silk dresses and stockings. I found also an invitation to attend a ball that evening which one of the dignitaries [in Goliad] was giving and I accepted it with delight, since it will give me the opportunity to observe closely the customs of the people.

As darkness was falling, Mr. Beales, Mr. Power, Mr. Plunkett, Captain Little, Mr. Paulsen, and I set out to go to the ball.[26] Mr. Power's light carriage, built in the style of our Holstein carriages and drawn by four mules, was able to hold all of us easily.[27] Uncertain about whether it would be worth the trouble, I did not want to unload my trunk [out of my wagon] and my attire therefore was not quite appropriate for a ball. I had merely replaced my traveling jacket with a jacket of Nanking fabric, and over this I was wearing my *Carbonari* [coat]. I was determined to pretend if necessary that this was a German style of dress, from which I could not deviate. The other men were dressed more in their *gala* attire. Mr. Little played coachman and in the darkness, as luck would have it, he tossed us down a small slope leading to the road. No one was hurt, and we continued on foot down the ravine. Then we got in the carriage again and, protecting our clothes as much as possible from the water running through the carriage, we reached the opposite bank of the river unscathed. Then we had to get out of the carriage again in order to help the mules pull it up the hill over the rocks. We all pushed the wagon uphill until at the end of the street we were shocked to realize that we were already very near the house where the ball was being held. Quickly we jumped into the carriage again in order to arrive at a trot with all the appropriate fanfare. Upon arriving, we had to push our way through the spectators standing at the door. Unfortunately, the christening of a child, which was the occasion for these festivities, was already over.

Like the other houses here, this house was *oblong* [in shape] and inside it was painted white. Lights had been installed along the walls and at the rear of the house a small room was partitioned off with a sheet where the *collation* was concealed from view. All around the room there were benches for the ladies, and the men were trying as well as they could to find a spot in the remaining space. Altogether there must have been about a hundred and twenty people present.

Then the dance began: Two men, one with a violin and the other with a guitar, were seated in front of the curtain and were playing the *fandango*. Curious now to see this famous dance of the Spaniards, I used my elbows to thrust myself into the front row of spectators. But how disappointed I was! After the *maître de plaisir* or the *maître de danse* (I do not know exactly what

---

[26] The ball was given by the young men of Goliad in celebration of Christmas Eve. Kennedy, *Texas*, 396.

[27] The term "Holstein carriage" could not be identified, but a light carriage accommodating six grown men (as Ludecus says this one did) was either a two-seated surrey or the more luxurious cabriolet. See Joseph J. Schroeder, Jr. (ed.), *Sears, Roebuck & Co. 1908 Catalogue No. 117. The Great Price Maker* (Northfield, Illinois: DBI Books, Inc., 1971), 104–107.

he was.) had led a lady to the middle of the dance floor, he brought a flabby young boy forward, placed him in front of the lady, and the cockfight (the word "dance" would not describe it accurately) began. I am still amazed that the dancers did not trip over each other and bruise themselves. During this revelry there was a terrifying scream that gave me a scare. As I turned around, I saw a fat fellow standing in front of the musicians with his back to the dancers and screaming the lyrics to the *fandango* in a terrible falsetto voice. With each new dance, after a pause, I was startled by him again. The custom to sing only falsetto appears to be commonplace here and at least until now I have not heard anything else. For me this is proof that these people, who speak the most beautiful language, apparently have absolutely no appreciation of musical beauty. Looking over the ladies present, one after the other, I found that the one who was dancing was the prettiest and was dressed in the most tasteful and most expensive clothes. In response to my inquiry I learned to my astonishment that she was the daughter of the priest in attendance. Of course, it is a well-known law here that priests are not permitted to marry. But that they have children and often a number of them is also a known fact. This fact does not appear to be affected by that law, nor does it appear to be detrimental to [the prestige of] the priests. I am told that one is tolerant on this point toward the priesthood all over Mexico.

At such social events there does not appear to be a distinct segregation of the classes. Judging from their dress, there were some individuals present from the richest as well as from the poorest classes. Every woman appears to acquire for herself a ball gown for her whole life: The dresses that they were wearing fit them so poorly, I can hardly imagine that they were made for them. The cut of the dresses is very old-fashioned with an extremely short waistline. The women appear to like pretty combs a great deal. There were also many golden chains to be seen there, but they may have been of alloy.

I was overjoyed when the hopping and jumping was over, and I was quite astonished to see that dance followed by a waltz with minor variations which did honor to the Mexicans' [musical] taste. Adapted to the climate here, it is danced slowly like our slow waltz. With this dance they turned out to be better dancers, and the commandant and the priest's daughter made a very nice couple. During all this there was some heavy drinking going on behind the curtain. I made the mistake of not taking a look around back there, although there was no lack of invitations. People seemed to be having a lot of fun back there and the *whisky* may have been having its effect on their senses. The ladies were being regaled with *whisky* and water as they passed the same glass all around the room. In response to a noisy disturbance in front of the door, the armed portion of the guests immediately rushed forward with drawn sabers and quelled the outburst.

About ten o'clock we left the party, climbed into our carriage, and drove away at a trot the same way we had arrived. Then we got out again, brought the wagon down the slope, and had gone two-thirds of the way across the river without mishap when we got stuck. The mules could not or would not take the guests from the ball any further across the current in spite of the lashes on their backs. The coachman was squatting on his seat, for the river was running through the bottom of the carriage, where our coats, caps, hats, and all the other things were swimming around in the water, but no one could move us forward. A quarter hour passed with invectives, cursing, laughing, and repeated futile attempts to drive the mules onward. As near as our camp was, no one came from there to give us assistance. We decided to help ourselves by making the wagon lighter. Marzelino, who had gone on horseback ahead of us, took me on his horse and brought me safely across the river. Immediately I hurried to the camp in order to fetch some men and some tow ropes. Upon my return I saw Captain Little, who is sort of an amphibian, already in the water. Marzelino was trying to help Mr. Hartman, a master carpenter [in our expedition] whom we had picked up on the other bank, to leave the carriage the same way he had helped me and take him across the river. Unfortunately, however, the girth on Marzelino's saddle broke, and he and his elegant burden, for Mr. Hartman was dressed very elegantly, fell into the water. Due to the lightened load and with the tow ropes I had brought, the rest of the ball guests were pulled from their wet cloakroom. Upon my return to camp, I took the watch and that is when I began writing this long *epistle*. This morning I continued it, but I have to close now, since I have to get everything ready to get underway at twelve o'clock. My next letter will be from [San Antonio de] Bexar and I will hopefully have something new for you.

San Antonio de Bexar, February 6, 1834

Here I am in the metropolis of Texas and with a joyful heart I shout: Thank God! That was a sad journey, crawling along like snails. By the end of the trip our poor oxen could hardly drag themselves along, and a third of them are running loose on the prairie, if they can still run, for we had to let them fend for themselves.

On the twentieth of last month we set out with mostly newly rented carts. My hope of recovering the oxen that I had lost remained fruitless. However, a few moments before our departure I heard that they had been found and that the finder had promised to bring them to me. In anticipation of their return I did not buy any more and traveled on with my single yoke of oxen. After two hours on the road we made camp and on such a glorious evening as this one I felt compelled to sleep outside in the grass. But in the middle of the night the weather changed with a rapidity such I had never before experienced. A strong north wind came storming through with rain and forced everyone to run for shelter. After a few hours the cold had become so severe that, almost frozen stiff, we left this windy campsite. Several people were not feeling well and Mr. Power was having a relapse of his former ailment.

We had been traveling hardly a half hour when the rear guard caught up with us with orders to make camp at the first water we found. We found some in the vicinity and before long camp was set up again. The entire day remained cold and rainy, and toward evening we were visited by two rich Mexican men. One of them was the owner of large estates and the spot, where we were camped, was his property. It was magnificent land and the *nopal* there had grown to a height of fifteen feet, a sure sign of rich soil. Magnificent groves of *sycamore* trees are found there, covered all over by long moss trailing down from the branches, which is a glorious sight to see. My compatriot, Herr Wetter, had caught a cold and was complaining that evening of the same trouble that Mr. Power was suffering from. He was having intense pain. So, a warm bath was immediately prepared and he was placed in it. Of course, this gave him some relief right away, but he remained in it too long and when he started feeling bad, he was taken out, but immediately he became unconscious and was put to bed. I had the watch from nine to twelve and I was startled by the family's cries calling to me that I should bring the doctor. He was on the spot right away and in a short time Wetter had been brought around enough that, although he was delirious, he soon fell asleep. The next day he was as good as before except for some residual weakness. At half past one I went to bed, but at three o'clock I was awakened again to go on watch. Mr. Beales, who is no great friend of standing watch, especially during bad weather, asked me to let him take the remaining half of my watch and in return I would take over his watch since he had been called to Herr Wetter and had been required to stay with him for some time. I did not refuse his offer, but I do not believe that he would have made this *proposition* to someone who had Englishmen or Americans under his command. The Germans did not get any rest all night long.

The next day was better. For ten pesos we bought a fine bull for slaughtering from one of our guests. The herd was rounded up by his servants. Both Mexican gentlemen remained on their horses and had the oxen driven past them. Every one of the Mexicans had in his hand a tightly twisted rope of horsehair called a *cabestro*[28] After Mr. Beales had selected the bull he wanted, the herd was driven past again and as the chosen animal in the mid-

---

[28] A *cabestro* is a type of halter or lead for cattle and horses. See Roger Steiner (ed.), *Webster's New World International Spanish Dictionary. English/Spanish. Spanish/English.* (Hoboken, N. J.: Wiley Publishing, Inc., 2004).

dle of the herd rushed by the catchers, one of them was swinging over his head one end of the *cabestro* that he had tied into a loop and he flung it with extraordinary accuracy around the bull's horns. At the same moment he tied the other end to his saddle horn, turned his horse, and spurred it forward, causing the bull to be stopped in his tracks. Then the other rider galloped up behind the standing bull also swinging his *cabestro* and as the ox resisted and raised his hind leg, it was caught in a noose also. Like the first rider, this rider tied the other end to his saddle. Both riders moved forward and the bull fell to the ground. The riders executed this maneuver as elegantly as they did swiftly from a distance of about twenty-five feet. The riders tied the bull down, slaughtered it, and skinned it out on his own hide without allowing it to become at all soiled while they butchered it. That evening they all left.

During the days that followed, we made a good day's progress each day and traveled through some magnificent territory. Mr. Beales lent me a pair of his oxen, which were of course also very worn out. I traveled along well with them, but had still not yet given up hope that someone would still bring my oxen to me. On the evening of the twenty-fifth, we stopped on a hill or on a rise in the prairie. It was a pleasant day and evening, but again during the night the weather took a turn for the worse. It stormed violently and by turns it rained and snowed. The next morning I found my wagon covered with ice. In this weather it was impossible to go on, so we had to wait three days before the weather finally improved. During this time our camp was transformed by the incessant rain into a marsh and it seemed hardly possible to go on through all the deep mud. Although the mud was cleaned out of our tent several times during the day, we were still standing in it up to our ankles. Several in the expedition remained in bed all day. People ate breakfast, lunch, and dinner on Mr. Power's bed. A large pile of coals was placed in the small space between the beds leaving the people standing there no room to move about. For hours they were limited to one spot and after a while they had sunk so deeply into the muck that it took a lot of effort just to work their feet loose again. The worse our situation became, the more everyone joked about it. At night it became so cold in camp that we could hardly bear it. In the wind and rain we could not keep a fire burning, so we all ran into the surrounding brush, took cover there as snugly as we could, and no one thought of going on watch.

Here I must mention a matter that again concerns the man for whom I feel such an extraordinary affinity. It is a matter that again casts a stain upon his otherwise so charming character. However, no one is perfect and I would not tell this if I did not hope that by doing so, many things in these letters will be published and they will be a warning to my compatriots: They should not entrust their fate so unconditionally to people and especially to a country they do not know, as the German families on this expedition with us have done. It is lucky for them that Herr Paulsen and I are here, so that we can look after them. It is only natural that Mr. Beales shows a preference for his nation over another and when it is kept in moderation, I would not say anything about it. But the following incident will demonstrate how things have gotten out of hand.

Since the beginning of the journey there has been constant strife between the women of these two countries: The English women, and especially the wife of the distributor [of food], who is a real she-devil, have done everything to annoy the German women, and they [in turn] are too hot-tempered and have not behaved judiciously in the conflict. Consequently, there is an uproar every day. The chief bone of contention now is the wagon in which the English women are usually the first to get seats and then they spread out and take up so much space that only a few of the German women can find a seat there, and the rest of them must walk. Until then Herr Paulsen and I had kept the situation under control through persuasion until it unfortunately erupted the morning before we came to our marshy campsite. It was an extremely romantic spot, very close to a deep chasm that had thick brush and trees growing all around it. About twenty Indian huts showed that they had also recently camped there. The Germans, who were already annoyed at always having to be the ones to yield, brought the beds of their wives early that morning to the wagon and placed them inside. But as they were leaving the wagon, they saw one of the English women already approaching with her beds. Herr Schwartz followed her and when he got to the wagon, he saw his bed thrown out and the woman standing on the wagon shaft placing her bed inside. He picked up his bed and shoved it past her back into the wagon. His movements may have pushed her to one side and, as she lost her balance, she grasped Schwartz's hair. As she fell on the other side, she was caught by a German girl and came down safely on her feet from the shaft. In her initial fright that she might fall, she had screamed. The cook, who is a nimble and hot-tempered fellow, came running, saw the woman in the aforementioned situation, and without investigating further, he struck the frail Herr Schwartz in good English style with both fists in the face and chest. Not knowing what was happening to him, Herr Schwartz stepped back. The clamor had brought me running and from a distance I saw Mr. Beales already at the scene of the trouble. At the same moment the cook stepped in again and displayed his bravado by again striking Schwartz, who was not even defending himself. Mr. Beales finally called out to him, "*it is sufficient*" (that is enough), and the cook stopped. These words, which the Germans had understood, were interpreted by them as coming after an earlier order to the cook to strike Herr Schwartz. As well as I know Mr. Beales's character, I do not believe that he is capable of such. Tallör, who had witnessed the scene from nearby, described to me the course of events and, as I later learned from face-to-face conversations with others, his description was truthful.

A short time after the incident I went to breakfast and Beales said jokingly the following to me: "One of your soldiers behaved badly this morning." I was ready to take the matter very seriously, however, and asked very tersely, "In what way?" [Beales answered,] "He hit a woman." [And I countered,] "Who said so?" "I did," [he replied]. This unequivocal declaration held my own comment, which I had wanted to make about the incident, in check for the moment. However, I described to him the sequence of events as I had heard it. Then I went to the source itself and asked the woman whether she had been struck and her answer was "No." During this time the wagons began to get underway, and Schwartz refused to go on with us. He insisted that he would prefer being killed to being treated as he had been treated. His face had been disfigured in a disgraceful way and his chest was causing him a lot of pain.

After much persuasion, I took him into my wagon. Even the Mexican drivers, who had witnessed the scene also, were so outraged that they offered to assume the costs if Schwartz wanted to charge the cook [with assault]. Schwartz speaks French and some Spanish, for he was a soldier for a long period of time in both countries. The humiliation he suffered here seemed to have affected also his morale very deeply. The next day he was not able to get up out of bed, and that evening he was still complaining a lot about his chest. I went to Beales to tell him this and to remind him that something had to be done about the matter in order to prevent more incidents. Then there was an exchange of words between us out in the open which included Herr Paulsen and Mr. Power. The former was on my side and the latter on Beales's side. Mr. Beales stated finally that he had no power to punish the cook, and he was not able or willing to do anything. I told him then that under these conditions I would never make an attempt to attract Germans to his colony. Then he tried, of course, to make amends by giving the Germans some more attention. But he did not concern himself at all about Herr Schwartz's health.[29]

The oxen that had been lent to me also became unserviceable on the last leg of the journey, and I even had to leave one of my own lying by the road. Therefore, I rented another pair from a Mexican who was able to get along without them. Finally, the weather cleared up somewhat on the nineteenth and we hurried on. During one long stop, which had been caused by two lost oxen, we killed twenty-eight rabbits. They are extremely abundant in this country, especially where there is a lot of *nopal* growing. They usually

[29] Beales mentioned Mr. Power's illness of January 10 to 12, but made no mention of the attack on Herr Schwartz. Kennedy, *Texas*, 399.

live there in droves. Some of them were caught by our dogs and we killed others with clubs, or we caught them alive among the trees. Captain Little was chasing after one when he saw it disappear down a hole. He reached in after it, but when he grasped something smooth that immediately started rattling, he recognized the sound and quickly pulled out his hand. He had grasped the tail of a rattlesnake, which we then killed with a lance. It was about seven feet long and had fourteen rings in its rattle, indicating that it was seven years old. The rats and mice were even more numerous there than the rabbits, and in those areas of the country where we were they were countless.

We were hoping to reach by the thirty-first [of January] the *rancho* (farm) that lies on our route, but our oxen were able to move us only a few miles. We stopped halfway along the road at a watering hole and made camp there. Several of the men had hurried on ahead. So, I got back on my horse to go catch up with them, and found them already at the *rancho*, where I found lodgings also. For several days I had not been feeling so well and I was afraid that the weather, which was again growing worse, could be having a bad influence [on my health].

This estate belongs to a rich man in Bexar. It lies on the San Antonio River and was established here just three years ago. We have seen here a cotton plantation and many other new things. That evening we were served coffee, a chicken, eggs, beans, and milk by Don Antonio, the manager, who speaks a little English and who has spent some time in the United States. We had not seen such food for a long time, so we savored every delightful bite. We spent the whole evening talking. Mr. Pepin, who speaks Spanish, played the role of translator. Our host told us a lot about the Indians, but he has not yet been molested by them. His dwelling and those of his servants and workers are completely enclosed by a heavy palisade of tall tree trunks that is like a fortress. Don Antonio is a handsome man who embodies all the qualities of the old Spanish *grandeza*. From him we learned a great deal about the institutions and laws of this country. I was particularly displeased to hear about this law: If a debtor cannot pay his creditor, then he is required to work for him until the loan is paid off. The creditor can then give this servant for his needs as much as he wants, and when he has no work for the servant, then he can sell him to someone else for the amount of the loan. On the other hand, if the servant can find an employer who will pay him more than his present employer and will pay the amount owed, then the servant has the right to force his creditor to give up his claim on him. This is to me a modern form of slavery. The servant has no money and is compelled to borrow money from his creditor for clothing and everything else and by the latter's high charges the servant can be kept in debt all his life. As much as I have learned until now about these laws, they seem to me very disadvantageous for the poor, and therefore [I think] it is not advisable for such people to come here.[30]

The next day I went walking along the banks of the river and I was astonished at the density and size of the grapevines I saw there. Those vines, as thick as a man's arm, were growing to the highest tree tops. Unfortunately, everything was shrouded in the bleakness of winter, but I could imagine in my fantasy the splendor of this wilderness in the summer. Along the river there is an abundance of timber, which is very rare elsewhere in this country.

Around noon the wagon caravan arrived and we made our camp on a small hill among the brush opposite the *rancho*. In order to let our animals rest up, we decided to remain there two days. Don Antonio, with two servants behind him, came to pay Mr. Beales his respects. He was invited to eat, but he declined the invitation for that day. He left then and, according to custom, he sent Mr. Beales a portion from his [own] dinner table. The afternoon was spent cleaning our firearms in preparation for competitive shooting the following day. The Mexican [estate manager] had challenged us all and, as Americans do, had promised to beat everybody. And really, he seemed to be the man to keep his promise. The next morning brought pretty weather, and the first thing we did was measure off a hundred and fifty feet. With the aplomb of a Wilhelm Tell, Don Antonio shot and was beat by me and Mr. Beales, who had the best shot. Then the target was enlarged, and our marksmen called for me to fetch my Turkish pistols, which were known to be excellent firearms, in order to teach our opponent a lesson. I did so, tried out the powder in two [practice] shots, then I fired and beat my opponent, for it was an exceptionally lucky shot. He thanked us for his loss and did not seem at all piqued about his defeat.

On February 1, we continued on our journey. Nine pairs of rented oxen were necessary to get us underway again. I had two pairs of them. Not far behind the *rancho* we entered a forest that may have been a half hour across. It was the only place we had seen until then that deserved to be called a for-

---

[30] Ludecus and the other men in the caravan stopped at the *rancho* of Don Erasmo Seguin, described by Beales as "admirably situated on a rising ground about 200 paces from the [San Antonio] River . . ." Kennedy, *Texas*, 403–404 (quotation). In 1834 [Juan José María] Erasmo Seguín was living in San Antonio. Jesus F. de la Teja, "Seguin, Juan José María Erasmo," Tyler et al. (eds.), *New Handbook of Texas*, V, 966.

est. However, one should still not imagine a German forest here. Only thick, low brush and now and then a small tree is all it takes to qualify here as a forest. The road went through a marsh that caused us some problems, but soon it got better. In the vicinity of our camp we saw an abandoned *rancho*. Its abandonment is said to be the reason that Indians now plunder [in the area]. The prairie wolves that made a lot of noise every night seemed to live there in especially large numbers. The whole night through there was an infernal commotion [from them]. The *polecat* or skunk is also very abundant there and a lot of them are killed. The *opossum* is rarer. The next day we found a good route and passed by a very deep chasm. Beautiful cedar trees were growing on its steep walls. Going through such passes affords a highly grotesque sight. The pass itself is enclosed by beautiful, tall trees, and in the valley there is a stream. The oxen, horses, and mules are going downhill [on one side], and on the other side the long trains of oxen are pulling a wagon up. Teams of oxen are being driven down to hitch them up to other wagons, while the cries of the drivers are amplified by the echo there. All of this produces the most interesting scenes before the viewer's eyes.

Yesterday, on the fifth [of February] we came up on a hill at noon from which we could see Bexar lying [before us] in a broad and barren plain. To our left on the far bank of the San Antonio River there was another mission to be seen which in its extent seemed to exceed the former one [at Bahía].[31] Mr. Beales had hurried on ahead in order to secure a place for our camp and to obtain permission from the *alcalde* for our stay there. Unfortunately, he returned with the news that within a range of several hours [from the city] there would be no food available for our animals except at our present location. These were sad prospects for our animals. In recent days we have been forced to leave some of them behind. My last ox was among them. It no longer had the strength to continue on for even the last two hours of the journey. Tomorrow I will go and look for it. Our stay here had at first been planned for only three days in order to rent new carts. But the time is approaching to begin working the fields and that makes it difficult to get them. Our stay here has already been extended to a week. Before we leave, I will write again from this city. Until then, etc.

---

[31] In 1834 there were five missions in the San Antonio chain of missions, all of them founded and built before 1750. Ludecus could have been looking at any one of them. See Marion A. Habig, *The Alamo Chain of Missions: A History of San Antonio's Five Old Missions* (Chicago: Franciscan Herald Press, 1968), 29, 80–81, 84–87, 119, 122–125, 158–161, 202–204.

NINTH LETTER
Sojourn in San Antonio de Bexar. Wedding of a German Couple
San Antonio de Bexar, February 18, 1834

Tomorrow we leave finally. How little have the leaders of this expedition known about this country that they were going into! It has been one problem after another, and if Mr. Beales were not a man with enough talent to deal with even the most difficult situations, we would now be in the worst predicament in the world. So, we have come this far only to pay our teamsters the rest of our money. Whoever had some money gave it up. I do not know the exact amount that Mr. Beales brought along, but I do know that we have not yet covered half the distance to our destination, and the provisions are running low. Nothing has been done yet to stop the waste and theft of them, and we have to buy five more pairs of oxen in order to continue on. Then we will have nothing left to establish the colony at our destination and to sustain ourselves there. I brought along as much money as Mr. Beales had advised me to bring, and [some of] that had been set aside to pay my passage back to New York or New Orleans if I did not like it here. And now I cannot even get along on that! I have bought four new oxen. I am leaving the last one of mine here, since it has not been able to recover. It will remain here with several others and be used to bring along the things we are leaving here. We have lost a total of some twenty oxen and four horses along the way. At first Mr. Beales had tried in vain to negotiate a loan, but the only man who could have lent him money was unfortunately away. So, for a week we were in a quandary, when finally this individual returned and gave him a thousand pesos on a letter of credit on [a bank in] New Orleans. This got us on our way again. But what would we have done if Mr. Beales had not gotten the money? He said the following to me in reply to this question: "We will have to leave behind what we can get along without, and continue on as well as we can." That was easily said, but difficult to do, and I would not have wanted to take on that responsibility.

I was disappointed in Bexar. It has about three thousand inhabitants, many of them Blacks. I had expected to find a city resembling more a European city, and yet, it was little better than Bahía. It lies on the western side of the San Antonio River and its name is actually San Antonio de Bexar. The river originates at a distance of about an hour and a half northwest of the city, where it flows with a considerable volume of water out of the earth. For its short course, it has a great deal of water. Like Bahía, Bexar was for the most part destroyed in the revolution of 1813, and even today there are clear signs of that [destruction] still to be seen here.[1] Several streets and plazas are

---

[1] No record of widespread destruction in San Antonio de Béxar during the Mexican Revolution (which occurred in 1811) could be found.

laid out in a regular pattern and I have also seen houses here which have floors, even wooden floors. In the middle of one of the plazas which joins another plaza there is the church. It has fallen into ruin and on the inside it looks very shabby. I have made two drawings from different sides [of the church], but I had to sketch them too quickly since there was a whole flock of curious onlookers standing around me. These people, who were otherwise not timid, were now extremely reticent, watching me silently and speaking in hushed tones with each other. Then they went away just as quietly. Drawing does not seem to be well known here.

I found a German boy here, a blonde boy who was about nine years old. He is the son of Elizabeth Shuk from one of the southern German states. I have forgotten his father's name. Both parents died from the cholera when they came over here as *settlers* with Baron von Racknitz's expedition.[2] Only a few members of the expedition are still alive, for all the others were taken away en route by the cholera. A priest has taken in the boy as his own child. I made the acquaintance of the former and found him to be an amiable old man and a native Spaniard. He spoke some English and he spoke French quite well. But there was nothing to be gotten out of the boy. He said nothing but "Ja" and "Nein," and that only rarely. Otherwise, he left all my questions unanswered.

The inhabitants [of Bexar] annoyed us quite a bit. They came in groups [to our camp], mainly after the *siesta*, sat down at the entrance to our tents, and made it impossible to go in and out. They gathered also around our campfires and not a single one of our cooking pots escaped their investigations.

On February 12, we celebrated [Peter] Dippelhofer's marriage to [Elizabeth] Corbé. The marriage couple, Mr. Beales, Herr Wetter, the [girl's] stepfather, Herr Schwartz and his wife, and I walked to the church at seven in the morning.[3] The priest was not there, so we sent for him. He then sum-

---

[2] Johann von Racknitz led a group of German colonists to Texas in 1833, but most contracted cholera in New Orleans. By the time they reached Texas, there were too few survivors to form a colony so they fled to other settlements. See Louis E. Brister, "Johann von Racknitz: Ein Württemberger an der Spitze der deutschen Auswanderung nach Texas, 1832–1841," *Zeitschrift für Württembergische Landesgeschichte*, 53 (1994), 227–261; Louis E. Brister, "Johann von Racknitz: German Soldier of Fortune in Texas and Mexico, 1832-1848," *Southwestern Historical Quarterly*, 99 (July, 1995), 48–79.

[3] At the time of Dippelhofer's wedding to Elizabeth Corbé, the marriage registry of the archdiocese in San Antonio was not being maintained. Thus, the registry contains no record of this marriage. Ed Loch, Archivist, San Antonio Archdiocese, letter to the author December 5, 2005.

Ludecus writes that the wedding was performed in San Fernando "church" (*Kirche*), the only church in San Antonio at the time. In 1834, San Fernando cathedral (*Don*) had

moned us to his house. It had a passageway to the courtyard, and from there an entrance without a door led into the study of the pious man. We were met there by a man of rather ordinary appearance. He asked to be introduced to the marriage couple. Then he spoke a few words with Dr. Beales, put on his vestment, took his place before us, and began a speech in Spanish which was translated by Dr. Beales into French, and that in turn was translated by Herr Schwartz into German. So it went, sentence by sentence. One can imagine how much of the edifying speech must have been lost [in the translations]. The ceremony lasted ten minutes, during which time Schwartz's wife was kept busy at the entrance to the study, where she was standing, keeping the pigs away that were constantly running up and down at the entryway. I signed my name as a witness, and the young groom pressed six pesos, the wedding fee that had been negotiated down from sixteen pesos, into the hand of the spiritual merchant, and we left. All the way home I tried to figure out why the groom had paid these six pesos and could not find any rational explanation.

We are beginning this leg of the journey now with renewed strength. The Presidio de Rio Grande is the next goal of our journey.[4] Before we reach it, we have to cross the Rio Bravo del Norte or Rio Grande, and I am curious how this will be carried out. The river is low at this time [of the year] and it is said that one can cross it in a wagon. How deprived of water the western regions of this country must be that one can wade across a river several thousand miles downstream [from its source]. In Presidio we hope to meet Captain [Fortunato] Soto, Mr. Beales's brother-in-law, and Mr. [William Henry] Egerton, his friend. We have heard that they are staying in Monclova in order to hurry to meet us at the first word of our arrival. The latter has traveled over the country there several times and is said to be interested as a [land] speculator. Mr. Beales got his unfortunately rather superficial information from him. However, they will be all the more welcome since, as Mr. Beales says, they will have money with them.

We have been busy the last few days making bullets, since the news that we have gathered about the Indians is of the sort that we must always be ready to react. We are going now into the areas often ravaged by them. The sentries must be vigorously monitored, the outposts stationed further from camp than before, and they must be visited every quarter-hour by the officers. A few days after our arrival [in San Antonio de Bexar], the owner of the

---

not yet been built. Ed Loch, Archivist, San Antonio Archdiocese, telephone conversation with the author, December 5, 2005.

[4] Presidio de Rio Grande was located near San Juan Bautista on one of the two roads linking Bexar to the Rio Grande. See Stephen F. Austin (comp.), Map of Texas, . . . (Philadelphia: H. S. Tanner, 1831).

rancho where Don Antonio lives received word that all his horses had been driven off by the Indians. The *ordre du jour* [order of the day] is: fire at every redskin. That is terrible, but when it is either me or him, what else can I do?

I do not know anything else to say about this city, and I am truly happy that we are finally traveling on. There is no variety here, just as elsewhere in this whole country it is always one and the same thing: boring to the highest degree. I will write more from Presidio de Rio Grande.

TENTH LETTER
*An Adventure. Continuation of the Journey. Rio Frio. Shawnee Indians
Trapping Beaver. Crossing La Leona [River]. Presidio de Rio Grande.*
Presidio de Rio Grande, March 7, 1834

One more station [on our journey] has been reached! But for heavens
sake, what a journey of horrors it was! But what is the use? Oxen are not
hippogryphs.[1] I must have patience. Here I sit today out in the open and all
around me are my clothes, linens, and everything that I have lying in the
grass and hanging [to dry] over ropes in the much too ample sunlight. Why?
In the course of this letter you will learn the answer. I wish you all could see
the colorful groups of Mexicans who, filled with curiosity, are standing here
all around me and my belongings. They are very bold and they walk all
around and touch everything. Therefore, I look up furtively from time to
time from my writing to observe their long fingers that have a somewhat
notorious reputation here. You all may find this pardonable.

I wrote to you all the last time in Bexar on the day before our departure.
That evening we received some bad news. Two Americans (one understands
everywhere in America the term "American" to be someone from the
United States, but the Mexicans use this name for everyone who does not
speak their language), who were residents of Bexar, came and asked for our
help in the following incident: Mr. Mac Neil coming from Austin's colony,
had been traveling through Bexar to Saltillo.[2] He had stopped in Bexar for
several days where we had made his acquaintance, and then three days
before our departure he had continued on his way. That same evening a
young man who was accompanying him had returned to Bexar alone and
on foot with an arrow wound on his cheek and on his arm. He reported that
at a place called Tawakonis they had been attacked in the evening by Indians of the same name as they were going back to camp. [Mr.] Mac Neil had
received a serious wound on his neck from an arrow and another wound in
his side from his own pistol which had discharged as he fell from his horse.
The young man himself had not remained unscathed. To be sure, Mr. Neil
had driven off the savages by shooting at them several times with his pistol,
and he thought that he had killed their chief. But their horses and baggage
had been lost and had probably been taken by the Indians.

---

[1] The hippogryph (or hippogriff) was a mythical monster with the hindquarters of a
horse and the head and wings of a griffin. Victoria Neufeldt (ed.), *Webster's New World
Dictionary of American English*, 3rd ed. (Cleveland: Webster's New World, 1989), 639.

[2] The identity of Mr. MacNeil could not be established in the context described by
Ludecus. In his fourteenth letter Ludecus reports hearing that Mr. Neil had died of his
wounds. Ludecus, *Reise*, 222.

They [Neil and his companion] had started back to Bexar, but Mr. Neil had not been able to go more than a few miles. At that point they had turned off the road into the brush, where the young man had left the wounded man behind in order to find help in Bexar as quickly as possible. The *alcalde* had promised assistance, to be sure, but not with the haste necessary, for a number of soldiers were not going to be sent out until the next morning in order to retrieve the wounded man under their protection. The friends of Mr. Neil were afraid that the delay, compounded by the difficulty of finding their horses on the prairie, would put the life of the wounded man in danger. Immediately, we promised to go with them if it was possible to round up some horses [for us] that same evening, because it was impossible to use our own horses on such an expedition. They promised to try to find some, but they did not come back and we heard the next morning that they had prevailed upon some Mexicans to accompany them. The negligence and laxity of the Mexican government in matters concerning the Indians is unbelievable. But it is even more astonishing to learn with what indifference the inhabitants [of Mexico] tolerate their harassment by the Indians. They can rarely be persuaded to pursue those who steal their horses and murder their neighbors. So, it has now gotten so bad that if the people of Bexar had the will to go after the robbers, they could not find enough horses to do so, for the Indians have taken them away.

Our first day's journey was very short. We had the pleasure of being able to make camp in a place covered with new grass. The horses, oxen, and mules were savoring the quality even if not the quantity. We kept sharp watch, although a camp such as ours probably had nothing to fear, at least from the Tawakonis, who have no firearms. Since leaving Bexar we have had in our party a surgeon from the United States who intends to travel on foot through Mexico and South America. I wish that I could accompany the man, for it will no doubt be a very interesting journey. It is a shame that he is lacking one resource for the journey, and the most important one in fact in order to be able to get much out of his trip—he does not understand the Spanish language.

On the second day [of travel] we were met by Mac Neil's rescuers with the wounded man. He was sitting slumped over on the horse belonging to Mr. Smith, who was leading it. Two Mexicans were riding beside him, one on either side. The others were following along behind him. He displayed extraordinary composure, not complaining and answering [questions] with extreme calm. He recounted to me the course of events plainly and certainly truthfully, and comforted our women with the assurance that our numbers eliminated any danger of attack. He was placed under a tree where Mr. Beales investigated his wounds. He found that the one on his neck was not dangerous and he cut the bullet out [of the other wound]. He [Neil] endured the operation without uttering a sound from the pain. [Meanwhile], the Mexicans had collected probably forty arrows and only a few of them had iron points. The number of Indians were estimated to be about twenty-five. We bade them farewell, wished the wounded man a rapid recovery, and about three o'clock we reached the Medina River. Not far from that spot the Medina flows into the San Antonio River, and probably it is actually the larger of the two. The water of the Medina is extremely clear and its banks look romantic with growths of oak, cedar, and sycamore.

We crossed the river without further difficulties and a quarter hour beyond the river we made camp. The somewhat narrow river valley offers splendid sites for *settlement*. The soil is loose and there is beautiful timber available in abundance. But I do not know whether the land there is subject to flooding. The next morning the weather showed promise of being fair and I hurried out of camp very early. Peter Dippelhofer went with me. We turned off [the road] to the left into the prairie. About one and a half hours later, as we were veering to the right back to the road, I saw in the distance a rider galloping toward us. It is completely natural that in this endless prairie the sight of another human being calls forth a lot of suppositions and security measures. The rider stopped. He was riding a white horse, but I could not make out anything else about the dark figure. I thought at first that it was Marzelino on Dr. Beales's white horse looking for some lost oxen. But his [Beales's] horse was lame. Then I thought that I had been traveling in a circle and was now meeting our own caravan of wagons, but one look at the sun convinced me that this could not be the case. Meanwhile, the rider had gone galloping back and at that moment I noticed a lot of horses' heads and dark figures behind a hill. I had no more doubt then that they were Indians. Our situation was not the most advantageous: no trees and no bushes were nearby that could shelter us from an attack by riders. Unfortunately, my companion was no hero either. Immediately he stammered something about making a run for it and wondered in what direction we could go to meet the caravan. Refuting that idea, I explained to him that to make a retrograde movement now, to borrow a term from Napoleon whom I like to imitate, would be the worst thing we could do, since someone on horseback could catch up to us in the blink of an eye. I showed him the direction to go and revealed to him my decision to go straight toward the riders, for a bold move is often a better strategy than either iron armor or swift legs. Then I planned to duck off to the side into the brush and wait for their attack. We were superbly armed. I had a musket, a dagger, and two good pistols. My companion had a double-barreled shotgun loaded with buckshot and a pocket pistol. But he still had not recovered [from his initial fright]. Consequently, I had to get his firearms in order and put them in his hands ready to fire with the order, not to fire until I told him to. Meanwhile, the mounted men had gathered around the rider who had ridden back to them. They seemed to be deliberating, but at that distance nothing could be clearly made out. We continued on our way and the lone rider came galloping back toward us. He stopped then and signaled with his hand to his companions. In the expectation then to see the whole band of them racing toward us, I realized that only determination could save us. Therefore, I started straight toward the rider who stopped and I signaled with my hand toward the area behind us in order to make him believe that I was only the avant-garde [of a larger force]. This was a military tactic I had learned as a boy in youthful scuffles. I continued to approach so that now I could recognize a mule loaded with baggage. The procession of riders had begun to move too and more of them could be seen as they came over the hill. The error was now clear. As I learned later, it was the governor of Texas who was traveling to Bexar and he had also thought that we were Indians.[3]

After this innocent adventure we climbed the hill and saw at a great distance our caravan approaching. We turned off to the left again and soon I found a herd of deer, about a hundred of them, and I set off running after them. After an hour's time I shot a beautiful buck, hung him on a pole, and we loaded him on our shoulders. Then we tried to get back to my wagon as quickly as possible. We walked on, for an hour and a half, but to my surprise we could find no trace of our fellow travelers. Undaunted, we continued on our way, but when we did not find the road after the passage of another hour, we threw our burden aside. Seduced by the sunny weather, I had not brought along my compass that morning. Now I was severely regretting that failure. For hours now the sun had been hidden behind clouds and I did not know in which direction to set my sails. I hurried on in the confidence that I could not possibly be far from the caravan. But several more hours went by and still no road came into view. The day was humid and we were suffering a lot from thirst. About noon we saw some fresh horse tracks and assumed there were Indians in the vicinity. Soon we saw also their well-worn *trails* and continued on very cautiously. Around this time the sun came out for a moment and I immediately took my bearing to the west in order to find the road or the Medina River. Unfortunately, we now came into such a thorn thicket that we could not possibly stay consistently on course. One could get through there only by force, and several times I was of a mind to give up altogether, go back, and find a way around the thicket. But finally, after a half hour we finally reached a somewhat open area. Our clothes were torn and

---

[3] At the time Ludecus was in Texas, the governor for the Bexar District was J. M. Berrimendi. The acting political chief was Manuel Ximenes. See Eugene C. Barker, *The Life of Stephen F. Austin Founder of Texas 1793–1836. A Chapter in the Westward Movement of the Anglo-American People* (Austin: University of Texas Press, 1990), 368–369.

we were bleeding all over. Again the sun came out from the clouds for a while. In order to be sure of our direction, I checked the course of the sun against the shadow of a stick that I stuck in the ground. I found that I must have miscalculated at the sun's first appearance, because the course of the sun at noon is very difficult to judge. In these regions the sun is then almost directly overhead.

I set my course again to the west, and soon I began looking for a watering place more than for the caravan, but I did not find either one of them. The sun was now getting nearer the horizon and we went marching on as fast as we could. The heat was oppressive and our thirst was beginning to become unbearable. And yet, for that day at least, I was not about to give up hope of finding either water or the caravan. My companion had become completely discouraged and, not knowing how to calculate directions from the sun, he insisted that we were going in the completely wrong direction. He wanted to go off in the direction opposite from our present course, and I had to summon up all my arguments to dissuade him from this insidious decision, which obviously would have been fatal for him. I tried in every way possible to convince him that the path we were on was the correct one, but points on the compass, the course of the sun, and all of that were Greek to him, and I just gave up. I still had hope, albeit a faint hope of reaching camp even that night. I was nurturing the hope of catching sight of our campfires if they were not too far away. But in the course of the day's travels the face of the landscape had changed drastically. The plain had disappeared and in its place there were now small hills overgrown with low thorn bushes, which blocked our view into the distance. I set out for one of the hills in order to discover from there perhaps either a watering spot or the caravan. My companion began hanging back and complaining a lot about his thirst. By his words I soon became convinced that he had completely lost heart. He was whining like an old woman and showing me that his morale was spent. Every minute I was afraid that this large twenty-six year old man would begin to cry. I scolded him thoroughly and continued on my way.

I must admit that the barometer of my own courage was also falling rapidly. My thirst was becoming from minute to minute more unbearable and I was not able to suppress the thought that our situation could come to a bad end. Then I found a *trail*, and I did not care whether it led to redskins or to some other dark-skinned race of people. I followed it for a while and then the password was uttered—water! When a person is walking alone in the twilight (and I was truly alone, for my companion was not quite present) with nothing but a desert facing him, with a thirsting throat, and an empty stomach, sober and foolish thoughts alike occur to him. That is what was happening to me as I was trudging along on this uncertain path. When I thought about how I would perhaps quench my thirst soon in camp, which gave me strength, I immediately remembered also that it was much more likely that a savage would quench his bloodthirst with my life, and that thought did not give me much strength at all! So it was with my hunger too. The head of the buck that I had shot was still hanging over my shoulder and when I thought about roasting it in hot ashes, I imagined also my own *scalp* being dried in the smoke of an Indian's *wigwam*. In short, that path seemed somehow enchanted. As the path under my feet ended, those foolish thoughts vanished also from my mind and with certainty I formulated the very rational decision to continue on as long as my strength held out, and then to rest until the next morning. I was hoping that the dew would bring us some refreshment in order to be able to keep on with our search, or if everything should be in vain, to do what I . . . I will leave that to everyone to guess what [I would have done], for I really did not know that myself, and since then I have not been able to figure it out. However, in reality I had made the decision to wait for my companion who had fallen behind. Consequently, I fired a signal shot with my pistol, but there was no answering shot, and then suddenly I heard a sound like the lowing of cattle. I listened intently, but the noise was not repeated. But I had hardly gone a hundred paces when I heard someone talking and off to the side of my path I saw through the brush two of our fellow travelers sitting on a tree stump. This discovery brought the straggler running in a hurry. The hunt was over, and the hunters they had been hunting for were home again.

The others had been quite worried about us, but had not wanted to send someone out to look for us too soon in order not to expose several others to the same dangers that could have befallen us. This narrative may seem to have been perhaps too detailed, but it seemed to me necessary to show all the difficulties that one can get into in the wilderness. It is too easy to get lost on the prairie and one does not need a degree from Göttingen to do it.[4] The worst thing about our experience was that [even afterwards in camp] we could not quench our thirst without satisfying our hunger at the same time, for the water was so thick [with mud] that it would have satisfied both. But necessity knows no prohibitions and the slimy water had to suffice. Our animals got nothing.

The next morning we got underway early, for the Mexicans had told us that the water was quite some distance away and in addition, we had to make a crossing at a very bad place. We reached that spot about noon and found that it was not so dangerous. We crossed [the Arroyo Hondo] rather quickly. As soon as my wagon was through, I hurried to the head of the train,

---

[4] The meaning of this remark is unclear, but Heinrich Heine, in his satirical travel account, *Die Harzreise* (1826), had portrayed the University of Göttingen as a center of esoteric learning.

because I had the day watch and I was responsible for keeping order in the train. But I had hardly dismounted from my horse, in order to use the spare time for a little rest, when we heard a sound as from a trumpet. In a second everyone was on his feet, because no one had any idea where the sound was coming from. Of course, one of our first thoughts was that the sound was being made by Indians. I ran to my horse to investigate the situation. But just as I was standing with one foot in the stirrup, my horse leaped forward and took off with me at full gallop. At the same moment I saw two riders, one with the North American flag, the other with the Mexican flag, galloping past me among the trees as one of them called out to me, "Where is Mr. Beales?" My position at the time was too *uncomfortable* to be able to give them any information about him. On the contrary, I was busy enough trying to keep my hide from being ripped off or my neck from being broken. Consequently, I did not answer them. When I finally did have the opportunity to get completely in the saddle, I brought the horse to a halt. Then I made it clear to the riders that I was, of course, a European and a German, but I was not one of those people who fear the tricolor of the [Mexican] Republic. On the contrary, I was hoping to live under this flag. I do not know how this aristocratic fear came over my horse, who was born in a republic, but every time I tried to approach those flags, I had to teach him with my quirt to love them.

Mr. Egerton and Don Fortunato Soto, whom I mentioned in my last letter, were the two riders who had come riding toward us. After they were quickly introduced to all the other people there, we hurried on our way, and for good reason, because Mr. Egerton had notified us that the distance to water was considerable. He expressed the doubt that one day would be sufficient to get there. Soon the baggage of the two gentlemen arrived also with their carts, horses, and servants. When the two gentlemen had learned from a few men who had hurried ahead on foot that we were nearby, they had sent the men back in order to surprise us. Unfortunately, Mr. Egerton's prediction proved accurate. We did not reach the watering place until eleven o'clock that night and whoever had a horse, rode ahead to bring back water in containers for the others who were thirsty. Twenty voices greeted them as they came back with one question, "How far is it?" Everyone wanted to know exactly how many minutes it was [to the water] and how long they had to endure the torture of thirst. Finally, we reached the pool and everyone rushed forward to gulp down the water thick with scum. We had been underway for seventeen hours and our crew was extremely tired.

I was compelled to take over the watch alone, but it was impossible for me to keep the sentries awake. I finally gave up after I had to wake up one of them four times in a half hour. I spent my watch patrolling constantly around the camp, for the night was incredibly beautiful such as they are only in tropical countries. Since I had been riding on horseback all day long, I was not so tired. At supper everyone was very happy. Mr. Egerton is a very sociable person and was constantly joking. Captain Soto understands only Spanish and could not therefore participate in the conversation since no one but Mr. Beales and Egerton know the language.

The Rio Frio was the goal of our next day's travel. We did not get underway early, since the distance there was only a half day's travel, and in order to let everyone get some needed rest. Then everyone hurried along in order to get there as quickly as possible in order to quench their thirst for once without revulsion. We had all been forced to skip breakfast since the oxen, horses, and mules, about seventy animals in all, had turned the pool into a puddle that was seasoned so strongly with excrement that it seemed impossible to drink that water, even when it had been boiled to make strong coffee. Nevertheless, several had been driven by the torture of their thirst to try to drink the coffee, but immediately they had been forced to throw it up again.

As soon as the caravan had begun the march, I hurried ahead with the Mexicans who were driving the loose horses. Others had already begun the march at daybreak and although it was only a two-hour ride to the river, when we got there we found two people already there who had come on foot. Their thirst had lent wings to their hurrying feet.

I do not know who drank more, my horse or I. The Rio Frio (cold river) is a beautiful stream. It has high banks and good timber, especially beautiful cedars. The water is clear, with a good taste and plenty of fish. But it is not a major river, for one can cross it almost anywhere without being forced to swim. The ford where we crossed was not over two and a half feet deep. Nevertheless, one can see on the trees, in which masses of moss and brush were hanging, that the river rises at times to a height of about thirty feet. However, the banks are even higher. The surrounding land is very fertile as one can see from the size of the *nopal* cactus and *mesquite* trees. In general, there has been a change in the vegetation of the country since yesterday. It is taking on more of a tropical character, and we have now found some new plants, especially the large numbers of agave that are beginning to bloom.

Around noon the [wagon] train arrived and crossed the river with little effort. Camp was set up a hundred paces from the river in a beautiful green area. As soon as everything was put in order, we hurried to the river with our fishing nets, but Saint Peter was not with us and our efforts were not rewarded. The stony bed of the river protected the inhabitants so well that we did not pull out a single fish. After working with the net for two hours we gave up. Although fishing with hooks yielded some fish, it was not worth the effort. The hunt yielded much more. Whoever had a rifle hurried out in the evening to hunt turkeys which had gone to roost in large numbers in the trees growing along the riverbank. In a short time twenty-eight of them had been killed. Among those turkeys, I saw some that in size far exceeded the tame European ones, but rarely do they taste better than the tame ones. It is incomprehensible to me where they get their food from, for I do not believe that they can live only on insects because I have seen too few of them. No one could tell me anything about these turkeys.

Our departure had been set for the following day, but suddenly at midnight a storm came up in the west. A strong wind began to blow and came sweeping toward us in a few minutes and then passed over us. But it lasted long enough to turn our campsite into a pond. Water was falling like a torrent from the skies. The storm blew two of our tents over and it was extremely funny to see how the people under the tent came crawling out one by one through the water and mud. Nevertheless, they were all happy, laughing and joking. No one had a single thread of dry clothing on his body. One person was running around in his shirt, another [only] in trousers, and a third one in a wool blanket—girls, women, and men, all in complete disorder. In a short while the rain let up and we immediately made a fire. First we dried ourselves and then our clothes, and passed the time as well as we could until morning. It was impossible to get underway that day because as soon as the sun came up, everyone was hurrying to unpack all his belongings and dry them out. The covers on our wagons had not been able to repel the torrent. Everything was as wet as if it had been pulled out of water. As we were eating breakfast, everyone was joking a lot. Each one was telling his own story of bad luck, when suddenly the cry, "Indians!" put a sudden stop to all that. We ran from the tent and saw four Indians on horseback with several pack horses. They were from the friendly tribe of Shawnees and were coming back with a rich haul from their beaver hunt. They also had buffalo and deer pelts with them. Mr. Beales purchased several beaver pelts from them, but not their secret for trapping beaver. We gave them something to eat and then they bade us a friendly farewell. They were going to sell their pelts in [San Antonio de] Bexar or in Natchitoches.

Beavers have their lodges usually on the banks of a river and live in communities. Consequently, hunting them is always rewarding. They are trapped in several ways. The most common method is to dig down into the lodge and catch the beavers with snares and traps, and [on lakes] through holes in the ice. When they come to the hole to get air or to look out of the hole, they are pulled out with hooks. Beaver pelts sell here for three *Thaler* a pound.[5] The Indians were well armed and were carrying Mexican muskets.

[5] The *thaler* was a silver coin in common use in Germany until the introduction of the *mark*. In Mexico a silver *thaler* was accepted as roughly equivalent to a silver peso and in the U.S. as equivalent to a silver dollar. Garland and Garland (eds.), *The Oxford Companion to German Literature*, 847.

The chore of drying clothes was soon done and the rest of the day was spent fishing and hunting. I brought back from my hunt a stalk from an agave plant with the flowers in full bloom. It was so large and heavy that I had to carry it on my shoulder because my hand grew tired from carrying it. Everyone marveled at the beauty of this flower which resembles a three-foot high pyramid of white bell-shaped blossoms. Of the thousands that I have seen since that day, I have not found a single one as beautiful.

On the twenty-sixth [of February], after a long day's travel we reached the La Leona River, a narrow but deep stream. Mr. Egerton had hurried on ahead with several other men in order to make the bridge that consisted of several tree trunks a little [more] serviceable. Darkness fell while they were working, and we managed to cross over by the light of a number of large and small fires which were ignited on both sides of the river. It was an extraordinarily romantic scene: All around us was a dense forest of trees, some of them tall and majestic trees, and flowing through the forest was a peaceful river. There was a small bridge of tree trunks covered over with a layer of green tree branches, and on either side [of the river] wagons and carts [were moving along] drawn by long processions of oxen. All of this was illuminated by the fires burning on the high bank, while people were swarming around these fires, coming and going, appearing and disappearing, as they came into the light of the fires or withdrew into the darkness of the night. The furious activity of these creatures contrasted sharply with the deathly silence of nature. There was no rustling breeze or lapping of the waves [against the riverbank] to be heard. Instead, the silence of the night was pierced only by the blows of the woodcutter's ax, by the cracking and rattling of tree branches, by the lowing of the oxen, and by the [exclamations] *Arriba!* [Up!] and *Carajo!* [Bastard!] of the Mexicans, the *Get along!* and *God damn!* of the English, the *Hott* and *Hie!* [Gee up!] and *Canaille!* [Devil!] of the Germans, the commands of the wagon master, and by the curses of everyone. The first four wagons and carts went over the bridge quickly, and mine was among them. But then the Germans' cart got stuck on the bridge. One wheel had run off into the water, and all of our efforts to pull it out of its precarious position with teams of oxen were unsuccessful. It had to be unloaded, which caused a long delay. I wanted at least to get the animals on the first wagons out of their yokes and take them to our camp a quarter of an hour away from the river. But the darkness made it impossible to distinguish the oxen and wagons just a couple of paces ahead of me and even more difficult to see the road. So, once I happened to be walking too closely behind one of the oxen and with just one kick he threw me to one side, probably just to let me know none too gently that I should keep my distance from him. The aroma of an ox is rather strong too. I had smelled it several times before. I was alone there with Tallör and a Mexican, and we were supposed to keep four wagons and twenty oxen under control. But the oxen, driven by hunger, wanted to go eat and did not want to follow the road. Finally, after much effort we succeeded in getting them all to move along. I was riding in front of the oxen and letting my horse find the road, [a tactic] which soon enough brought us to the right place. We were not far from camp, however, when I saw by the light of the campfires that the oxen in front of the herd were no longer following my horse, but were heading toward a steep slope. I jumped from my horse to drive them away from that dangerous spot. When I came back for my horse, he was gone, which was not customary for him. Driven probably by hunger, he had walked off without first allowing me to remove his saddle and put the hobbles on him. I was afraid for my pistols too which he could lose when he rolled himself on the ground. I looked for him for a long time but without success. The next morning I got up early and found him wandering along behind Mr. Power's mare. My eyes went immediately to my pistol holsters. My worst fears were realized—one pistol was gone. The horse's bridle was missing too, which a Mexican found later. But my weapon was lost and remained lost, even though the prairie was searched over by a number of people on foot and on horseback.

I must admit that a loss of this kind really put me in a bad temper such as I had not experienced on the whole trip. This will be very understandable even to any European who ever had a good rifle and lost it. It was even more painful to me to lose such an excellent weapon in a country where one is engaged in a war of extermination with the original inhabitants. One must be prepared every minute to use these weapons to defend one's life, weapons which one cannot replace for any amount of money! The excellent quality of these pistols made it possible to use them effectively at a distance almost equal to that for a musket. They were of Turkish manufacture and a gift from my father. Unconcerned about any danger, I could go out into the prairie with them and my musket and be fully confident of being able to turn back with these weapons any attack by a band of Indians.

We were late setting out on our march that morning, and I looked back once more with annoyance at the beautiful meadow covered with countless yellow flowers which were concealing a treasure [of mine], and then I hurried on. As we were approaching the peak of a hill, we saw Luna, one of our Mexican servants who had ridden on ahead, motioning eagerly to us. Immediately, all of us spurred our horses to a gallop, but instead of seeing Indians as we had expected, we found that we had been taken for Indians. Three Mexicans coming from Presidio had seen Luna's naked form and had thought that he was an Indian. In spite of his beckoning gestures to them, they had immediately ridden into the brush. But soon they realized their mistake; then they came forward and after a short conversation with us, they continued on their way.

Everyone here is constantly fearful of being attacked and robbed. The next day brought us after a long day's journey to our camp on the bank of the Nueces River. It was already completely dark. We were supposed to enter Mr. Beales's grant the next day and we agreed to have a little ceremony that was carried out as follows: The day before, a group of men had ridden ahead and had begun repairing the bridge. The next day they were still working on it. But the road leading down to the river could not be much improved. So, we had to lower the wagons down the slope with ropes ourselves and then pull them over the bridge and up the hill [on the other side]. In spite of all these difficulties, the work went rather swiftly. Before long Mr. Egerton's carriage came along as the last vehicle to cross over, and Mr. Beales was placed in it. On the other side of the river he was greeted with a blast of a trumpet and with shouts of "Hurrah!" Both [the North American and the Mexican] flags were flying on the bridge itself, and on the hill we all fired a salute with our rifles. The carriage was drawn halfway up the hillside to a tree. In the tree's trunk our carpenters had carved out an area flat like a plaque and on its surface that jack-of-all-trades, Captain Little, had carved the following inscription in Spanish: "The first colonists of the town Dolores crossed here on February 28, 1834." As Mr. Beales was reading the inscription, a wreath was placed on his head by Mr. Power and then the carriage was pulled all the way up the hill. I do not believe that I was mistaken when I saw a hint of displeasure in Mr. Beales's face when he saw the inscription and did not see his name there. Pride and a little boastfulness are two conspicuous traits in the character of this extremely amiable man. It surprises me that Mr. Egerton, who arranged these festivities, had not been somewhat considerate of Mr. Beales and included his name in the inscription. I would also be very mistaken if Mr. Beales had not even induced his friend to arrange this ceremony so that he could include in his account of the expedition and [the reports in] the New York newspapers a nice story about entering his colony lands. In any case, I must conclude from his behavior that he knew about the ceremony, for he had beforehand carefully avoided going to the other bank of the river. It was a pleasure for me to observe the republican character of the North Americans on the occasion. These sons of the United States displayed a thoroughly impassive attitude and even made disapproving comments about the wreath. "*What they are going to do* [*sic*]," I heard them say, "*we don't want a king*." (What do they intend to do; we do not need a king.)[6]

[6] The colonists were traveling on the main route from Bexar to San Juan Bautista near the Presidio de Rio Grande, a portion of the old Camino Real. For a depiction of the route, see Austin (comp.), *Map of Texas*. For a description of the crossing at the Nueces River by an earlier traveler on the same route, see Jean Louis Berlandier, *Journey to Mexico*

We continued on our march with the most beautiful weather. Everyone was happy and filled with hope. The land around us resembled a garden. The luxuriant vegetation gave testimony to the great fertility [of the soil]. We were seeing some new plants now too, among them an especially beautiful type of aloe. Everyone was wishing that we could settle in the vicinity of this river. After a short hour we reached a large pond which was fed by the river at flood stage and was enclosed by beautiful large oak trees. Behind the pond we set up our camp on a delightful spot of meadow that resembled a large yellow carpet of flowers. The fragrance exhaled by those flowers was most pleasant, but almost too strong.

The camp area was soon bustling with activity. Our pretty campsite was filled with carts, wagons, and tents, and in front of it waving [in the breeze] were the two flags that today had been carried at the head of the train. The horses, mules, oxen, dogs, and the busy people filled the colorful scene with activity. Over here some men were felling trees, and over there some women and children were gathering dry wood to burn in the campfires. A couple of Mexicans were racing on horseback through the cactus, swinging the *cabestro* over their heads as they chased after a runaway mule. Other men were putting hobbles on the front legs of their restless animals that did not want to be still because the grazing was too delicious. The oxen especially were already feasting on the beautiful blossoms of the agave, which were on display there in extraordinary numbers and size. The pond was swarming with swimmers. Others came with their fishing nets, which the swimmers pulled through the deep water, and all around one could hear shooting. Only the poor rabbits and fish had cause to mourn that day!

I was among the fishermen and swimmers myself. Although the fish we caught were in terms of quantity nothing to be sneezed at, they were definitely lacking in quality. In addition to several nice turtles, we had caught a number of fish that, after a lot of work to remove their armor-like scales and to cook them, were hardly fit to eat. These fish, some of them weighing from eight to ten pounds, have a long snout-like mouth filled with two rows of extremely sharp teeth. Their skin is so hard that it is difficult to penetrate even with the sharpest knife. In English this fish is called an "alligator gar."

The hunt had not yielded much either and so our dinner that evening was very meager. We eat only in the morning and in the evening here in order not to be held up when we are on the march. Since we left Bexar, game has become very scarce. But our hunter may share some of the blame

---

During the Years 1826 to 1834, trans. Sheila M. Ohlendorf (2 vols.; Austin: The Texas State Historical Association, 1980), I, 275.

Beales recorded in his journal a less detailed and less cynical version of this event at the Nueces. Kennedy, *Texas*, 408–409.

for that, for his enthusiasm [for the hunt] appears to have diminished somewhat. He is an American who was staying over in Bexar and who came to us with an offer to accompany us and for pay to provide us with meat [on our journey].

The Nueces River is narrower but deeper than the Frio River and its water is said to have a salty taste, but we could not verify that. Its water is somewhat murky and the riverbanks are muddy. As far as timber is concerned, it is very inferior to that on the Frio River. I have not seen here any cedar nor any good stands of timber. On the other hand, I have noticed that the Nueces River, like the Frio River, must rise at times to an extremely high level.

The next day we continued on our journey. We were not happy to leave our beautiful campsite and we were hardly underway for a half hour when we found ourselves again in the desolate prairie. We could see nothing [before us] but thorn bushes and small mesquite trees. At times the territory resembled a veritable desert where there was not a tree, a thicket, or much grass to be seen. One morning I observed the same manifestation that Professor [Hinrich] Lichtenstein saw in southern Africa and which he mentions in his travel report.[7] It was between eight and eleven in the morning, during which time the countryside all around us, a boundless plain, seemed transformed into a sea. As far as the eye could see there was nothing but silver-colored, quivering waves and beyond them, a distant coast marked by a row of treetops, the tallest ones portruding up like the masts of distant ships. The cause of this phenomenon was easy to determine. A heavy dew had fallen during the previous night and had saturated the land with moisture. This moisture was now being drawn up by the powerful sun's rays and set in motion by a barely discernible current of air.

Without encountering any other remarkable phenomena and after taking a day to rest, we arrived on March 4 at the Rio Grande and we set up camp just short of the riverbank. Everyone was extremely anxious to see the river where we thought we were going to settle, and even more anxious because we had heard the most contradictory reports about the river. But the reports were all in agreement that there was little or no wood at all to be found there, least of all for the construction of homes.

A few days after his meeting with Mr. Egerton, we were called together by Mr. Beales in order for him to inform us that after consulting with Mr. Egerton and Mr. Power, they had decided not to *settle* as originally planned southwest of Presidio in the vicinity of Laredo, but instead to go up the river

---

[7] Hinrich Lichtenstein was probably a minor writer of travel reports. His name does not appear in either the chief biographical compendium of his age, *Allgemeine Deutsche Biographie*, or in the contemporary encyclopedia, *Meyer's Konversations-Lexikon*.

to a spot Mr. Egerton had found on his inspection of the territory. This place was a bit more removed from the [Rio Grande] River on a stream called Las Moras and it would meet all of our expectations. On the other hand, the land downstream was suitable for ranching to be sure, but it was not suitable for farming. Moreover, there was no timber there. But if we should reject this [new] place, although that was not anticipated, we could always seek out the other areas. I cannot yet grasp [the significance of] this new situation, but I have noticed this much—since his meeting with Mr. Egerton, Mr. Beales has become a little subdued and does not talk anymore about his grant in such exalted terms. I think that much about this will become clear very soon, but this much seems clear now—they are not being entirely open with us. I will write more about this soon.

I want to return now to [the subject of] the Rio Grande. Whoever might trace the extraordinarily long course of this river on a map, which is called the Rio Bravo and the [Rio Grande] del Norte, would be greatly surprised to learn that this river can be crossed by wagon most days of the year. This is not true everywhere on the river, but it is positive proof of the lack of water in this country. Although we were hardly a quarter hour away from the river, we looked in vain there for some sign of its existence. But there were no tall green trees and no luxuriant vegetation to be seen there, which elsewhere in this land are to be found near all the rivers. We were still doubtful that there was a river in our vicinity when we saw it hardly a hundred paces in front of us. The sight of it, its murky, sandy water and its bare banks with only fifteen- to twenty-foot high cane and willows growing there made a very depressing impression on me and on all the others too. Everything is bleak and dead in its vicinity. Nature seemed to have died there. This much was sure—if this river did not have any better areas to offer, then it would not be seeing me for very long in its proximity.

It was already too late in the day to begin crossing the river. But I rode through it to investigate the depth of the ford there. I found the bottom of the river to be good rock and sand, and the water, which was rather swift, was no more than three feet deep. The road up on the other bank, however, was bad beyond imagination, and would definitely have to be made serviceable before we could try driving up the slope. It was about twelve to sixteen hundred feet wide.

The next morning at daybreak a group of workers was immediately sent over to prepare the road, and about nine o'clock the first half of the wagons got underway. The wagons could not be driven to the other side, however, without any difficulties or loss of time. Then they were unloaded there and they were sent back, for in order to protect each wagon's load from water, we had to leave part of the load behind and the baggage was piled on top. My wagon was tall, so I needed to elevate it [the baggage] in the front only a half a foot. In the back it would not have been necessary. I had measured the depth of the water with a measuring stick and I could say with certainty that Tallör's baggage, which was in the back, was in no danger. But in spite of my remark that, due to the narrow wheelbase of my wagon, it could easily tip over, Tallör nevertheless insisted on placing something under his baggage. Being familiar with his anxious nature, I unfortunately gave in. We reached the other side of the river safely, but as we were about to ascend the bank, I saw that little had been done to improve the road there and that I had little hope of driving safely up the bank. As I was thinking about what should be done and not realizing that the other wagons had been prevented from tipping over by the use of tow ropes, several men called out to continue on. I did so, and the outcome was that my wagon was lying on its side in the water.

Luckily, the wagon did not float very far downstream before it became stuck. It was unloaded and the contents brought to safety. To be sure, I did not lose anything, but everything was wet through and through. As soon as I had everything on the riverbank, it was hung out to dry, and in this chore the Germans and the sun helped me most kindly. By evening all my linens and my clothes were dry. I spent the night on the riverbank with Tallör. We made a large fire and dried out all the other things, the books, etc., which unfortunately had suffered quite a bit. The next morning at daybreak we loaded everything up and drove to the camp that was some distance away. There everyone was ready to get underway. They were just waiting on the return of a missing ox. Immediately I rode out into the prairie to help find the fugitive animal. After a half hour had elapsed I returned to camp only to find that the caravan had already left. I was just about to hurry after it when I saw through the thick mesquite trees the dark form of an Indian who seemed to be following my *trail*. He was coming along on the path that I had just come on, and his eyes were fixed steadfastly on the ground. He had not yet noticed me, so I stopped and prepared to shoot. He was coming nearer and I noticed that he was armed with a musket. Having no desire to wait for him to attack me, I raised my musket to my shoulder and was just about to fire a ball at him when I saw the lower part of his body, which before had been hidden by the bushes. Then I recognized him as one of the oxen drivers with the Mexican carts. His striking resemblance to an Indian had been often noticed by us and there is little doubt that he was a descendant of the Indians. This man had just warned me that same morning when he found me unarmed out on the prairie looking for my oxen. He had told me not to ride out without my musket and as a sign of my gratitude, I almost shot him down. I gave him some advice then, namely to wear something on his upper body in the future or at least to put on a hat, so that he would not be exposed to the same danger again. He was quite shocked when I told him what I had almost done. He had ridden out with the same intent as I that morning. But the departure of the caravan seemed to us proof enough that the missing animal had been found and we set off after it at a gallop.

Soon we reached the *mission*, the ruins of a former monastery [near Presidio de Rio Grande] and now a *rancho*. It must have been a work of extraordinary dimensions. It was built with the help of the Indians and later destroyed by them. It is located only a quarter hour away from here. Presidio de Rio Grande★ is a new town with a regular street plan, but it is a poor place. The inhabitants can hardly grow a little corn. The soil is very barren here and beans, which are hardly edible, are the only thing it produces. The inhabitants live mostly from ranching.

★ In order to protect the inhabitants of the border provinces against the attacks of the wild Indian tribes, some military posts, the *presidios*, were built by the Spaniards at certain points. The troops at these posts were obliged to come to the aid of the inhabitants in [times of] distress. But there were too few of them and they were located too far apart to achieve their objective. The *indios bravos*, like the Bedouins, knew the tactics of limited warfare too well for the military posts to be able to prevent their attacks. Their help usually came too late. The wild Indians were called *indios bravos* by the Spaniards to distinguish them from the *indios de paz*, which are somewhat civilized. They raise corn in the areas where they live and lead a quiet existence.

[*Author's Note*—Eduard Ludecus]

Today is an extremely warm day. I have hung up all around me all the things that did not dry out the day before yesterday. I hope they are not too badly damaged. Our camp, which we have set up near the town, is swarming with Mexicans. We are being especially honored by frequent visits from the fair sex, but one must keep a sharp eye on them because their fingers do not fully respect the difference between what is mine and yours.

I just came back from dinner where we had company: one of the dignitaries from the town was eating with us and he enjoyed it very much. He made no use of the forks and the knife provided. In their stead he used his fingers. While he ate, his wife and daughter sat behind him and did not accept our invitation to join us at the table. It does not seem to be the custom here for women to dine with their husbands.

Tomorrow we are planning to move on. The journey is being held up more and more, and we must hurry now to get to our destination, otherwise we will miss the time for preparing our fields. Here that time is already past and I am afraid that we will not be able to do much this year. Only God knows where I will date my next letter. We are going into the wilderness now.

ELEVENTH LETTER
Continuation of the Journey with a Mexican Escort. Taming Mustangs.
Preparations to Cross the Rio Grande. Rattlesnakes and Trapping Bears.
Shawnee Indians. A Dangerous Crossing of the River. Arrival and
Journey's End.

Villa de Dolores, March 16, 1834

Two large bruises and two small ones on my leg have provided me with a good opportunity to be able to continue my report. Without these bruises it would hardly be possible. You can politely thank them therefore for this report, for who knows how long it would have been before I would have found time to put pen to paper and satisfy your curiosity about my new residence if I had been able to work. Why? I do not need to give more explanation.

This morning Tallör went back to the Rio Grande in my wagon to bring along the baggage of the Germans. Their baggage and a large portion of other things had to be left behind [on the bank] because the Mexican carts had been contracted only as far as this side of the river. I am lying here under the open sky and my possessions are lying all around me. However, I have already begun building my hut and I hope to be protected soon from any rain that may come. But I will hurry to fill in the gap between Presidio and Dolores, and report what has happened since then.

We got underway as scheduled on March 8. Two Mexicans were hired as guides since they had earlier shot buffalo and caught *mustangs* in the area which we were now entering. We followed a path that had been worn down by the comings and goings of men catching horses. One of these guides was a great supporter of Santa Anna. Why? He did not know that himself, and I know therefore much less. He had never seen the general, but about twenty times a day he raised his voice to cry "*Viva Santa Anna!*" He was riding a *mustang* mare. He had caught the horse just recently and we had the opportunity to observe the Mexican method of breaking a horse.

When the catcher of the *mustangs* comes to a broad open space where there are few trees, he throws his *cabestro,* the *lazo* of the Brazilians, over the front legs of the horse to be trained and ties them together. The horse is already wearing a bridle without a bit. Fastened to the bridle is a wide piece of leather that one can push down over the horse's eyes. As soon as that is done, another trainer throws things at the horse's head or legs. The horse reacts wildly and tries to flee. It arches its back and kicks with its hind legs, but it is held fast by a second *cabestro* that is fastened around its neck and it falls to the ground with every violent exertion. As soon as the horse has learned in this manner that man is his master, the leather band is drawn down again over his eyes and a saddle is placed on his back. This does not happen the first few times without the animal resisting. Then the rider mounts the horse and carefully removes the leather band from its eyes. At that moment the dance begins and it does not end until the horse and his rider fall to the ground. This is continued as long as the horse resists, but soon the animal becomes tired and more patient. His rider who until then had always let him feel the spur now treats the horse with more kindness. Soon the horse catches his breath and the chase begins all over again. It goes on like this day after day until, if one of them, horse and rider, does not break his neck, the first phase of training is over and the more refined phase begins.

Our first day's journey extended past nightfall and the weather, which had recently been so extremely mild that it was a pleasure to sleep under the stars, changed during the night. A north wind brought rain and cold, and made the second day [of travel] very unpleasant. In the course of that day we saw many wild horses. About three o'clock we reached the river valley of the Rio Grande again. It is about three to five miles wide, one hundred to two hundred feet deep, and it resembles an enormous gorge. In the middle are several small channels that serve as a riverbed. The slope [down to the river] is in most places so steep that it makes the drive downhill impossible [for wagons]. Several hours work cleared a roadway for us through trees and brush and we put the slope in such a condition that it was, of course, difficult but not impossible to descend. Everything went along fine. The difference between the vegetation growing on the plain above and in the riverbed is striking. At the river level, the trees, bushes, and other plants are twice as tall as those on the plain. Below, everything looks more vital and vigorous.

Only a few thousand paces from here we found the Rio San Juan and set up camp there. An investigation of the ford revealed it to be very difficult and troublesome, due in part to the river's depth and due in part to the mud there. Consequently, another ford located a few miles upstream was investigated by our guides and found to be good. While they were there, they saw some Indians on the opposite bank who were busy trapping beaver. Our guides spoke to the Indians, but since they spoke no Spanish, they were not able to get an answer. The next morning we set out early in order to get to the Rio Grande. I was not happy to bid farewell to this beautiful valley. I was wishing that I could have such a place as this for a farm. (The valley forms here a semicircle, and on the front of the curve the river is enclosed by beautiful, tall trees. The land is as flat as a tabletop and as fertile as one could wish for.)

After several hours we crossed the San Juan River at a very good spot and immediately paid the Indians there a visit. They belong to the same tribe of Shawnees as those we had seen on the Rio Frio. There were four of them and a Scotsman who had been living with them for some years. They were distinctive for their large, powerful, and good-looking physical build. I estimate that all of them were six feet tall. They are the mortal enemies of the

Comanches and they give no quarter to each other [in battle], but they are greatly feared by the Comanches. They are brave and well armed. Each one had a long American musket, a *tomahawk*, and a long knife. Mr. Beales tried to strike a bargain with them to trap beaver for him, but they did not want to agree to it. Instead, they promised to follow after us later and to spend some time with us in camp.

We continued on our march then, following the river basin upstream and keeping the higher region on our left. It was not separated from the valley here by a steep slope like it had been the day before. Here it consisted of several hills that were covered by pebbles of all different colors. On the other hand, there were very few trees there, but the ground seemed to consist of very fertile soil. Our oxen were very fatigued, so for that reason we abandoned the effort to reach the [Rio Grande] River that same day, and also, because we were still uncertain about the condition of the ford across the river. Two places had to be examined first in order to choose the better one. The next morning Mr. Beales hurried off at daybreak with the guides, but they came back after a few hours with the report that the one ford would require days of work just to get down to it. The other one was bad, to be sure, but it would be easier to use for crossing. Consequently, we set out on the road to the one a few miles higher upstream. Our *hunter*, [Mr.] Duty, shot a large black female bear while she was in her lair nursing three young ones. The dead bear and the young survivors were all loaded on the carts and brought along after the train. I was curious to see the river and my thirst was also urging me to hurry. Consequently, I rode ahead with Antonio, one of our Mexican servants. He is the favorite of everyone in the caravan. He is extremely eager to please and is helpful to everyone. He is always amusing and cheerful, always giving us something to laugh at and to talk about. He is especially friendly to the ladies, to whom he pays court with the gallantry of a thirteenth-century knight.

We found a lot of rattlesnakes and killed several of the larger ones. Each time it was a fun time for Antonio and very amusing [for me] to watch when he spotted one and jumped from his horse to go jumping and dancing after it, calling after it with his nice expressions to stop and coil. And then, as he approached it, he struck it several times with the handle of his *kantschu* [knout] which he was holding by the braided end. When it lay stunned upon the ground, he placed his foot on the snake's head, pulled off the rattles, grasped the body, and pulled on it until the head separated from it.

That is the same maneuver that I use myself to kill snakes, but in view of the danger involved, I have a great advantage in my cowhide boots over Antonio, who was wearing only a few scraps of rawhide tied to his feet with thongs. If the snake has just enough room to turn his head a little, Antonio would get bitten for sure. He showed me several scars on his arm where he had been honored with bites, but he had healed them himself with an herb. He promised to show it to me, but he has not yet kept his word. I had the good fortune to kill a snake of extraordinary size. It had fourteen rings on its rattle and was very fat. I skinned it in order to dry the hide and Antonio remarked that the snake was good to eat. Until then I had no idea that the Mexicans also eat them. I gave it to him so that it could be prepared that evening and invited myself to supper with him. There were two new dishes awaiting me that evening—roasted bear and roasted snake. On account of the first dish I might be envied by many people, but on account of the second one probably by few. About three o'clock we reached the Rio Grande and dropped anchor just short of the riverbed. Right away Mr. Beales rode along the river with the guides to find the ford and they did not return until after nightfall. He was not particularly satisfied with the result and the guides, although they were on horseback, had been up to their necks in water.

Everybody was called on to help out the next day making the way down to the ford passable and to expect a hard day's work. In the meantime, the bear was skinned and the meat distributed. Everyone was busy trying to prepare his portion as well as possible. It yielded, by the way, an extraordinary amount of fat, all with a pleasant taste. I would probably prefer the meat from a young bear to the best beef, and I had to force myself to stop eating it in order to save some room for the second dish. We had put the snake on a stick that we placed at an angle over the fire so that most of the fat, which had a bad taste, ran down [and dripped off]. The meat itself was very dry and I cannot recommend it to any gourmet.

On March 12, the bell called us all early at daybreak from our sleep. Breakfast was quickly prepared and everyone hurried off to work with axes, shovels, mattocks, and spades. First of all, the two slopes that formed the top portion of the riverbed were cut down. Then we had to cut through a dense thicket of vines and willows which were growing in hundred-foot wide strips along the river. Then the road went through tall grass, six to eight feet high, that had been mostly burned down the day before. Then it went upstream to a wooded spot, where our axes again cut a way two to three thousand paces in length through vines, willows, and other trees. We had to fill in some deep holes and again there was another slope to cut down. The last obstacle was a thick patch of willows. As we came out of this thicket, we found ourselves on the narrow riverbank, which consisted of two ridges of sand thrown up there when the river flooded. We cut through them in a few minutes. So, in less than three hours we had made the whole stretch passable in a makeshift fashion, about an English mile in its length. The Mexican carts, at the front of the caravan, had to do the rest.

Then we broke camp. Half of the wagons were brought down to the river, and a portion of each [wagon's] load was removed. Each of the wagons was given one extra pair of oxen and they entered the river being led by one of the guides who was riding ahead of them all. The route went at first straight ahead, but then it turned to the right and went onto a long sand-bank that ran along in the middle of the river. From there the ford went some distance downstream in the middle of the river. Then, after traversing the deepest part of the river, it angled off to the left toward the opposite bank. The ford must have been two to three thousand feet in its length. In order not to have another misfortune, I decided to investigate the river myself before I went through there with my wagon. [During my inspection] I noticed that there was a dangerous spot where the wagons left the sand-bank. One Mexican cart had come dangerously close to overturning there, and my own wagon, without a doubt, would have tipped over at that place. So, I unsaddled my horse, rode out there and back, and found that every-thing would go well if the oxen could be kept under control. The greatest depth was three and a half feet. I left half of my load on the bank, but took a few of the Germans on my wagon and did not accept the extra pair of oxen. Tallör was standing on the wagon shaft [as we set out]. I rode out ahead of the oxen, and everything was going well until we were beyond the sand-bank and had entered the deep water. The oxen, as they saw the firm land to their left, wanted to turn off in that direction, but I was trying everything I could to steer them back, because the wagon and the oxen would have cer-tainly been lost in the deep water. I succeeded too, but then they turned to the other, more hazardous side. I had to ride around behind the wagon to that side, which was very difficult due to the strong force of the current. It was very slow going, but I made it all the way from one side around to the other. By now, my horse and I were both fatigued. With half of my body wet from the water and the other half bathed in sweat, I could not master the sit-uation alone. Tallör, who could not swim, was terribly afraid of the water. Notwithstanding that, he was of even less help in such situations, since he easily loses his head. Finally, after ten minutes of sustained effort, during which time my wagon was in danger several times of breaking or of being overturned, I succeeded in getting the oxen under control and moving again. I arrived safely on the riverbank and then at the place chosen for our campsite. I had just arrived there when a young Mexican came running up calling for help for his father who was about to drown. We rushed down to the river and saw that he had already been rescued on the other side with two of his oxen. The other oxen, however, had been lost with the cart. He [the Mexican man] had met me on the bank as he was coming back to bring along the rest of his load. He had dared to drive his oxen alone in the expec-tation that they would follow the cart ahead of them as they usually had done. But they did not like resisting the strong current, and at the same spot where I had had such trouble with my oxen, they had continued on straight ahead and he had been unable to keep them on the right path. In order to save himself, he had quickly cut the traces on the lead pair, grabbed onto them, and let them bring him back to the bank.

Some people were immediately ordered to cut down the twenty to thirty foot high bank of the river, in order to create an exit path for the oxen and their driver who had been rescued. This incident did not make a good impression on the others. When I went back through the current to pick up the other half of my baggage, I took the precaution of placing a pair of Mr. Beales's oxen in front of my wagon in the expectation that they would lead better than the front pair of my own, one of which was skittish and the other one was weak and lazy. But I was disappointed in them, for they refused to go directly against the current and I was even less capable of controlling this lengthier team of three pair of oxen as well as I had the original team of two pair. I worked my way back over the sandbank, where every effort to drive the oxen any further proved futile, and my horse, which was tired now of all the toil, was trying with all his might to throw me off. He would not let me do anything with him. In my moment of distress, Marzelino, the hero of the lagoons, came to my aid. Five minutes later I was safely on the other bank. Quickly I loaded up the rest of my baggage and several passengers, among them Mr. Beales, and I moved on this time quickly and without further delay with the rest of the wagons. The Shawnee Indians were riding now at the head of the column. They had caught up with us the day before and camped in our vicinity. It was a beautiful sight the way these tall dark figures went striding through the rushing current, one behind the other with their packhorses between them. They went along silently and apparently indifferent to everything that was going on around them. They camped in our vicinity again [that night].

The next morning, since we were having a day of rest, I paid them a visit and talked for a long time with the Scotsman. They were just preparing to leave and travel deeper into the interior of the country. Their faces had been painted with a sort of rust color as a sign that that they were now in the enemy's territory, committed to a war with the Comanches, and were expecting to encounter them. Konukop, the chief, had ornamented his long, black, curly and wavy hair with the feathers of a white predatory bird.[1] Another Indian, a younger man, had wound about his head a white cotton cloth in the style of a turban. They were busy cleaning their weapons when the tranquility was interrupted by a weapon being carelessly fired in our camp. The bullet whizzed closely by over our heads and suddenly, like a stroke of magic, I saw the living figures [of these Indians] transformed into statues. They were sitting there without a sign of life. Only their keen eyes

---

[1] No information could be found to identify Konukop in this context.

were searching all around through the surrounding countryside for a concealed enemy. Slowly they lowered their arms and hands to their knees and leaned forward again with their upper body. After a brief pause, which passed in silence, they discovered the true cause of the shot and each one went back to his work without saying a single word about the incident. Soon afterwards we saw these proud figures traveling fearlessly into the prairie, unconcerned but not carefree, as they braved the thousands of the enemy tribe whom they hold in contempt, but they do not expose themselves needlessly either to danger.

That day several Mexicans arrived who had been hired as guards to see after security in the colony. Another hunter arrived also, a North American by birth, who was supposed to shoot game for us. His wife, a Mexican woman with her small son on her arm, [was with him and] accompanies him on his hunting expeditions. She was riding also, of course, for no one travels on foot in this country. That same day we ate the last of our cornmeal. We had run out of wheat flour already in Presidio. So, from then on everyone was going to have to grind his own cornmeal with the handmill. Meat had become a rarity in camp long ago. The hunters' attempts to procure some meat for us were for the most part unsuccessful. It was the same situation with other food items: sugar, coffee, tea, and lard. There was a shortage of corn too. We decided not to give any more to the horses until the arrival of some food supplies for our households that had been purchased in San Fernando, a town about seventy m[iles] from here.[2] So, the food supplies here, that according to Mr. Beales's calculations were supposed to cover our needs for three months after arriving in Dolores, are already used up.

The Mexican carts had already left, and consequently, we had to carry all of our baggage the rest of the journey [from the river] on our own wagons. That portion of the baggage that we could do without most easily remained on the riverbank under the supervision of Mr. Addicks and some Mexican guards. It will be picked up as soon as the first load is delivered to its destination. Our guide is now Zapata, the commander of our escort. I never come into this man's presence without becoming lost for a short while in his appearance. His proud, lean, six-foot frame, his extraordinarily delicate and yet masculine, handsome, and pale features, together with his carefully parted raven hair falling down to his shoulders in natural curls gives him the most perfect Christ-like appearance. That image and his noble bearing

---

[2] San Fernando was a small farming village on the south side of the Rio Grande. In the fourteenth letter, Ludecus recounts visiting the community, which he thought might serve as a model for San Fernando. San Fernando had a complete irrigation system and a considerable stand of tall protective trees. Ludecus, *Reise*, 220–221. See also, the fourteenth letter.

inspire in everyone who approaches him respect and, I would almost say, subservience. But when this clear, sincere face and his quiet, gentle eyes are once aroused by some passion, they blaze with fire. When the evil intent of his soul is written in the expressive features of his face, those around him turn away in fear. They recognize probably that in this man both God and the devil dwell. He is lame, and when he rides, he places his left foot under his body and sits on it, but rides along confidently and boldly. Earlier [in his life] he had been captured by Indians. When they spared his life, he pretended for three years to serve them submissively and married a *squaw*, until he lulled them into relaxing their vigilance over him, and then he fled. His absence was discovered, of course, and they pursued him and wounded him, but then he escaped successfully. He speaks the language of the Comanches and is supposed to make an attempt to establish a friendly relationship between us and them. I am sure he will succeed. Indeed, the Comanches will be our friends until they see some advantage in cutting all our throats or just get the idea to do so.

Our course lay to the northwest and soon we reached a tableland from where we could see the hill Las Moras. At its base originates the stream by the same name. Some distance to one side we could see the Piedras Pintas and more to the north another hill.[3] In this area one of the loyal guards of our caravan was bitten by a rattlesnake and he died in spite of the measures taken. Strangely enough, a young hunting dog that had been bitten first by the same snake survived. Our march that day was short, and in order to avoid a lot of unnecessary wandering around, it was decided to investigate the entire length of the stream and then to go immediately to the best spot.

The next morning all the men left the caravan and I was given the responsibility of leading the wagons by the shortest route to the stream. I would have gladly gone with them if the bruises [on my body] that had become aggravated during the incident on the Rio Grande had not prevented it. About two o'clock we reached the stream at a brushy spot. The riders came back before nightfall and they were all very satisfied with the place chosen by Mr. Egerton. But the next morning they rode out again downstream to investigate that end of the stream while I went upstream with the wagons. There was no doubt that the upstream site would be selected. A few hours later the riders caught up to us again. Everybody continued now merrily on their way. Scattered stands of trees marked the course of the stream and everybody was happy to see finally the end of our weari-

[3] Beales describes the hills of Las Moras and Piedras Pintas as the source of the Nueces and Rio Frio rivers. "The Moras is composed of a very dark granite, and a fine species of soft limestone. It is situated about four miles from the head waters of Las Moras, and twelve from our village." Kennedy, *Texas*, 416 (quotation).

some journey. Every five minutes one could hear someone calling to Zapata, "*Adónde está la villa?*" (Where is the town?) In response, he would point to a distant wooded spot. Others called out: "*In what hotel are you going to stop at—the hotel of clear sky?*" And others asked: "*What are they going to play tonight?*" Jack Clops's answer to this was: "*Poor life in Texas.*"

So, the joking went on until we turned off from the prairie down into the valley and reached a brushy area. After traveling for a half hour among scattered wooded spots and savannas (meadows that are at times under water), we finally came out onto a large meadow. It was bordered on the right by a small patch of woods and on the left by the stream, or rather it was enclosed in a circular fashion [by the stream]. The small patch of woods was designated as the spot where the town was supposed to be built. We set up camp off in the brush a bit, and we had hardly finished with that chore when a thunderstorm passed over us. Was this perhaps a bad omen? For quite a while I have been seeing stormy temperatures in the faces of many of the people arriving and should more of such heated vapors gather, a thunderstorm could form and a windstorm could blow everything away. But I do not want to make any predictions, for my nurse used to tell me that such stuff was all nonsense and she was a wise woman.

After the rain had passed, everyone went quickly to work clearing the designated spot. A square was cut clear and the thorns, bushes, and trees were piled up in a wall around us to protect us from an Indian attack. We arrived here yesterday morning and today we sent the wagons back to the river [to fetch the rest of the baggage]. Right now *dinner is ready.* The *ladies and gentlemen* are very hungry. So, *adieu* for now.

TWELFTH LETTER
*Emergence of the Town Dolores. Swearing Allegiance to the Mexican
Constitution. Election of a Town Council and the Resulting Intrigues.
Celebrations of the Indians and Mexicans. Dr. Beales's Trip Back to
New York, in order to bring Money and Settlers.*

Dolores, March 30, 1834

Today is Sunday. The inhabitants of the town of Dolores are strolling on
the boulevard. The ladies are discussing the latest fashions and the gentlemen are talking about the state of affairs at the royal residence. But here I
sit in my *parlour*, with my mattock, spade, and ax standing in the corner. But
I am not spending the day of idleness loafing about. On the contrary, I have
decided to be very busy and write a lot of news for you all. I hope this letter will make a boring Sunday afternoon hour pass more quickly for you.

What a strange creature man is! When I look up from this writing paper
and see through the holes in my wall of tree trunks the finely dressed people outside, I feel compelled to suppose that the hot Mexican sun has damaged their brains. Why have these foolish people searched through their
trunks and boxes, unpacked and put on their black frock coats, their embroidered shirts with the tall stiff collars, and their round felt hats which after a
few hours they will just put away again? As I see them parading around in
their formal clothing and dripping with sweat (for it is quite warm today),
they remind me of turkeys that have been scalded in hot water [for plucking]. Six days of the week they go about so dirty that one would think Circe
had been practicing her [magic] arts of transformation on them.[1] But on the
seventh they put on their best caparison so that they can show the ragtag
commoners that they are better somehow, although they have all been wallowing in the same dirt for the [other] six days. I just heard Mr. Plunkett say
that all he needs today to be completely happy is to be able to go to church.
The good man forgot to bring along the church from New York. But it does
not occur to him here in nature's magnificence and under the clear blue sky
that he is standing in the most beautiful church in the world, nor that one
can pray just as well here and even much better than within four walls and
among a thousand curious people. But here his piety is not on display, his
prayer is not overheard, and others do not catch the scent of his perfumed
handkerchief. The foolishness of these people follows after them like the tail
of a comet. I believe they are afraid that they will not be blessed if they cannot be dressed better on Sunday than on Saturday and Monday. On the

---

[1] Circe, daughter of Helios and the Oceanid Perse in Homer's *Odyssey*, was a powerful sorceress who lived on the island of Aesea and turned men into swine. Hornblower
and Spawforth (eds.), *Oxford Classical Dictionary*, 332.

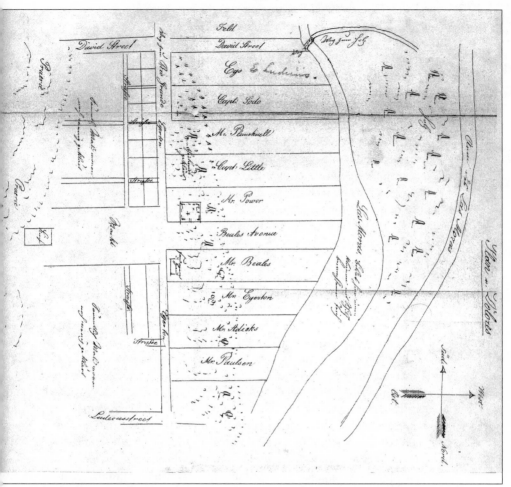

This sketch of the layout of La Villa de Dolores, drawn by Eduard Ludecus, is affixed to the rear cover of his personal copy of his published letters. *Courtesy of S. Stemmons, Dallas.*

other hand, I am an awful free thinker and for sure I am going to be condemned in all eternity because I put on clean clothes when I need to. I leave off my jacket and frock coat and I go about only in my shirt sleeves unconcerned about what day the calendar says it is while others are stewing in the sun. I wanted to write something new for you all, but this is something you can observe for yourselves every day. So, I am going to break off here in order to report what has been happening here since my last letter.

Our first chore was to get a roof over our heads as quickly as possible. A lot of huts went up quickly in the *square* (quadrangle); they are constructed of tree trunks and branches and covered with grass or reeds.[2] The immediate area around the *square* was completely cleared and the old grass on the meadows was burned in order to allow new grass to grow. Mornings and evenings one can hear the report of rifles and shotguns along the stream. Hundreds of wild turkeys live in the trees here and provide us with tasty roasted meat, although they have lately become scarce because so much gunsmoke has driven them away. Several of the men undertook an expedition to the stream's source and to the top of Las Moras mountain in order to survey the [surrounding] territory.

Unfortunately, I was prevented from going with them by my bruises which bother me now and then. Mr. Beales, who originally intended to stay here a few months, has been hurrying to take care of the most urgent business, so that he can go immediately via Matamoros to New York, partly to send back some money from the the former city and a second expedition of *settlers* from the latter. Both seem to me very necessary to keep this young colony alive. I fear, however, that his departure will have dire consequences, for his personality did a great deal to maintain the trust of the somewhat discontented settlers. Mr. Egerton, who is now managing the whole enterprise in his place, does not seem to me the man to replace him.

Several points were quickly marked off in a survey, in order to demarcate the first streets and plazas which will be named after the [colony's] officers. I have not yet visited *Ludecus Street*. I will do so when the street is lined with beautiful palaces and when it is as long as the Friedrich Straße in Berlin.[3] Without a doubt that will not take long if I can believe the exalted opinion of certain gentlemen [here].

So, the twenty-seventh [of March] drew near, the day when the cornerstone of the church was being laid. It had been brought here by horses. I do not know how far it had been brought, for there is no stone in the vicinity.

---

[2] See Note 17 to the eighth letter.

[3] In 1834, the Friedrich Straße in Berlin was noted for its extraordinary length. Ludecus is convinced that his street will never be as long or as famous as the street in Berlin. Ludecus, *Reise*, 180.

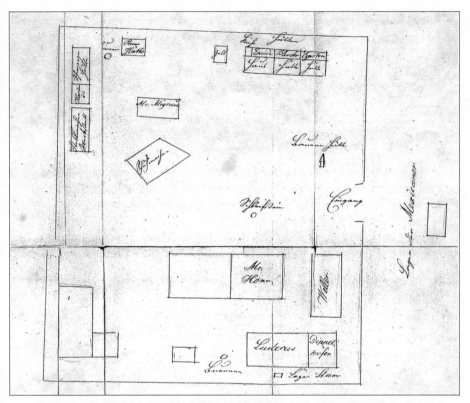

This sketch of the layout of La Villa de Dolores, drawn by Eduard Ludecus, is one of the drawings affixed to the rear cover of his personal copy of his published letters. *Courtesy of S. Stemmons, Dallas.*

Each of the *settlers* was going to swear allegiance to the constitution in order to be recorded as a citizen of Mexico. Early in the day, about nine o'clock, the bell began ringing to call all the inhabitants of the town together. Following behind the flags and the cornerstone, etc., the men marched to the church plaza, where, consecrated by our prayers, the cornerstone was laid and Mr. Beales made a short speech. Then came the dispensing of the Madeira wine that had been saved for this celebration. Each one of us received several glasses of wine that we drank as we toasted the happiness and prosperity of the small colony. Then Captain Soto, as the government's commissioner, accepted the civil oath from each one of us as we knelt before him. Then, after spitting out our tobacco wads, we raised our voices in a *Viva!* to Mexico and its inhabitants. In return, the members of the Mexican guard who were present responded with a *Vivan los Americanos!* They were joined in their salute to us by the Shawnee Indians present whose numbers had [recently] been increased by another Shawnee band.

Then everyone hurried back to our interim town, for the municipal council was supposed to be elected. According to [Mexican] law, the council consists of an *alcalde*, a *regidor primo*, a *regidor segundo*, and a *syndico*. This varies according to whether a town has many or few inhabitants. Thus, there can be two or three *alcaldes* in one city. Court is held publicly. The [two opposing] parties appear with their *hombres buenos*, [that is], their mediators, one of which has been chosen by each of the two parties and whose job it is to bring about an amicable settlement. If they do not succeed, then the trial commences. The two parties interrogate each other and the witnesses for and against each of the parties. The *alcalde* or a clerk records the proceedings and when all that is finished, the court makes its decision. A majority rules. In the case of a tie, the *alcalde's* vote is decisive. The *alcalde* can also hold court and make decisions alone, and this is what happens most frequently. Appeals are heard before the supreme court of the province. Furthermore, the *alcalde* has the power to delay the court's decision by a half hour, if he believes that the hot tempers will cool off and be amenable to making a settlement. Then he proposes first of all what he considers an appropriate compromise, and only after this has been rejected does he pass judgment to the full extent of the law. Although there is much to praise about this method of justice, the power the *alcalde* possesses to influence the process and to make decisions without consulting his colleagues is reprehensible. The situation is made worse by the extreme difficulty of appealing a judgment to a higher court. It is a lengthy and expensive procedure if the appellant does not live by chance where the supreme court is located. In general, too much power is given to the *alcalde*, and according to what I hear, it is often abused.

The elections were extremely lively, as the aristocrats and the democrats squared off for the contest. But there were few voters present who were not directly dependent on Mr. Beales and Mr. Power for giving some of them work or paying the annual salary of others. The few independents among the voters were afraid that these two gentlemen and their relatives, that is, the company and the owners of this land, would have this position [of *alcalde*] and all the judicial power in their hands. In order to prevent this, it had been made known already the day before the elections, and in our tent that same evening, that there were plans to elect Mr. Pepin as the *alcalde*. Mr. Beales was nevertheless too popular for there to be any real concern that the attempt would succeed. On the other hand, there was no doubt that Mr. Pepin would get one of the other posts, possibly the position of *regidor primo*, and he would act as deputy *alcalde* after Mr. Beales's departure. But Mr. Beales had intended for this post to go to Mr. Egerton and the second one to Mr. Plunkett. There was yet the last post to be filled also, and Mr. Power, the presumptive choice, was not particularly popular with one party or the other. I believe that Mr. Beales was not unhappy to see that he [Power] might fail to be elected, so that he could present this to the company in New York as proof of Mr. Power's unpopularity among the settlers. Mr. Beales himself wished to see Mr. Egerton instead of Mr. Power as company commissioner, for already during our journey there had been some differences between the two men, not insignificant differences, but lately they seem to have been smoothed out. On the other hand, it would have been unpleasant for Mr. Beales if Mr. Power were completely rejected, since he could feel insulted as a result. The cause for Mr. Power's lack of popularity, however, was his personality more than his politics, for overall he behaved more like a democrat and often exhibited too great an affinity with the lower classes. The greatest contributing factor here may have been that one wanted to make him unpopular for the very reasons cited above. I had planned to remain neutral during all the elections, for I was to some extent still unsure whether I would stay or not, and the whole business seemed to me to a certain extent unimportant, since in a small, new colony like ours laws and their enforcement are beyond discussion. Of course, there can be and have to be adequate laws. But who is going to be there to enforce compliance or to punish the transgressors? On this point, extreme forbearance is needed to maintain a colony.

Even the manner of voting was the subject of a debate. The aristocrats wanted votes to be cast orally before the government's commissioner. The democrats, on the other hand, wanted to write down their votes and place them in an urn. Preparations had already been made for the latter procedure when Captain Soto stepped forward and declared the former method to be the one prescribed by law. Then Mr. Pepin stepped up to the *rostrum* and began haranguing the people by suggesting some candidates for office. But the people were not satisfied with them and shouted back several times with a thunderous "*No! No!*" and shouting that he was trying to have illegal influence on the elections. That drove our Cicero from the stage. Then, a tailor who had come with Mr. Egerton from the capital jumped up to speak from his own rostrum, a clumsy old wagon that could carry about twelve people. "Who buys votes?" he shouted. "Here I have a whole load of them for six *reales* apiece. What? Are there no takers? Do you think that I have riffraff here? These are nothing but refined gentlemen here," and so on. With that he pulled from the wagon one of the young bears such as we raise [in Germany]. "There is not a *bull* among them" (an obvious reference to the *bull* and the bear at the London stock exchange). A roar of laughter greeted the tailor as he sprang from his wagon following his clever joke.

In the meantime, the elections had begun. Mr. Beales was elected *alcalde* and the announcement was received with a shout of "hurrah!" But then the contest began again. Mr. Egerton and Mr. Pepin each received an equal number of votes for first *regidor*. Mr. Wilson, the [Georges Jacques] Danton of Dolores, had quickly counted the party members of the left and called out that there must be eighteen votes for Mr. Pepin instead of seventeen.[4] But no one paid any attention to him. The matter between the two candidates was to be decided by a drawing of lots. The democrats suggested that the decisive vote should be cast by an absent settler who was expected [to return] that evening. They were sure that he would vote for Pepin. But this suggestion was rejected. Captain Soto declared that the law determines the procedure for [a tied vote]. The procedure was that both candidates turn to a page in a book. The first letter on the left-hand page determines the winner. The candidate whose letter is nearer to the letter A beats the other candidate. That was the law. Pepin lost and the aristocrats gave loud voice to their pleasure at the outcome. Captain Little expressed his pleasure in a way that was insulting to Mr. Pepin and the two had an exchange of words. This persuaded me to toss aside my neutrality and side with the offended party. Pepin was elected second *regidor* and drove Mr. Power from the field. Captain Little was punished by losing several bets that he had made on Mr. Power being elected.

Then the last post came up [for election]. Mr. Power was again a candidate. Herr Paulsen came to me and told me that the people would elect me. I asked him to prevent it, but he seemed to be already arranging it himself. I was not able to do anything about it and was proclaimed *syndico* or people's magistrate. I thanked everyone for their confidence in me, and with that the elections in Dolores were concluded. Everyone gathered for the noon meal which was begun almost in silence. But the wine soon loosened up the tongues. The gentlemen who had not been elected put on a good face about it and played the fox who could not reach the grapes. Delicious treats had been saved for this day, and the goose liver, the chicken pies from Paris, with the Madeira and finally the champagne put everyone in good spirits. After dinner we had the Indians come into our tent and they sang their *war song* and other songs, danced, and drank Madeira. Everyone was quite *tipsy* when we broke up to go our separate ways.

That evening there was a concert and a ball. Huh, I see your long faces and your turned-up noses that seem to say, "That must have been a beautiful concert and an even more beautiful ball." But just keep quiet. If I had in some measure the talent to depict for you with half the vividness necessary what my eyes saw and what my ears heard, and were it possible to give you

---

[4] Beales records only the results of those elections that were "received by cheering." J. C. Beales was elected *alcalde*; W. H. Egerton became first *regidor*; V. Pepin was elected second *regidor*; and E. Ludecus was elected *syndico*. Kennedy, *Texas*, 417.

the choice, you would for sure leave the concert where [Nicolo] Paganini was playing or the ball where [Henriette] Sontag[-Rossi] was singing and dancing in order to be able to be present at our events.[5] I will try to give you a vague image of them.

First of all, imagine yourselves under the eternally clear and celestially pure skies of the tropics. It is night. There are countless stars in the heavens. Thousands of fireflies appear and disappear, illuminating the air and making it grow dark again. A slight breeze, scarcely perceptible, keeps the temperature of the air moderately cool and disperses the almost excessively strong perfumes of the countless sweet-smelling flowers and plants. In the middle of a small forest of oaks and nut trees with a luxuriant growth of wild grape vines and other vines trailing among the branches, shading the treetops with their leaves, you see by the light of a large fire that is blazing up near a thick wall of thorns and tree branches the prominent thatched roofs of a small village. Around the fire you see sitting, standing, or lying in a semicircle some men and women, boys, girls, and children, the masters and their servants, Englishmen and Scotsmen, Irishmen, Germans, Frenchmen, and North Americans in a colorful blend. Also, there are the Mexicans, Zapata and his subordinates: they are lying there half-naked on their animal hides. Behind them are their huts with thatched roofs, and hanging on the walls of the huts you can see their saddles, bridles, *cabestros* and *calabazas*. Painters could find here in Zapata and his companions some striking models for biblical figures, for Abraham, Jacob, and their servants must have also enjoyed their leisure in this way too after a day's hard work. Their sunburned faces and bodies form a natural transition from the whites to the Indians sitting next to them and completing the circle. One can see these tall dark figures sitting on recently cut tree trunks. The bright light of the fire is hardly able to make the dark brown figures distinguishable and visible before the dark background. They are singing their *war song*, as they beat a rhythm with wooden sticks that they hold in their hands. In the distance one can see dimly illuminated a couple of sentries posted for safety against hostile Indians. They have horses tied there ready for momentary service, and nearby dogs and a couple of tame bears are playing. In the middle of the small circle, the Indian chief,

---

[5] Nicolo Paganini (1782–1840) was an Italian violinist and composer, renowned throughout Europe, including Italy, Germany, England, Scotland, and Vienna. In Vienna he was named royal Chamber Virtuoso. Brockhaus. *Die Enzyklopädie*, 24 vols. (Leipzig: F. A. Brockhaus, 1996), XVI, 463.

Henriette Sontag-Rossi (1806–1854) was a soprano soloist in Vienna who also performed in Berlin, Paris, the U.S., and Mexico City, where she died in 1854. Gitta Günther, et al. (eds.), *Weimar: Lexikon zur Stadtgeschichte* (Weimar: Verlag Hermann Böhlaus Nachfolger, 1998), 403–404.

Konukop, a famous warrior and dancer of his tribe, is dancing the war dance with short measured leaps around the fire. He is tall with a lean, but powerful body. His head is covered with a wig made from the mane of a horse. His gleaming eye, like the eye of a falcon, is shaded by heavy, prominent eyebrows that are already beginning to grow gray. His aquiline nose, the delicate mouth graced by a thin mustache, and the copper-brown skin of his naked torso that is vividly illuminated by the fire lend his whole appearance a demoniacal and dread-inspiring quality. In his right hand he is holding a *tomahawk*, a small hatchet, in front of his chest poised for attack or for defense. His left hand is braced against his side. Keeping every member, every muscle in constant motion, for herein lies the beauty of the Indian's dance, he moves, turning first to the right, then to the left, and often turning back, he moves around the fire until he returns to the same spot from where he started. Here he suddenly stops and with all the force he is capable of, he erupts in a war cry. The other Indians and the Mexicans who have learned it in captivity among the Indians join in. The others who are lying nearby jump up startled, for it sounds as if hell itself is threatening to erupt and release its captive spirits. Words are not able to describe these sounds. But whoever hears them once will never forget the impression they make. The human speech organs can scarcely produce anything more terrifying, more horrible than this *war whoop* uttered by a dozen Indians and which can be heard over an incredible distance.

After the chief has repeated the dance two or three times, another Indian suddenly leaps forward from among the huts of the Mexicans. In stature this man is every bit the equal of the chief, but is not as lean. He is in the prime of his life—possibly twenty-four years old and resembles the image of Achilles. As a model for that youthful hero of antiquity, the symmetry of this man's limbs and his handsome facial features leave nothing to be desired. He is scarcely of pure Indian ancestry. He has the build of an Indian, but the head of a European. He is painted with the war paint of a hostile Indian.

Then the dance begins anew. One dancer following the other, they circle the fire. Their song and their dance grow constantly more intense until one or the other dancer leaves the circle exhausted.

Now the Mexicans take their turn, and the *fandango* commences. However, I must admit that this is the weaker portion of our *soirée*. The rules of the art of the French dance have not yet penetrated the desolate regions of the Rio Grande. Their song consists of recitatives and is performed in a falsetto voice with a terrible tremelo. It is astonishing that a people who speak such a beautiful language can abuse it so in song. The dance is followed by games. The evening is concluded with a few English, French, and German songs. Then each person steals away to his hut, in order to fly away to his homeland in the arms of Morpheus. There in his dreams he tells [his friends] about the dream that brought him to the wilderness of Mexico to live under her beautiful skies and among her hideous savages.

But not everything is so pleasant. The innocent pleasures are very often spoiled by the thought that a Comanche is sneaking up out of the nearby brush to fire a fatal arrow into the circle of unsuspecting settlers. Over there a buzzing rattlesnake is threatening with a deadly bite the person jumping back in fear. In the grass there is a poison tarantula walking along, and here is the even more dangerous scorpion. Meanwhile, maybe there is an ambling bear or a cunning panther prowling around the woods and threatening to attack the person who goes out there alone. But familiarity makes these things in time acceptable. The Indians are the only living beings here who can still inspire fear and, commensurate with our expectations, will present great obstacles to the flourishing of the colony.

This was our concert and ball. Whoever thinks that he could like it is invited to some similar celebrations a year from today. But I must tell you beforehand that if the weather is bad, you all must go back home, for my palace is too small to shelter many guests. On the other hand, whoever sleeps out in the open as is customary here can stay as long as he wants.

The day before yesterday Mr. Beales called each of the *settlers* into his tent to present to him the papers of his *installation*. One hundred and seventy-seven acres or one Spanish *labor* in addition to a lot in the town, called a *town lot*, 300 feet wide and about 1,300 to 1,500 feet [in length] down to the creek were granted to me by the company. Every *settler* coming into the colony at his own expense is entitled to the first piece of land, but the second one, intended for one's farmstead, consists actually of a piece of land only ninety feet long and sixty feet wide. Those of us who acted as officers on the journey here received some preferential treatment. Given the local circumstances, this second piece is obviously too small. Once a house and a farmyard are established on it, there is very little room for planting [foods to eat]. Given the lack of personal safety here, how can the farmer be expected to go far from the town alone or even to live on his *rancho*? I have to confess that in general the views held by the owners of the colony are somewhat incomprehensible to me. How can they expect [to attract] *settlers* when they place conditions on colonists here that are much less advantageous than for colonists in other colonies that are far better located with better living conditions than ours? Other colonies that are located nearer to the sea and to civilization give a family one square mile of land and a single man a quarter of that in addition to two acres as a town lot.[6] Now for what reason would

[6] In 1824, the legislature of Coahuila and Texas passed a colonization law that allotted one *labor* (177 acres) of land to a married man who wanted to farm, and twenty-four *labores* (4,251 acres) if he wanted to raise cattle. Altogether, he could receive one *sitio*

he [a colonist] prefer that? Certainly they will be able to bring enough people here who are ignorant of these conditions, but it is equally certain that those people will leave as soon as they learn about the other colonies.

When Mr. Beales asked me whether I wanted to remain here as a *settler*, I was able to give him only an indefinite answer. I shared with him my opinion that my expectations had not been satisfied here. I stated further that I needed to become better informed, which I had not yet had an opportunity to do, but my decision to go or to stay depended upon that. As the chief conditions [for my staying], I stated 1) that the Rio Grande become navigable for steamboats; and 2) that I be allowed to choose the thousand acres that I was of a mind to buy one English mile from the town; and 3) that I wanted timber and water there. The latter condition was granted to me immediately, and Mr. Egerton was supposed to ride out with me the next day to look over the land. But it did not happen. On the other hand, I did select my *town lot* at the southern end of town and Captain Soto is my neighbor. On the other side of my lot is a street that leads down to the creek. But it has not yet been accurately measured and I cannot report any details about it.

Yesterday Mr. Beales, Addicks, and Herr Paulsen left. They took the colony's last shillings with them to pay their travel expenses as far as Matamoros. Since the latter [Paulsen] is supposed to bring the money up here that they will draw [from a bank] there, we have to get along for five weeks without any money. We will probably have enough corn for that time, but if we cannot get anything in San Fernando on credit, and even if we can kill something with our shotguns, we will still be on short rations for a while. For my part, I am not counting on credit, for it is not known out here.

Just before Dr. Beales's departure, the cornerstone of his house was laid, and just as he had mounted his horse, he was handed a speech which expressed our gratitude and our recognition of his merit for having brought us out here safely. I was able to sign it with a good conscience in regard to his having led us here. But if it had said "for bringing the colony forth," I would have asked for six months to think it over, and—I fear—I would not have signed it. Time will tell whether my misgivings are justified or not.

At this opportunity I want to conclude this letter with a few observations about Dr. Beales. An Irishman by birth, he studied medicine at the

---

(league) containing 4,428 acres. Yet Beales granted the colonists only one *labor* for farming; perhaps he did not expect any of them to have cattle or possibly the Rio Grande and Texas Land Company was simply ungenerous in its distribution of land to the colonists. See Carl Coke Rister, *Comanche Bondage: Dr. John Charles Beales's settlement of La Villa de Dolores on Las Moras Creek in Southern Texas of the 1830's*, . . . (Lincoln: University of Nebraska Press, 1955), 79; Mary Virginia Henderson, "Minor Empresario Contracts for the Colonization of Texas, 1825–1834," 31 (July, 1927–April, 1928), 297.

University of London. Then he went to North America, and later to the capital of Mexico where he practiced medicine for seven years and married a rich young widow. He had investments in several mining companies, but he probably did not get much out of them. His excellent physical build is complemented by his strikingly handsome and interesting facial features. He combines good manners with pride, and friendliness with majestic bearing, and a knowledge of human nature with ingenuity. In social situations he is lively, almost eccentric. This is expressed chiefly in his extravagant plans. He constructs castles in the air and then abandons them, forgets them and never mentions them again, and then builds them up again when the slightest occasion presents itself. A great facility, almost carelessness in the execution of his designs are the result of the confidence he has in himself to be able to help himself in difficult situations. In all of this he is generous, somewhat vain, and perhaps even cunning. This is the man whose charming personality aroused in me the desire to be able to spend my whole life in association with him. Soon I will know more. Until then I salute you all, etc.

THIRTEENTH LETTER
Sunday Celebration in Dolores. Mode of Living and Activities of the Settlers. Entertainment. Shortages in the Colony. Discontent of the Colonists.

Dolores, April 26, 1834

It is Sunday again today. The bells of the church of *Notre Dame* began announcing it early today, and our ladies, laced up very snugly, are now strolling along like mobile church towers. The tongue of our neighbor, Mrs. Migrains (the *Xanthippe* of Dolores) has been chiming all morning.[1] Her husband, a true Socrates in patience, has another day of repentance before him. He has to do penance 365 days a year for having taken her as his spouse. But today everyone who approaches her is compelled to do penance. *Go to hell, go to hell and damnation* is a favorite exclamation of the English and the Americans; it rings through the streets of the town, penetrating even into the most private chambers of the houses. All the sinners grow pale and await the moment with trembling and trepidation when her vengeance might strike them. Even now the darkest clouds have been gathering over the house of Mr. Horn. There is a lightening flash and a strike! Who could have been less deserving than this faithful couple? The woman, who is eager to assuage the sufferings of others, grants to him who asks for it everything that such a pretty woman can give. And there is her husband who bears with such patience the burden of such heavy horns that the others have given him. Who could boast of a greater right to bear his name than Mr. Horn? Nature itself furnished the cause for Mrs. Migrains's tongue to be firing harmless shots between his horns which are still standing as immobile as a rock. Her shots are hardly able to entice even a loud bellow from this bull. This material is nonflammable. So, the source of this storm is moving on, more enraged now to wreak new devastation. Before it had pursued only individuals and families. Now it is raging over entire nations!

Then I saw my whole nation in the path of the hurricane. Fortunately, I saw the attack coming and held fast to the central pillar of my palace, which is a good oak post. I was listening fearfully to hear the whimpering of the good Germans when I suddenly realized with great joy that, contrary to their usual manner, they had drawn their swords in effective self-defense. The battle was brief, for the attack was repelled and the attacker withdrew with the loss of most of her available ammunition. Only Captain Little, who just sailed onto the scene, had to withstand some high breaking waves

---

[1] Xanthippe was married to Socrates and was a prototypical nagging and quarrelsome wife. Harry Thurston Peck (ed.), *Harper's Dictionary of Classical Literature and Antiquities* (New York: American Book Company, 1896), 1671.

and a strong groundswell which he handled by taking down all his sails.

Now everything is quiet, and peace has returned. I would continue with my report about my activities if the babbling a couple of paces away in the house of my compatriot and my neighbor, Herr Wetter, did not keep me from doing so. But I must digress a little to condemn a matter that unfortunately in my fine fatherland is more or less customary and detrimental to true piety. For example, I can see at this moment through the wall of my house and the wall of Herr Wetter's house (They are both perforated structures in the Gothic style.) a five-year old boy standing in front of his father who is holding a rod in his hand. With a blubbering voice the boy has already rattled off a prayer for the fourth time while keeping his eyes fixed on the rod in the other's hand. As soon as the man's hand moves, the boy's hands that are held together in prayer part to parry the coming blow. This is called raising children in the fear of God. For heaven's sake, what nonsense!

Children have so much fear just because of this sort of thing, but I really do not know why people confuse God with a thrashing. The teacher tells his pupil: "God is a loving God. Nothing happens that He does not want. He gave man free will and man is made in his image. If you do not want to believe that, and if you do not pray the Lord's Prayer every day, then I will give you a sound thrashing."

When I was in the ninth grade [at the *Gymnasium*], I was compelled to feel the sting of the rod, but under different circumstances.[2] When I did not have a valid reason for failing to go to church, the boy below me was advanced over me. I was punished for roaming about in the outdoors and for doing no good, but for doing no harm either, and the other boy was rewarded for his sanctimoniousness by being allowed to sit bored for two hours or as was generally the case, to pass the time with a kind of game of numbers in a corner of the balcony of the church where he could neither see nor clearly hear the pastor. Such a place had been wisely assigned to us so that we would not be disturbed in our devotions. This impression is still vivid in my memory. The diligent churchgoers are unlikely to have complained about me, that my profane presence was oppressive to them or that I obstructed someone's view of his dearest or his sweetheart. As long as the fear of God, like marching drill, is taught to the beat of a drum, it will always be a puppet-show. If one wishes to lead people to God's love instead of teaching them empty rituals, then heartfelt religion will come about and with it the return of the golden age.

---

[2] Ludecus probably attended the Wilhelm-Ernst-Gymnasium, which was founded in 1712 in Weimar to prepare young men for university study or a professional career. Gitta Günther, et al. (eds.), *Weimar: Lexikon zur Stadtgeschichte*, 496.

Fortunately for you all, the boy has just stopped crying and I can get back to my report. I would have been about ready to share with you all the tenets of my new religion. Of course, I am the prophet of this religion. Religion is a good business in America and very lucrative. On October 27, my birthday, I will open up shop. I hope the renowned alliance will not have anything against it. The freedom of the alliance, which it proclaimed twenty years ago, shall not suffer any thereby.[3] But I am really curious as to whether my fine [German] compatriots will be waiting as long for their redeemer as the Jews have been. They are still singing now: "Lend me patience, Lord." It is a very beautiful song, but rather old, and I wish they would postpone their plea. What difficulties would they get into if they had to give free rein to their impatience! God save them, these good people! I give them my blessing. Amen.

Here I am now, sitting on a stool that I made myself, resting up from working for six days as a day laborer. I signed on to work for myself and yesterday I paid myself four and a half *reales*. The day laborer Eduard Ludecus works in the service of the landowner Eduard Ludecus. Both men are very satisfied with each other and the pay goes regularly to the former while the latter is consistently satisfied with the work he does. Today the former has a day of rest and the latter is taking pen and paper in hand to describe the work that has been going on in his vineyard, in order to help you, dear friends, while away a boring, rainy autumn evening. Hopefully, by then this letter will be in your hands.

Our life is very simple now. Early every morning I get up with the sun, pull on my trousers and shoes, put my straw hat on my head, take my mattock and axe in hand, and with Tallör, who brings the other tools, we walk out of our fortress of thorns to my *lot*. We are working there to build an enclosure, a *fence*. We dig holes until eight o'clock and then the bell rings calling us to breakfast (Mr. Egerton, Captain Soto, Mr. Pepin, and I are sharing domestic expenses.) Breakfast consists now of cornbread, corn coffee (roasted corn), and corn mush (gruel), with which, if the cows choose to show up, we have some milk. The colony actually owns two cows already that we brought from Presidio, but since they have never been milked before, they give little milk, and if not boiled, it is of poor quality and unhealthy. It is even disdained by the Mexicans who prefer goat's milk. We eat this frugal

---

[3] Ludecus appears to be referring to the Vienna Congress, which convened on September 18, 1814 to put the affairs of Europe in order and to draft a German constitution after the defeat of Napoleon. The members of the German committee at the congress were Austria, Prussia, Hanover, Bavaria, and Württemberg. Gerhard Taddey (ed.), *Lexikon der deutschen Geschichte. Personen Ereignisse Institutionen* . . . (Stuttgart: Alfred Kröner Verlag, 1979), 1298.

breakfast, which we must admit it is, amid a lot of joking, and at nine o'clock, when the bell rings again, we go back to work. The previous evening Zapata had received the order that the landowner Don Lodrigos—that is what people here call me—needed a pair of oxen. The day laborer Ludecus accepted them, hitched them to the wagon, and drove out into the prairie. Tallör and I chopped the long thorny branches from the short trunks of some mesquite trees, loaded them up, and drove back to the garden with them. Another time we went out into the woods to cut trees for posts, and once we had piled up a suitable number of them, Tallör continued digging holes while I set the posts and began weaving the branches between them.

At noon we interrupt our work, for at one o'clock dinner is ready, which for variety's sake consists of corn mush, corn coffee, and cornbread. For the second time someone will remark to me that this food is simple in a republican way. It is strongly reminiscent of the soup of the Spartans, and our privation is our Lycurgus.[4] I would recommend to the ladies of New York who are learning Greek to come on down here. They could soon experience here what they need to learn. Jokes about our temperance have to provide the best spice and everyone is eager to live here according to Spanish custom and await the *siesta*.

After a little sleep everyone hurries back to work, and just before dark the bell signals quitting time. Then we go to supper. For additional variety there is some corn coffee, corn mush, and cornbread on the table. Who will not concede that while we are on this diet we will not die of a migraine headache. Yet I have to honor the truth here: such frugal meals are the exception, for usually the hunt yields just enough game that we have some meat on the table. Only lately nothing has wanted to come in front of our sights. For four days we have been limited to corn, and today, I hear, we can wipe our mouths clean again. As soon as the money gets here from Matamoros, this diet will be over. Everyone is waiting with great anticipation for it, the proprietors of the colony probably most of all. This wretched life arouses a great deal of discontentment among the colonists. Nevertheless, everyone gathers in the evening at the entrance to the small *villa* or a short distance away in the camp of the Mexicans, where there is usually some fun to be had, especially on Saturday. Everybody sits there under the bright stars mingled all together around the fire. The Mexicans dance the *fandango*, play party games, or act out scenes in pantomime that are usually scenes about the Indians. We have three Mexicans in our service now who understand the language of the Comanches. One of them was in captivity for one and a half

---

[4] Ludecus's reference to Lycurgus and the soup of the Spartans is unclear. Lycurgus is traditionally credited as the founder of Classical Sparta's "good order." Hornblower and Spawforth (eds.), *Oxford Classical Dictionary*, 897.

years, the other for seven years, and the third for nine years. Usually they had been rescued from death by a *squaw* who was in love with them, whom they married and then abandoned at the first opportunity.

Yesterday they presented a pantomime show for which they had painted themselves black with charcoal and covered themselves with animal skins. The men looked like half devil, half wild animal. At the end two of them had a conversation in the Indian language, and following that they made a speech to the spectators around them. It was a love declaration by a Comanche to one of our ladies. He had left his people in order to warn us that we were going to be attacked. He described the atrocities that his people practiced and at the end he advised us to flee in swift flight, or we would all be murdered and our town burned.

Among the competitions the following one was memorable for its comical aspect: Two people are restrained in the style of a "Polish billy-goat" (the hands are tied and drawn down over the knees and a heavy stick is inserted between the elbows and the back of the knees). The two people are then seated directly opposite each other on the ground. Each one has a pointed stick about one foot in length placed in his bound hands, and each player, with his toes braced against those of his opponent, tries to force the other over on his side. As soon as one or the other succeeds in this, and the enemy has no possibility of moving, the victor slides behind him and as quickly as possible pokes him with the stick in what [Heinrich] Heine in his *Reisebilder* calls a person's "legitimacy." The constrained position of the two players produces an extremely comical spectacle and the laughter does not stop until one of the spectators takes pity on the loser and helps him up again. The loser tries his luck again and is perhaps beat a second time. Bets are won and lost on this game, and after each failed attempt, the wagers are doubled.

Another game goes as follows: A number of people sit in a tight circle so that all their feet are together. A *frazada* is thrown over their feet and legs and one of the players steps into the middle. Everyone pushes his feet as hard as he can against the feet of the person standing who lets himself fall down stiffly onto one of the people sitting, and he is then propelled around like the blade of a windmill [on the legs of the people sitting]. The person who made him fall must take his place in the next game.

The Negro Henry gives us a lot to laugh about each time this game is played. He spends a lot of time with the Mexicans and is the butt of their jokes. As a joke they have made him their private *alcalde*. With all of his physical lethargy, intellectually he is quite the opposite. He is the one here who has made the most progress learning the Spanish language.

As concerns the location of the colony in general, as well as I can judge the circumstances now, it is nothing less than brilliant. If some particularly favorable circumstances do not arise, I would like to set out from here before winter to travel north to Austin's colony that is located nearer to the sea, and live there under better circumstances.[5]

The soil near the creek and in the lowlands can, of course, be called good. It consists of one and a half to two feet of humus on a base of yellowish white clay that is found everywhere in Texas. But that soil diminishes considerably six hundred to a thousand feet from the creek to a rise on the prairie and there the plow turns over only clay.[6]

Along the creek one can see extensive lowlands consisting of savannas which are flooded during every heavy rain. Good grass grows there, and with some outlay good sugar cane plantations or even rice fields could be established there. Moreover, the water that can be found at a depth of five to fifteen feet is of a superior quality and is the best that I have drunk in this country. Finally, I must mention the climate, which leaves nothing to be desired. Of course, it is quite warm already, but a constant breeze that comes up and abates with the sun rising and setting cools the air. I have not yet experienced a day that would have been as unpleasant as I remember having experienced in Germany. This is the only good thing that I have discovered until now. Other disadvantageous circumstances are in part factual, in part very probable, which I list now as follows:

First of all, it can happen that it does not rain at all for about six or seven months, namely from the beginning of March to the end of September. Of course, at first during the first few of these months a heavy dew moistens the earth, but not adequately. Two hours after sunrise, none of this moisture is any longer noticeable. The same grass that early in the day looks fresh and green resembles hay by noon. Already now the dewfall is becoming less frequent and later, they say, it will cease altogether. Then there is an eternally cloudless sky stretching over these areas. Only rarely does a thunderstorm come along, and then, propelled by the winds, it races on by. The fields on which it bestows some of its moisture are the lucky ones. This lack of rain makes it necessary for the needed moisture to be brought to the soil through ditches, as it is done here, I am told, in San Fernando. I am going to ride over there very soon to look at the situation.

Now, as soon as there are hands available to do the work, a main ditch will be dug at company expense, of course, from the creek at a point a mile

---

[5] Having read Mary Austin Holley's book on Stephen F. Austin' s colony, Ludecus decided he would soon leave the Rio Grande colony, and he let the other colonists know of his plan. Ludecus, *Reise*, 200.

[6] The knowledge that some 600–1,000 feet from Las Moras Creek the plow had turned up only sterile clay should have prompted the colonists to leave Dolores much earlier. Ludecus, *Reise*, 200.

upstream from the town down through the town to an equal distance below the town. Everyone can then run a small ditch from the main one to his *lot*. However, an annual fee must be paid for it [by each landowner]. The amount of this fee has not yet been determined, but it will probably give the company a good return in interest. By doing this, the town and surrounding area would likely be helped, but who will bear the costs of this irrigation project? Who has the desire, the time, the energy, and the money to expend on the project, when there are other places where adequate rain saves the *settler* all of this trouble? Now it is a question of whether there are other favorable circumstances prevailing [here] that will reward the *settler* for these considerable expenses? One may conclude from the following description of other deficiencies that the *settlers* will hardly be able to exist here under the prevailing conditions if the good Lord has not hidden a few veins of silver in the soft clay.

There is also a serious lack of good timber. Of course, along the banks of the creek there are oaks and [pecan] nut trees, but the wood of the former is so hard that it is almost impossible to work it. The [pecan] nut trees are better, but one can find very few that in length and circumference are suitable for cutting boards from them, and these few, after they are cut, often turn out to be rotten in their core. There are supposed to be cedars growing upstream at the source of the creek. In a few days an expedition will be leaving here to look for timber on the Rio Frio about seventy or eighty miles from here. It is needed for the construction of Mr. Beales's house. I do not doubt that some will be found, for the Rio Frio is richly wooded. But who has the desire, the time, the energy, and the money to spend transporting wood by oxcart over so great a distance? For my part, I am not one of those persons. Now, in order to conserve the little timber that is in our vicinity and to assure the company of an income source, the company commissioner has issued an order that no one shall cut wood here until the commissioner gives his permission and indicates the trees for cutting. This order has the force of law and entails a punishment for violating it. We were just barely able to achieve this much [latitude], for at first the commissioner wanted to hold back the timber altogether or to release it only in return for payment until he had obtained instructions on this point from the company. Under this ruling everyone would be limited to cutting only the timber growing on his own property, which in most cases are only some dry mesquite trees. The *labors* and about a fourth of the *lots* have not yet been surveyed owing to Mr. Egerton's tardiness. [7]

---

[7] The scarcity of timber for construction and the difficulties the carpenters encountered working with what little timber was available should have convinced the colonists that Dolores was an inappropriate site for establishing a village.

For God's sake, I would like to know what these gentlemen are thinking. They want to populate their colonies and they bring the first colonists out here and then they want to make them pay for timber and water. Mr. Egerton did all that he could to make the absurdity of this notion clear to Mr. Power, but to no avail. As one can imagine, this measure caused great dissatisfaction among the *settlers*. I agreed to take up the matter again at the first occasion and soon the opportunity presented itself: Mr. Power got the intermittent fever and was compelled to remain in his tent. I needed some posts for my fences and went to him to report it to him. He promised to assign me a place for cutting, but several days passed without this being done. Nevertheless, I was in a hurry because the cows, the oxen, and the horses were eating my young corn and the young corn of my neighbor. I reminded Mr. Power of my request and he apologized due to his indisposition and several more days passed. Finally, tired of waiting, I went into the forest and cut posts where I found them. The next day he was walking past my *lot*, saw the freshly cut posts, and asked Tallör where he had gotten them, who pointed to the little thicket on my property. Tallör [later] told me about it. Annoyed that Tallör had not told the truth, I sent him out the next day to cut quickly a few posts when I saw Mr. Power and Mr. Egerton going to the woods. I positioned myself at the edge of the woods. As I expected, when Mr. Power heard the blows of the axe, he came up to me and asked me in his typical officious, crafty manner how I as a member of the municipal council could violate prevailing law. I responded in kind and then an exchange of words took place. I told him finally that if he wanted to add new obstacles to the existing ones, then I felt it was my place to say in my own name and in the name of the other settlers that we had no reason to continue living here. If there was not sufficient timber available here, then we should not have been brought here. But if the timber is here, [I said], and if he had not assigned wood for me to cut only because of his indisposition, as he had said, then I sincerely apologized for cutting the posts. Nevertheless, I did not want to lose my crops due to his indisposition, because the proposed arrangement to have the cattle kept away from the fields until all the fences were finished had not been successful. [I said] that he should understand that as a result, I was ready to go back [the way I came]. This remark was effective. He assigned me a place to cut wood, which I did not use, however, since I had found other means of getting posts. There has been no more talk [from him] about the law. These little official disputes have not, however, caused any trouble in our circle.

The third issue to consider is the location of Dolores in relation to the outside world. This is for me the most important point. Where will the farmer be able to sell his produce? This is a question that no one has been able to answer for me. Of course, they [the owners] want to have a steamboat built that will be able to bring produce to Matamoros, but we need a navigable river for that—and there is the snag. I have been gathering information about the Rio Grande from whomever I thought might know something. One person told me that the river is not navigable, that waterfalls and boulders all along the river made navigating it impossible. Another person said that it was navigable, but only in the summer months when the river rises due to the melting snows of the *Cordilleras*. A third person disagreed with that, saying that the river would have to rise to such a level that it would cause floods, but that rarely happens. There are waterfalls and boulders in the river—that much is a fact. The question now is whether the river rises every year at all to a level that it floods over its banks so that one could navigate over the falls. The gentlemen who are invested in the company do not like going into this issue. They think that one could go down the river on rafts loaded with produce and then sell everything together. Wood is easy to sell in Matamoros too. Of course, this is more easily said than done. I just wish that these gentlemen would show me where I should get the wood for these rafts without having to pay as much for it as I can sell it for in Matamoros. And yet it is still not certain whether it is even possible [to navigate the river on rafts] and without danger. If it is not without danger, then who would risk throwing the fruit of his labor in the river? In San Fernando I hope to get some further particulars about the river, and I have halfway decided to go down the river with Mr. Power in a boat that is already finished. He is still waiting for the money to be able to pay for the boat that an American carpenter in San Fernando has built. In this particular case we do not have good credit there.

The overland route to the coast might be just as costly and as difficult, and that is not counting the time that would be lost. It is almost completely impossible, however, to sell anything in the interior of the country. In the first place, the Mexican needs [almost] nothing. The little that he does need, he raises himself. If he wanted more he has no money to pay for it. I am told now that the *settlers* arriving later would be compelled to purchase everything from us, and that only those would be accepted who would come here on their own account and who would have some money. That is a very good story under the prevailing circumstances, but those *settlers* ought to think it over first, and if a few who are not familiar with the circumstances here really do come, and if they have enough money, they would certainly use it to leave. Who would possibly burden his conscience with the reproach of wanting to invite someone to *settle* here? I am convinced at least that there has not been any such scoundrel among us who would have done so. Unfortunately, it happens too frequently that people who are forced by circumstances to remain in a place where they are established do deceive their friends and relatives by feigning contentment and tell untruths in order to entice them to the place where they are settled. And they plunge their friends into misfortune merely because they see some personal advantage in bringing several people into their vicinity. This is one of the reasons that such different rumors can be in circulation about one and the same place. Everyone praises the area where he lives and denigrates other places as much as possible.

But let us assume that all of these disadvantages here were present to a far lesser degree. Yes, I can assume they do not exist at all. But [let us imagine] a *farmer* who has beautiful herds of cattle and a productive farm and can convert to cash what he has produced here. But then a young Indian decides he wants to marry. He courts the girl he loves, but the ambitious beauty demands a true hero as her husband. Her suitor has only eleven scalps and she demands a full dozen, and until her suitor has them, his wish to marry her will not be fulfilled. So, he sets out with his friends to get what he needs. The *farmer* is coming back from town. He has done some good business, but already from afar he sees the smoke coming from his burning cabin. He finds his fields devastated, his livestock slaughtered, and his horses driven off. He thanks God that his absence has saved him the loss of his hide and hair, and in the meantime the young Indian brings his beloved the desired token of his victory, which he took perhaps from a servant left behind or possibly even from a wife and child.

These are the circumstances as I can judge them and must judge them at the present time. I expect to learn even more about these circumstances, but I am not expecting to learn anything good. One can easily imagine that there is a general discontent in camp and a short while ago we even had a small revolution. Six or eight young workers whom Mr. Beales had brought along at his own expense came forward and declared that since Mr. Beales was not able to give them land in the amount he had promised, and since there was no timber or water here, and since the circumstances were in general not such that they could be persuaded to remain here, they declared their resolve to renounce their rights to the hundred acres accorded them by contract. But without pay they would not work anymore, since they had with their labor more than earned their passage and board since arriving here. This statement caused the gentlemen [representing the company] quite a lot of embarrassment. They talked a lot about the law and the contract, but no one paid any heed to it, and Mr. Egerton had to give in and agree to their demands on the condition that if Mr. Beales did not approve, they would still have to work off the time they owed. In general, Mr. Egerton does very little to diminish the dissatisfaction, but in fact increases it with his neglect and indifference toward the *settlers*. Not long ago I had the opportunity to tell him this in a rather heated conversation in the open marketplace. The occasion was as follows: Mr. Beales had told the Germans at the time of their enlistment in New York that during the half year that they had to work for him they would have enough time to be able to plant properly their own crops. But since this was impossible due to our late arrival here, they were granted two days a week [to attend to their crops]. I advised them to have these days specified, so that someone would not change the days and make other arrangements for them, when they needed to work for themselves. In these negotiations I acted as translator. Mr. Egerton left the choice of days to the Germans and they selected the first [two] days of each week. I was quite surprised when Mr. Egerton came to me already in the second week and asked me to tell the Germans that they were supposed to build three log cabins and that they should continue working on them until they were finished. And then they could take the days all together that were due them to work for themselves.

I said nothing to him in response and just delivered the message, but I received the answer that I had expected. The Germans were angry that their *lots* had not yet been assigned to them, although they had requested them almost daily and had been forced to build fences and plant crops on others' land. They were annoyed that even with such wretched rations, they were still being given second consideration after the other nationality here. Often weeks passed before they received a piece of meat. They suffered shortages not only of fat and salt, but with the little food that was at times borrowed in San Fernando, the Germans were last in line. They became even more outraged when the company wanted to rob them of the time they needed to be able to quickly plant their crops and protect them with fences from the cattle that broke in there every day. They had to drive the animals out of the young corn almost hourly, because the Mexicans who were supposed to do it did not concern themselves with it. It would take up too much space here to list these and several other complaints of the *settlers*, but they had come to the decision to follow their contract very strictly and not to do any less or any more than they were obligated to do. They refused to work that day and the following day. I delivered this message to Mr. Egerton, to which he replied that he would force them to work, for according to the contract they had to work when he demanded it. I told them what he had said and did not concern myself with the matter any further. But soon Mr. Egerton looked me up again and told me that since the Germans could no longer be induced to work, he could no longer distribute rations to them if they were not going to make preparations soon to go to work.

At that time, when he gave some sign that he believed I approved of his conduct, I could no longer keep silent and told him flat-out, I could not view the Germans' refusal to work as anything but completely justified. Then the conversation began to become heated. I added that the reason they had a right to complain was that none of the promises made to them in New York had been fulfilled, and that one could not reasonably expect from them any inclination to be obliging. They would do what the contract demanded of them and nothing more. In response, he pulled out heatedly the contract and showed me the instructions left behind by Mr. Beales. He flatly denied that two specific days a week had been guaranteed to the Germans (which I had negotiated with them myself). He talked about ingratitude and slipshod work, and insisted that he did not know anything about these promises, but instead that he was here to safeguard Mr. Beales's interests. To this I replied tersely that if he wanted to have the terms of the contract observed so closely, then he should set the example and give the people food as he was required to do. [I added], moreover, he could not expect hard work with the kind of food that he was giving the people, and that he must also take into account the unusually hot climate. I said that I was sorry if he was not informed about the promises made and sorry too that he could not remember my conversations with him about the two days in question.

But as far as the ingratitude was concerned, [I said] that I was really curious to learn what the Germans should be thankful for. [Should they be grateful] that they had been brought here (and I included a description of the prospects that the *settler* encounters here), or that if Mr. Beales and his agents in New York had told the truth, then he would have been spared this ingratitude and would have more likely been certain of their gratitude? [I went on to say] that if someone were trying a very unusual method of keeping *settlers* in the colony, and if one thought perhaps that these people would certainly have to remain here because they did not have the [financial] means to come here at their own expense, then that person could be mistaken. On the contrary, the Germans might for that very reason have the means to leave at their own expense and I as a German would in that case not deny them my help. This time, I said, I thought that I had the influence to persuade them to cooperate, but in the future I wanted him to spare me these unpleasant assignments.

This scene had amused the whole town, because every word spoken could be heard from one end of the settlement to the other. I had been speaking for everyone because everyone was suffering more or less under the same circumstances. Another complaint, a justifiable complaint, was the price of groceries. Captain Soto had opened a *store* and was selling groceries for over twice the high price he had paid for them in San Fernando. These consisted of corn, brown sugar, salt, and fat. He had pawned his wagon and oxen to pay for them. Of course, every merchant has the right to get his price [for his merchandise], but this was not applicable here. These people had been brought into this country where it was difficult or impossible for them to get groceries for themselves. One was not able to pay them their daily wages, and was thus denying them any opportunity to obtain groceries for themselves more economically in San Fernando. And still one was making them pay the price that one demanded.

Compounding all this is the fear that the soil is not suited for agriculture. Unfortunately, it has proven to be so at least for this year, if some other yet unknown circumstances, which I suspect, are not responsible. Of course, the corn that we had planted among the grass immediately after our arrival sprouted quickly and nicely from the earth, but the sun burned it in a few days to such a yellowish color that it shriveled up. We were afraid that it would die. It remained that way without change for a few weeks until a thunderstorm brought some rain, the first rain in six weeks. We thought then that everything would shoot up, but we were mistaken. Not the slightest change in the plants could be observed.

Now the corn has begun to grow, but it gives us little hope for a harvest. It was the same with the vegetables, the beans, the peas, and the melons, in short, with everything that we had planted. The greatest part of it simply did not sprout at all. I had planted some apple and orange seeds in the shade of a small patch of woods in my garden, but not a single one sprouted, and there was not even one seed left to be found. They all disappeared. The same thing happened to Mr. Magnani, the gardener. The lack of water is to blame for all this, proven by the fact that I have several corn plants down near the creek where our swimming hole is. The soil of those plants is kept moist by the swimmers coming out of the water, and they are twice as tall as the other plants. If the seed had been planted earlier, the plants would be considerably taller than they are now and would provide some shade for each other. Again, it was a huge mistake of the [company] directors that they did not inform themselves well enough about the growing season here and the way of planting. As a consequence, we now have to fumble around in the dark. A year's work will probably be lost.

We are awaiting Addick's return from Matamoros any day now with the money. That will perhaps give one or the other [of us here] some new hope. At least Mr. Egerton is expecting a great deal to come from it.

In the meantime, the foundation for Mr. Beales's house has been dug and an attempt has been made to construct the foundation wall, but the materials needed cannot be found. There are no suitable stones in the vicinity and attempts to bake some bricks failed also. All the types of clay that were tried turned out to be too loose.

If I have written somewhat too many details about this topic, it was my intention to give detailed information and to make *settlers* as well as those who want to establish colonies aware of the care with which one should begin and carry out such an undertaking.

But it is growing dark now and I want to enjoy yet something of this Sunday. *Buenas noches caballeros y señoritas.*

*Scarcity of Money and Chicanery of the Entrepreneurs. Insecurity on
Account of Indian Tribes. A Trip to San Fernando. Description of the
Region. Sojourn in San Fernando. Return Trip to Dolores. Defensive
Arrangements. Snakes, Chameleons, Tarantulas, Skunks, Birds, etc. New
Discontent of the Colonists. Decision to Abandon the Colony. Visit of the
Lipan Indians.*

Dolores, June 12, 1834

My worst fears seem to be materializing sooner than I could imagine.
There is a peculiar cloud of misfortune hanging over our colony. I am
going to wait a few more days and then, when the Germans are released
from their work obligation, I am going to set out from here and take several
of them and another *settler* by the name of Wilson who also has a wagon and
oxen with me. We will go first to San Fernando and then probably to Matamoros. But I do not want to get ahead of myself. I will tell you everything
in the order that it happened. So, first I will return to the time when I left
you in my last letter.

I was busy at the time getting my fencing completed, but I was no longer
getting any pleasure from the work, for I could already see that my efforts
were fruitless. But I am happy, by the way, that I had the foresight to do the
work myself and not waste a laborer's wages on it. In this way I did not lose
any money on it. Otherwise, I ate my corn, went hunting some, played a
game of *whist* or chess in the evening, and like all the others waited for
Addicks and the money. Hunting here had become more difficult because
we had to travel a greater distance away to find the game that had been
frightened away from the immediate vicinity. Hunting was dangerous too
because of the Indians and could be done only by several men in a group. It
was on just such an outing that my horse played another annoying trick on
me. With one of our hunters and another American who was just about to
ride out on a hunt for buffalo we had found a very good watering hole
about thirty miles from here. We stopped for the night, hobbled our horses,
and turned them loose. The night passed rather noisily. Once we were awakened by the loud barking of our dogs. The hunter and I jumped up and we
could see by the light of the glimmering coals [in the campfire] that the dogs
were standing in front of a nearby bush and that something suspicious was
hiding behind the bush. Believing that it could be an Indian creeping up to
our camp, we immediately grabbed our rifles from the tree in anticipation
of the attack that never came. Carefully, we approached the bush and recognized there a wolf just as he was retreating. The next morning we told our
sleepy friend about our brief campaign who had neither heard nor seen
anything. As the day was breaking, we were in a hurry to continue on our

way. I went out to get my horse, but it was nowhere to be found, only the broken hobble and his hoof tracks going off into the prairie. There was nothing left for me to do but to turn back because the pack horse could not possibly transport me and my equipment in addition to the baggage he was already carrying. The hunter continued on with the pack horse, while the American fastened my saddle and equipment behind the saddle on his horse and started back with me. For a long time we followed the *trail* of my horse leading back the very same way we had traveled going out. But we soon lost his tracks over a stony patch and I had little hope of ever finding the horse again. I did not think that it would find its way over the high brushy banks of Piedras Pintas Creek that were covered with thick brush.[1] [On the way out,] we had had a lot of trouble bringing the horses through there. The creek itself has little water, but it is very clear water that forms here and there little pools.

It seems that a lot of bears live in the thick brush there. When we crossed the first time, the hunter found fresh tracks, but he had no luck following them. At the time I saw another bear that was near me several times in the brush, but I was unable to get a shot at him. Annoyed at my failure to get off a shot, I had gone to one of the pools to cool off my ardor for bear. I threw off my clothes and was just about to jump in, when I noticed in the pool a number of large snakes. I stopped and discovered upon closer examination that I had seen a plant's roots being moved about by the water. The same thing happened to the other American. He was approaching the spot where I was swimming when he heard some splashing and already had his rifle cocked to shoot when, instead of a wild beast, he saw my humble self in the water. I was swimming toward him when he called out to me to turn back because there were snakes in the water, but I convinced him plainly that he was mistaken.

Along the way back we came upon several skunks that we killed by throwing rocks at them. [In size] they resemble a squirrel a lot and make the same postures, but they hop like a kangaroo. Their smell is not as strong or as unpleasant as it is often described, but one must take care that this animal does not spray one's clothing. The Mexicans eat this animal. I have tried it also and I thought the meat was quite tasty.

We came to the creek, but we did not find a crossing in the vicinity. Our "Rosinante" had turned off somewhere along the way and so we did not find the horse's tracks.[2] The whole time our landmarks were the two mountains Piedras Pintas and Las Moras. Using them and with the aid of our

---

[1] Piedras Pintas Creek was likely a tributary of Las Moras Creek.

[2] "Rosinante" was the name of Don Quixote's horse, a mare of no great beauty, strength, or speed. *Brockhaus Die Enzyklopädie*, 24 vols., XX, 544.

compass, we finally came safely back to Dolores and found our horses grazing there. But my brown horse was nowhere to be seen and I was afraid that
he had joined the mustangs. But the next morning the Mexicans brought
me the news that he had showed up. While my traveling companion had
hurried on ahead to the *villa*, I had gone swimming in [Piedras Pintas]
Creek. When I came along later, I was greeted by people screaming: "There
he is! There he is!" My companion had played a joke by telling everyone that
we had been attacked by Indians and that I had been killed, but he had rescued our baggage. The hunter's hut was right at the entrance [to the settle-
ment] and his wife had broken out in screams of grief thinking that her husband had been lost too. The day after our return he came back also. He had
decided that it was too dangerous to continue on alone and had turned back
without bringing any meat. He had even not been able to get a shot at a
large bear that he had followed for a long time.

During the days that followed I finished my fencing and arranged with
the hunter to take a hunting party into the mountains to the northwest.
However, Mr. Egerton engaged the men to accompany the expedition to the
Rio Frio and tried to persuade me to go along also, probably in order to
show me some nice land and good timber. But it was all the same to me that
there was good timber to be found some seventy to eighty miles from here
and I stayed home. On the other hand, I decided to ride to San Fernando in
order to see the irrigation system there and to gather information about the
Rio Grande and various other things. Two young Americans wanted to go
with me, but Mr. Egerton forbade the Mexicans from lending horses to
them. He probably did not wish for us to go to San Fernando for several reasons. He did not want us to learn more about the place than he wanted to
let us know. He especially wants to keep one of the Americans, the blacksmith, here, for he likely believes that since the blacksmith is one of those
who broke the contract, he might not come back. Of course, Egerton was
justified in doing this insofar as the guards were required always to keep two
horses ready for the use of the [members of the] colony. And they had always
been made available without any objections from him. This prohibition
caused a great deal of grumbling among the guards. I did not let myself be
bothered by all of this and decided to travel alone. But so that Egerton did
not achieve his end, the others went along on foot. I carried their *frazadas* on
my horse and off we went. The blacksmith did not have a pass since it had
been denied him and I had not asked for one because I knew that I did not
need one. However, I did accept a letter to Captain Soto, who had been in
San Fernando for some time in order to pay his debts there immediately
upon the arrival of the awaited money. We were hardly out of the district of
the settlement when the Mexicans came hurrying after us, took the two
men on foot behind them on their horses, and we traveled on for an hour at

full gallop. At that point we caught up to several Mexican wild horse catchers who had spent the night in Dolores and were also on their way to San Fernando. They had several extra horses with them and one of them was rented for our two men without mounts. We crossed the Rio Grande at the same place as before, but this time we crossed it at an oblique angle. We took a far shorter and also a better crossing, for the ford we had used before was no longer passable because various new sandbanks had formed. At the San Rodrigo River, which has extremely clear water and good timber, we met Mr. Power with a Mexican and an American at a place called Morales.[3] He had been in San Fernando for two weeks, waiting also for the money, and had sold his wagon to the commander of troops there. He had received from the sale four oxen, four cows, a hundred and seventeen goats, one horse, and some cash. He was herding his riches along like Abraham. The goats had arrived in Dolores already the day before I left. So, at least there was some meat available there. Mr. Power was just releasing the hammers on his shotgun [as we approached]. He told me that he was just about to shoot the Mexican from his horse at the head [of our party] because he had thought the man was an Indian. He was still pale from fright. He seems to me to be a very fearful, indecisive man. We spent the night there and Mr. Power gave us a clear description of San Fernando. Then we talked about the situation in the colony. We complained bitterly about the inadequate arrangements that Mr. Beales had made. Mr. Power asked me why I wanted to leave the colony. Mr. Egerton had probably written to him about it. I told him that I had not decided completely, but that I was more likely to leave than to stay, and then I explained my reasons which he made only a weak attempt to refute.

The next morning everyone continued on his way. Soon we saw a herd of wild horses and the *mustang*-catchers declared that they wanted to go after them. So, we called a halt under some mesquite trees. Two of the Mexicans unsaddled their horses and led them away on foot in a big circle toward the herd, hiding behind them as they went. They were getting close to the horses when the herd bolted. In an instant they were up on their horses and chasing after the herd with the *cabestro* ready to throw. Soon we lost sight of them all. After a half hour had passed, they returned without having caught any horses. Usually these are the mares and their foals. The former do not like to leave the latter behind, and so they are soon caught by the catchers.

We continued on our journey then, and crossed the Rio San Antonio. Its water is also of an exceptional clarity. We arrived safely in San Fernando and I found Captain Soto at the market. I gave him the letter from Mr. Egerton, and then he asked the two Americans for their passes. When one of them stated that they did not have passes, the captain ordered them to return immediately to Dolores. He wanted to take them before the *alcalde* and

---

[3] Morales was a very small village on the San Rodrigo River.

made a terrible fuss. The scene was even more ridiculous because the one party understood Spanish as poorly as the other party spoke English. Finally, I stepped in and explained to the angry little captain in Spanish, French, and English that it would be highly ill-advised to execute such an arbitrary order given the way things currently stood in Dolores. I understood little of the first language, Spanish, and he understood little of the other two. I explained that the law did not require us to carry a pass in the interior of the country, for I did not have one either and therefore I would have to return also. [I added that] the American was not at all inclined to leave, and that I would vouch for him. The captain answered me then that I did not need a pass and that he would accept my guarantee [for the American]. He directed the two Americans to a house where they could stay but told the landlady to give them only a few days on credit. He knew that they had no money and were hoping to get some from Addicks. He offered me his own lodgings where he had been staying for some time on credit.

San Fernando or Rosas lies like Dolores near the border between the two provinces, Coahuila and Chihuahua. The first town lies, of course, on the right side of the Rio Grande and the second one is on the left side in an enormous flat plain that is bordered on the north by a mountain range which must be a mountain spur of the *cordilleras* [mountain ranges].[4] From a distance one can see the long green rows of trees that grow along the creek where the town is built. A mile from town one comes already upon the ditches which have been dug for irrigating the land here. The white houses are visible only from nearby through the beautiful green fig trees, mulberry trees, and [pecan] nut trees. My eyes that had been so long disaccustomed to this sight feasted on the richness and vigor of the vegetation as I rode along the road. Really, I have never seen more beautiful and larger trees than I saw there. The contrast between those there and those here [in Dolores], which look sickly and have thin foliage, is extremely striking. The roads are all straight and intersect each other at right angles. The houses stand along the roads, and behind and beside each house there is a more or less large garden planted with corn, sugar cane, and red peppers. Due to this sprawling style of building, San Fernando covers a large area of land. The irrigation ditches run right through the middle of the town at certain intervals and the smaller ditches lead to the different *lots*. The water belongs to the rich people in the town and they sell a year's use of the water for ten to fifteen *reales*. On the other hand, the land does not cost anything and one can plant as much as one wants. The water customer has the right to open the irrigation ditch every fourteen days. If he plants more than he is able to irrigate on the day he is allotted, then he must buy a second day [for irrigation] if he wants to.

---

[4] It is unclear which mountain range Ludecus was viewing at the time he wrote this statement.

The water is not conducted from the [nearby] creek (which is located too low in a valley for the water to be raised to the plain). Instead, the water is conducted from another creek several miles away.

With the exception of a few houses of stone, all the houses there are constructed of a type of burned clay, and as a result they are not very strong. Collapsed houses and pieces washed [out of the walls] by the rain provide clear proof of this. San Fernando was severely affected by the cholera [in 1833] and a lot of the houses are now completely empty.[5] Only a small number of the beautiful trees are said to be left now. A larger number of trees were cut down in order to allow the air to move more freely there and prevent the disease. In spite of the advantages that it has over other towns that cannot irrigate, it is the most impoverished town that I have seen so far. One sees hardly any cash there at all. Barter is the only form of commerce. Even in the homes of the wealthy who have hundreds of cows, oxen, and goats, one does not find even the most basic necessities. The town has suffered also because of the Indians. I was told that the *ranchos* used to stretch out all the way to the Rio Grande. Herds of cattle covered the prairie. Then the Comanches took it into their heads to put an end to this spread, and in a single night the *ranchos* were attacked by them, eighty people were murdered, their huts burned down, and their cattle killed or driven off.

That these Indians are not as fearful as they are usually described, and at times act with great courage, is proven by the fact that just two years ago about two hundred of them rode right through the middle of the town in order to steal the horses of the Lipans, an enemy tribe of Indians who were camping near the town. They raced back again right through the town. They often sneak at night right into the town, untie the Mexicans' horses, jump on the horses, and ride away on them.

On the road we were traveling, not far from the Rio Grande, we saw to the north a type of building that used to be a citadel, but the Indians attacked the garrison of eighty men there, besieged the fort for some time, and [finally] killed all of them. This was bad news for us poor colonists. What is our little group supposed to do when those red-skinned devils get the urge to take our scalps? Half of the colonists would run away and the other half would have to fight them with poor weapons or without weapons. Our Mexicans here are no heroes at all and would probably be the first ones to take to their heels. One torch thrown into our protective wall [of thorns] would force us to abandon our fortifications and for sure not a one of us

---

[5] In the summer of 1833, *Cholera morbus* raged in New Orleans and in neighboring Mexico. See Louis E. Brister, "Johann von Racknitz: Ein Württemberger an der Spitze der deutschen Auswanderung nach Texas," 1832–1841, *Zeitschrift für Württembergische Landesgeschichte*, 53 (1994), 241.

would escape with his life. I heard the sad news too that Mr. Neil, whom one will remember from my earlier letters, died of his wounds.[6] Now one will ask: What is the government doing? Is it not trying to put a stop to this mischief? I have often posed the same question, but I have never received a satisfactory answer. However, I believe I can give one easily enough. A government such as the one in Mexico can hardly be called a government at all. One government here has no sooner established itself than it is overthrown. Where should the power and the means come from to keep a group of people like these Indians in check?

These Indians in the hot and desolate wastelands who are "accustomed to hunger and thirst" mock the troops pursuing them on poor horses (because the good horses have already been stolen from them). The troops cannot follow their enemy retreating into the mountains because their rations are about exhausted and hunger forces them then to retreat. Meanwhile, the Indian merely buckles his belt [more tightly] around his body, or he slaughters a horse and satisfies his hunger from that. But once the campaign has been successfully concluded and peace has been made [with the Indians], it lasts only until the Indians are again equipped with firearms, with powder and lead. To be sure, the sale of such items [to the Indians] is prohibited on the pain of death, but there are always enough people who will risk it for the sake of the great profit. They trade stolen horses for these materials from the farmers in Austin's colony who are said to be giving the traders formal orders for horses.

My lodgings in San Fernando could not be called the most elegant. The ceiling threatened to fall in any moment where several support beams were sagging down under the pressing weight. The rain falling through the roof had washed fragments from the wall and deep holes in the floor. The furniture consisted of a large table, a bench seat, two chairs, and a double bed which Captain Soto had taken. I slept on the bench while the mistress of the house slept together with her son and daughter on a cowhide on the floor. She was an old woman with a skin so brown and wrinkled that it resembled the casing on an old smoked sausage. Her gray hair hung about her face like the dusty strands of a spider's web and her ragged clothes veiled less than they covered. Her daughter was about twelve years old and by local standards she was already a fledgling. For a Mexican girl she was not ugly. The brave captain was paying court to her, probably on account of her pretty eyes, and to her mother, on account of the credit he needed.

I made the acquaintance there of Señor Don Louisana de la Garson who was the postmaster. He was a very polite and refined man of about thirty-

---

[6] Mr. Neil was the MacNeil whom Ludecus wrote about in the tenth letter. See Ludecus, *Reise*, 138-140.

eight years of age. I obtained from him some information about the Rio Grande. He maintained that the river was not navigable, and he told me that the attempt had once been made, of course, with two ferry boats loaded with corn. One of them overturned on the rocks and only the other one arrived safely at Matamoros. I had to promise him that if I came back to San Fernando again, I would stay at his house.

So, I passed the time as well as I could. I looked over the farms, ate apricots, mulberries, and the repulsive tortillas while Captain Soto tried to prove to me in beautiful Spanish, very bad French, and even worse English, and for the worst of all reasons that Dolores would soon be an excellent place. He is, so to speak, a bit stupid and in San Fernando not very popular.

Since Addicks still had not come and my cash reserves had been reduced to a few *reales* (I had bought for myself a pretty dark gray mare), I was in a hurry to leave town and to do so with my honor intact, that is, without debts. I was just about to ride away with my two companions when a violent thunderstorm held us up. In a few minutes the living room [of my quarters] was filled with puddles. The mistress of the house and her daughter were kneeling before the puddles and scooping the water with their hands into a pot which they then emptied into the street. This work kept them busy intermittently until well into the night. Besides the place where the bed was standing, there was not a dry spot in the house. That night I slept in the bed with Captain Soto and the family lay closely around the bed with the chickens and two dogs. The next morning we were greeted by bright sunshine and we got underway. Incidentally, I had bought two chickens that I was carrying in my game bag.

As I was riding along the way I noticed at some distance a panther, or was it a jaguar? I stopped my horse and motioned to my companion to bring me my rifle, but he raced past me, aimed, and the animal jumped into the high grass and was gone. Several more times we caught sight of it for a few seconds, and finally, cursing my unlucky star, I gave up the hunt for it. Continuing on my way on foot, I soon saw another thing that attracted my attention. A large tarantula was lying on the path and was squirming under the power of a murderess, a beautiful, bluish, long-bodied insect with iridescent wings. I chased the insect away from the spider several times, but again and again it returned and climbed between the legs of the spider onto its body to complete its conquest. Since I had not seen the beginning of the encounter, I cannot say that the insect was the primary cause of her enemy's death, but it is not at all impossible.[7] We see so often in nature that a powerful creature is overcome by a weaker adversary.

[7] The bluish, long-bodied wasp that attacked the spider was no doubt one of the 290 species of so-called "spider wasps" found in North America. These long-legged black or

The woman [in] Morales gave us lodging again for the night. There I was awakened out of a deep sleep by a noise, and I saw in the darkness hardly six feet away a tall figure on a white horse. I grabbed the pistol lying beside me to put a bullet between the ribs of this "sleepwalker," thinking that it was an Indian. Then I heard in very audible English the words, "Who in the devil is here in my house?" It was the carpenter Allen from San Fernando who wanted to go with us to Dolores and had made this joke to frighten us. But it could have cost him his life. We brought the distressing news to Dolores that Addicks still had not come, and the fear was widespread there that he could have been robbed or murdered.

In a similar vein, an unpleasant event had transpired in Dolores during my absence that had kept the inhabitants of the *villa* in alarm and fear for several days. It had happened as follows: A shepherd had been needed to herd the goats. I had been asked before my departure to engage one of Herr Wetter's sons for the job and I had talked with the boy's father about it. I had described to him the danger involved, that the boy could easily get lost in the prairie or could fall into the hands of Indians. He had agreed with me and had turned it down. But the day after my departure a small pay increase had made him change his mind and the boy had been sent out with the goats. The first day everything went fine. But the next morning, after coming home to eat breakfast, he had relieved his father who had temporarily taken his place. Then he was reported missing by a boy who had immediately followed him [out to the herd]. The boy's father went out [to look for his son], but returned after a half hour without having accomplished his objective. However, Mr. Egerton and the other men did not want to believe that the boy was missing. They thought that he was merely sleeping or playing a joke by not answering. They failed to take appropriate measures immediately, but when the boy did not come in at noon, the Mexicans were sent out. Everyone went out with a firearm to search, but it was to no avail. They rang the bell all through the night, but the boy did not come back. His mother was about to go crazy. The boy's sudden disappearance led everyone to fear that he had been taken by savages. Egerton himself was no longer in doubt about it.

The next day the Mexicans were sent out in the area again, primarily to see if they could not discover some traces of Indians. But traces of neither the Indians nor of the boy could be found. On the third day the Mexicans rode out again in different directions when suddenly the lost boy came strolling cheerfully into camp at breakfast time. One can imagine what

---

blue wasps, one-half to two inches long, sting and paralyze spiders so they can feed them to their offspring. Pamela Forey and Cecilia Simmons, *An Instant Guide to Insects . . .* (New York: Grammercy Books, 1987), 88.

exclamations of joy this elicited from his parents, his siblings, and all the people in the camp. During the last few days no one had ventured out of the camp for fear that they could also be kidnapped.

As soon as the boy had eaten some bread and milk, he told about his adventure: He did not know how he had become lost. The first day he had wandered around all day. He had come to a large mountain, probably the mountain Las Moras. He had found water twice, and toward evening, since it was raining heavily, he had gone to sleep under a bush. The next day he had wandered around again until noon, when he had found fresh horse tracks. He had followed them until about evening and, fearing that he could lose them in the darkness, he had laid down nearby to sleep until the next morning. Then, following the tracks, he had arrived safely back at camp. He had nourished himself the whole time with berries that he had found on bushes. But he was nevertheless half-starved and covered with hundreds of scratches. For his age, eleven years old, he had conducted himself extremely wisely. Many others in his situation might have been forced to die of starvation. Like some others, I have had to experience several times how easily one can get lost in this brushy prairie covered by high nopal cactus and mesquite trees. Even if one is most diligently watchful, it cannot be avoided sometimes if the sun is not shining. As soon as one is out in the open here, the mountain Las Moras is a good landmark.

A few days after my return I put my old plan into action to organize a hunting party. But besides the hunter, Mr. Stover, and an American, I could not persuade anyone else to go. The preparations were quickly made, because they are very different here from the preparations for a hunt in Europe. We loaded a sack of flour, some salt, a small cooking pot, and a *calabaza* on the hunter's pack horse which was going to carry the dried meat and the hides on the way back. We did not need anything more; our rifles had to provide the rest.

We rode for several days in a northwesterly direction, then we turned more to the west, crossed several creeks, and wandered through the mountains as we headed along a higher mountain range that probably was a part of the *cordilleras*. The region resembled completely a wilderness, and as far as the eye could see, there was nothing to be seen but a long range of barren mountain crests. For days we rode up and down mountain slopes over loose stony ground where the horses could hardly move forward. In vain we looked for water or even for a tree where we could lie down. Along the way we crossed probably three or four dry riverbeds and some of these rivers must have been at some time of some magnitude, for in those stony riverbeds there was a completely different type of vegetation. There were different plants, bushes, and trees there. It was there that we came upon an extremely romantic spot: in the middle of this limitless wasteland on a hillside there was a small pond surrounded by oaks, [pecan] nut trees, and thick brush. In the brush there was a large oak tree shading a round enclosure of large stones. All kinds of [animal] skulls and bones were lying about there, piles of residue from the meals eaten there by savages as well as whites. At some time two Americans had hunted buffalo there and had constructed a small fortress of stones, but they had been murdered by Indians anyway. We spent the rest of the day and the night there, but the night was not very restful. First, the wolves awakened us with their howling. Several times one of them came close, probably to drink, but our dogs made a commotion and this drove it back. We were afraid by then that it might go after our horses and maybe run them off. So, we went out in the dark of night to look for the horses and bring them in to safety. The hunter's white horse enabled us to find his horses right away, but we looked in vain for mine. Finally, the wolf withdrew. Then we lay down again to sleep. But soon we were awakened again by a thunderstorm. I pulled myself, my saddle, my firearm, and hunting bag under a buffalo hide and let it rain all it wanted to. The next morning I awakened to find half of my body lying in water. With horror I discovered then that water had run into my powder horn and ruined the contents.

We were in a fine mess! The hunter had hardly [enough powder for] four or five shots and the American, to whom I had lent my shotgun, had brought along none. There was nothing left for us to do but hurry straight back home as fast as we could. This was all the more urgent since we had no means of defense if we were to be attacked by Indians, which could have easily happened. A discovery that we had made the same day of our departure from Dolores had convinced us of that. Hardly seven or eight miles from our settlement we had found on the prairie a fresh *trail* with the tracks of about sixteen or twenty horses that had been made since the last dew. All indications were that the tracks had been made by Indians who never ride abreast of each other, you see, but always single file. We also knew for certain that our Mexicans had not ridden out in this area that morning. Also, at our first campsite, a nice watering spot, there were clear Indian signs. But they had taken a direction a little more off to one side [of our trail] and so we surmised with good reason that they wanted to honor San Fernando with a visit and not Dolores. Consequently, we did not put off our trip because of them and rode on.

So, we set out on the way home. At times the sun was insufferably warm. We suffered from thirst frequently, and even more so than usual because the American had broken my *calabaza*. Our dogs, which could bear the heat even less than we could, usually stopped somewhere around noon and followed us into camp when it began to cool off.

After a few days we saw the mountains of home again, and I cannot say that I was not happy to do so. As little as life in Dolores can be called pleasant, I must nevertheless confess that I do not love hunting passionately enough to feel compensated by this hunt for all the deprivations I suffered. Basically, I had gone out more with a desire to learn about the region than about its inhabitants. In this respect I was amply satisfied. I had not expected to find a desert. The scarcity of game would have also left a hunter dissatisfied. Of course, deer are not scarce, but in that barren landscape it is difficult to approach them. Only scattered individual buffalo can be found there, but it is easy to shoot them since they do not run faster than our domesticated cattle and one can easily catch up to them on horseback. If one finds them in a herd, however, one must be very cautious, for Indians can usually be found in their vicinity. Since the Indians do not raise crops at all, but live on meat, they follow the buffalo herds.

On the other hand, the area is teeming with a small species of wild pig. But people rarely shoot them, because their meat has a bad taste. Our dogs fought with them all the time and often were carrying deep wounds from these encounters. One must be very careful around them in order not to feel the pain of their long tusks. My passion for hunting once misled me to attack a boar with the butt of my rifle. Two dogs had surrounded him, but by turning first to one and then to the other, he was keeping them at bay. In the same moment that I struck him on the head, he wounded one of the dogs so [badly] that we had difficulty getting the dog away from him. I had reason to regret my action too, because the stock of my rifle was badly damaged by his hard skull.

The meat of the buffalo is extremely delicious and fatty. But our [German] style of cooking is not suited to its proper tasty preparation: Once camp has been set up, a fire is made, and if water is available, some of the meat is boiled. The rest is placed on the hot coals, and after a time it is turned, and then it is pulled from the ashes with a stick. The meat is pulled apart or cut up and then fearlessly chewed and choked down, ash and all. If the hunt has been poor, then a snake or something else has to fill the need.

Upon our return to Dolores we found everything still unchanged. There was still no word from Addicks. The mail had arrived in San Fernando, but without the letters which, even with Addicks's delay, we had definitely been expecting the mail carrier to bring. I had no more doubt then that some misfortune had befallen him. The other *settlers*, on the other hand, maintained that Addicks had gone with Beales to New York and that they had no intention of sending money to us. Some of the workers stopped working and a general despondency settled over the colony. For some time now one had been able to persuade the Mexicans to stick it out only by offering them higher wages. Since they were also afraid of never getting their pay, they were talking about leaving.

Immediately after our return [from the hunt], we asked the Mexicans whether they had discovered any trace of Indians and we reported to them what we had seen. [They responded that] they had not noticed anything, which is what I had expected from them, for I had often seen how negligent they were in their duties. Twice I had come upon them on the prairie, but instead of patrolling the vicinity, they were playing cards in the grass. Egerton ordered them the next morning to patrol in a large circle [around the settlement] and to be more watchful in the future. The next morning, as I was sitting in my hut, I heard all at once a frantic ringing of the bell and saw Zapata go running pale as a ghost out of the entrance to the *villa* and shouting several times, *los Comanchos, los Indios!* This alarm had already been sounded too many times as a joke in order to frighten some fearful person for it to bother me at first this time. I thought, as so often before, that a prank was being played. I thought that some men disguised as Indians had silenced some braggart and that the farce would soon end in laughter. In order to be present for the outcome, I hurried outside and found everybody running around. I inquired among the Mexicans about what was going on and learned that someone had found a *trail* of [fresh tracks from] twelve to fifteen horses nearby and in a thornbush some hairs from a buffalo hide. We were also shown the evidence.

We were somewhat mistrustful of our Mexicans and believed that they had perhaps concocted this little story in order to demand higher wages again. It was decided among several of us, therefore, to investigate the matter. Egerton was supposed to ride out with the outriders to the spot located hardly a few hundred paces away, but with his usual tardiness he delayed doing it until three o'clock in the afternoon. I would have been happy to go with them if my left hand that was swollen had not prevented it. Some poisonous creature, a tarantula or a scorpion, had given me this injury to bring home as a trophy of my hunt. Shortly after nightfall the patrol returned and this was their report: The Indians had approached the *villa* from the side of the Rio Grande following the *trail* of our wagons, when they must have caught sight of Zapata and his Myrmidons. Then they had hurried off into the prairie that is covered there with mesquite trees. Under the cover of the trees they had passed by the town not far from our carpentry shop and then they had taken the route to the Las Moras [mountain]. The patrol had followed the Indians' tracks for a few hours which was done with some difficulty because the Indians had employed every trick possible to deceive or to obliterate their *trail*. This was proof that the Indians believed they were being pursued. On this day the courage of the colonists was crushed. We had hoped to remain undiscovered in our hide-out until our numbers had increased enough that we could repel a serious attack by Indians. But since our place of abode had already been discovered, we could have no doubts that the Indians would return in greater numbers. The love [of the colonists] for our Troy under these unfavorable circumstances was not so great, and everyone was talking about leaving the flesh pots of Egypt behind and seeking the blessed promised land, wherever it may be.[8]

This day had affected Mr. Power most of all. He had always spoken in a way as though he intended to make another Zaragoza out of Dolores and another Palafox out of himself.[9] He called me into his hut the next morning where I found him with Mr. Plunkett and Mr. Little. He asked me what I thought about the situation of the colony and what I was intending to do. His face still had the color of someone frightened. Immediately I saw in his face too that he was expecting and hoping that I would declare my intention of leaving as soon as possible, and that he had it in his mind to go with me. In order to torment him a bit for his boastfulness, I gave a very indefinite answer. I expressed surprise at hearing him talk that way since he had just recently vigorously opposed all of our reasons for leaving the colony. I had often declared that the Indians could not frighten me and [I said] they were not the reason that I would leave the colony. In reply he described the Comanches, their might and their weapons in such a way that I could almost see the Prussian army coming for us. Then Mr. Egerton, who had heard the same terrifying description as I, stuck his head in the window and asked Mr. Power rather curtly what kind of nonsense he was talking and whether it was not his job as commissioner of the colony to persuade the *settlers* against leaving. There was a heated exchange during which Mr. Power behaved like a very unrefined braggart. He asserted that he was not going to leave if the *settlers* would fight the Indians. But they had said already in response to his inquiry about this that they had not been recruited as soldiers and would not fight. If anything had been said in New York about wild Indians, [they insisted], they would have remained at home. It was the same situation with the Mexicans. They had in fact driven together all the oxen and horses and declared their intention of going home. Then all the animals were allowed to go into our garden lots. They were really the only ones that owed some

[8] Myrmidon was a son of Zeus and the legendary ancestor of the Thessalian Myrmidones. Peck (ed.), *Harper's Dictionary of Classical Literature and Antiquities*, 1070.

Ludecus refers sarcastically to Dolores as Troy, for he believes the Indians will return and destroy the settlement as surely as the Greeks destroyed Troy.

In the Bible (Exodus 16:3) the Israelites, starving in the wilderness on their flight from Egypt, yearn for the flesh pots of Egypt. In Dolores, at the time Ludecus wrote this letter, the colonists had very little meat to eat. He was confident that his German friends reading this would understand his sarcasm. See Ludecus, *Reise*, 233–234.

[9] This remark is unclear. Ludecus is likely referring to the town of Zaragosa in Coahuila, and to the Spanish general Francisco de Palafox y Melci. See Carmen Perry, "Palafox Villa," Tyler et al. (eds.), *The Handbook of Texas*, V, 21.

thanks to the Comanches for coming near us, because they were eating to their heart's content and to their good health all of our corn, beans, peas, etc. A number of the Mexicans actually left the *villa* a few days later with Zapata, their commander. Several others, however, were persuaded to stay. But before this happened, we received help in a very different way.

I was just standing in the camp of our "Swiss Guards," when we saw through the trees a wagon approaching.[10] My first thought was that it was Addicks. Zapata stood up and cast a quick glance at the wagon, then he cast a meaningful glance at his troops. His eyes almost burst from their sockets. "*Dinero,*" was the only word I heard coming from his smiling, silver-filled mouth, and then he disappeared inside the enclosure of the *villa* in order to bring Egerton the happy news. Unfortunately, our expectations did not come true. Captain Soto had succeeded only in obtaining some food on credit, and with the food there was also a cannon, a three-pounder, which in a letter Egerton had requested to be sent from San Fernando. Earlier, our carpenters had made a few cannons out of the wood from the live oak and [pecan] nut trees and reinforced them with iron bands. Two of the small ones did, in fact, have enough strength that they did not explode when we loaded them with sixteen to twenty shotgun pellets and fired them. Two larger cannon replicas were intended only to inspire fear. Every evening a shot was fired from the metal cannon as a sign our gunpowder was not in short supply. They began also to build a forty- to fifty-foot high platform on the market square in order to install an artillery battery on it. Everyday now some new plans [of defense] were made, one more inept than the other.

A white flag had been waving for a long time from one of the highest trees in order to show any Indians who might approach that we wanted to be friends with them. Then a contrary wind blew it down. It was supposed to be put up again and in fact on one of the trees among the huts. Mr. Egerton wanted to hang it himself and climbed up the ladder with it. But he suddenly came tumbling down with a loud outcry and waving his hands all about his head. Swarming wasps, perhaps French liberals transformed in the process of reincarnation, were resisting the raising of the white flag and had inflicted several red and blue spots on Mr. Egerton's deathly pale face. If he had shown himself [in that condition] in Germany, he would have certainly been brought to Mainz as an arch-demagogue. As painful as this incident must have been for Mr. Egerton, it was still funny and no one could keep from

---

[10] Ludecus refers to the small Mexican force recruited in San Fernando to guard Dolores as Beales's "Swiss Guard" because like the Vatican's Swiss Guard, they were mercenaries recruited to guard a small and vulnerable city (in one case Dolores and in the other, Vatican City). See "Swiss Guards," *New Catholic Encyclopedia*, 2nd ed., Berard L. Marthaler et al. (eds.), 15 vols. (Detroit: Thomson-Gale, 2003), 213, 642–644.

laughing. Our soothsayers saw this scene as a bad omen and declared that nothing now could any longer save our Troy from its fall. The flag was later put up outside of the enclosure. In a letter [to the colonists], Captain Soto said that we should be watchful, since the Indians had killed and scalped two shepherds near San Fernando. They had opened the man's veins and had taken out his heart. Still no word from Addicks. What pleasant news![11]

Day before yesterday we saw that the prairie north and west of here had been set on fire. Without a doubt this could have been done only by the Indians. Yesterday the German gentleman, Herr Wetter, came home with the news that he had seen several Indians very near his garden hiding behind a bush, and this morning the prairie was burning very near the edge of our little woods. We investigated the cause, but we were not able to find any trace of Indians.

Meanwhile, our little village is the scene of the liveliest activity. For eight days now everyone has been working on drawing up their accounts and settling with Mr. Egerton. Since there is not a farthing of cash available here, bills of exchange have to replace cash and they are drawn on Mr. Egerton for work performed. They have been in circulation already for several months and right now they have been terribly devalued, especially since the Mexicans are trying everything to get rid of them. One of the Mexicans asked me to accept a *bill* for one and a half pesos in exchange for about ten grams of tobacco. At first I did not want to do it because the trade was just too Jewish for me, but finally I had to relent. My surplus of clothing, etc. has put me in a position of selling some of it so that I could redeem my *bills* for foodstuffs, etc. I sold my clothes at a very high price because several of the workers here have really been forced by their desperate straits to go about half naked.

Mr. Egerton seizes upon any pretext to prolong his account settlements and he is still hoping that if the money arrives, then the colonists will stay. But he is very much mistaken, even if a few of them should let themselves be persuaded by a high wage to extend their residence here. Such measures

---

[11] The stings inflicted by the wasps created red and blue welts on Mr. Egerton's pale white skin, which reminded Ludecus of the colors of the French flag. He refers to the July 1830 Revolution in France, which was prompted by the July decrees restricting freedom of the press and the voting rights of citizens. The population of Paris and the liberal majority in the assembly rose up in protest. The revolution ended with the installation of a monarchy under King Louis Philippe. Brockhaus, *Die Enzyklopädie*, XI, 297. See also H. A. C. Collingham et al., *The July Monarchy: A Political History of France 1830–1848* (London: Longman, 1988).

Ludecus refers to the Zentraluntersuchungskommission (Central Investigative Commission), established in Mainz by the Karlsbader Beschlüsse (Karlsbad Decrees) in September 1819 to uncover and suppress revolutionary activity and allegiance to outside demagogues. Taddey (ed.), *Lexikon der deutschen Geschichte*, 235, 624–625.

taken by him to keep the *settlers* here are not very supportive of the objectives [of the colony]. The contrary is in fact true, for the final few colonists have lost entirely the little confidence they had in the leaders of this colony. I will cite just one example that may shed some light on this situation. [Mr.] Swansen, a cartwright by trade and certainly the most hardworking and talented tradesman here, had been instructed to cut trees in Mr. Beales's garden in order to make for him wagons or carts out of the timber, on the condition that he literally clear that land there. This was done, but Swansen, who had seen the signs of trouble, decided also to leave and he has made for himself in recent weeks a cart to transport his own baggage and the baggage of his friends. When Mr. Egerton learned of this, he declared that the cart did not belong to Swansen but to Beales because it had been made from the wood belonging to Mr. Beales. This could not be proven, however, because Swansen had received some wood also from my property. Since Egerton was now claiming the cart for himself [and Mr. Beales], Swansen demanded that he at least be paid for his work, and it was a very high price. But there was no money. Egerton maintained then that Swansen had promised to make wagons and not a cart. Hence, he was not bound to accept the cart. But he could provide no proof of that and Swansen denied it completely.

Although as a rule I do not get involved in such disagreements, I nevertheless considered it my duty to help as much as I could everyone who had decided to leave the colony and Swansen had come to me for some advice. Since the owners of the colony have not been able to fulfill their responsibility for our personal safety, our food supplies, and last but not least, some money, I thought it was ridiculous to refer to contracts that were not even in writing and were being contested by the second party. I advised him to settle the matter in such a manner that he paid for the wood, but to charge the owners for his wages to clear the land. I promised to assume his debt if he came out short in the deal. This was embarrassing to them [Beales's subordinates], because they wanted to keep Swansen since he is useful to them. They made all sorts of promises and applied all types of persuasion possible, but it was futile. Swansen demanded a settlement of his accounts, which was finally given to him yesterday after a long delay, and even without the disagreement over the cart being settled, it showed him being still nine pesos in debt [to the colony]. Everyone was surprised at this because since our disembarkation he has worked constantly for Beales. He has taken care of all the repairs on his wagons and carts, and even driven his oxen. When Beales left, he settled his accounts with him. The charges of both men cancelled each other out. So, Beales did not do badly in the deal.

This deception was poorly conceived, because Mr. Beales had forgiven every [other] *settler* the debts he owed. I do not know how the situation will end. The Germans have been told that their work requirement was moved forward by five days, that their time was not being counted from the day of disembarkation, but from the day that the baggage arrived on shore. I told them [Beales's subordinates] on behalf of the German families that they [the Germans] would consider their contract fulfilled tomorrow and would leave with me. There are a lot of such disputes in which I am involved, sometimes as the translator and sometimes as the *hombre bueno* when there is a formal complaint. It has made my stay here for the last eight days unbearable, and I want to free myself of this place as soon as possible. It is incomprehensible to me, why these people are trying to keep the *settlers* here—*settlers* who, as they can plainly see, are forced to seek their delivery in a hasty departure.

Tomorrow the mail from Matamoros is arriving in San Fernando and day after tomorrow we can have the news of what became of Addicks. If we are again left in uncertainty, then my wagon is already standing in front of my door ready to be quickly put in order. Then I will leave accompanied by the Germans for whom I have rented a Mexican cart that brought us some corn. Mr. Wilson and a few others, whose few belongings will have a place on my wagon, will leave with us. Not only some people are trying to make our stay here unpleasant, but also the vermin are oppressing us now unpleasantly. No sooner have we rid ourselves more or less of the ticks than the snakes are beginning to take up residence in our houses. For example, a rattlesnake was recently discovered in a child's cradle. Another one had caught a young chicken in our dining hut, but when we went after the snake, it let the chicken go. The week before, I was standing in the doorway of the hut of my neighbor, Mr. Dippelhöfer. His younger sister was standing on the other side of him and several other people were in the hut when suddenly a snake came darting out of my hut with a frog in its mouth that was screaming bloody murder. It went slithering out among the trees and across the girl's foot. We beat the snake to death and the frog, as it hopped happily away, croaked its thanks to us.

I have killed several rattlesnakes in my field, and once, when I was coming out of the creek where I had been swimming and was about to step out onto the bridge, I saw a snake below me on the dry spot where I was about to place my bare foot. I had no desire to play the pope and offer my slipper for kissing, since this kiss would have brought me eternal bliss instead of humble happiness. One hop took me safely out his dangerous vicinity. Altogether I have observed five or six species of snakes here, among them is a water snake that, as one Mexican told me, is poisonous. The rattlesnake is the largest and the most numerous. But this one does not appear to be the same rattlesnake, the *crotalus horridus*, that one finds in Canada and which is very much feared. This one has silvery gray scales and the rattles are whitish in color.[12] It appears to bite only when it is provoked.

---

[12] See Ludecus's remarks in the eighth letter about the rattlesnakes he observed.

We cannot complain about mosquitos, but we are plagued by a small fly, possibly a large species of gnat, often so badly at work that we have to leave the field. It appears with the rising sun and disappears a little before sundown. Once on a hunt we came upon several watering holes where the mosquitos attacked us in such numbers that we had to race away at a full gallop. Nevertheless, we were already covered by hundreds of them and they just seemed to enjoy the fast ride with us and we had to kill them all in order to get rid of them.

Another creature that populates the prairie and the woods in extraordinary numbers is a small species of lizard (*lacerta* in English). This small animal runs with such speed that one's eyes are hardly able to keep up with it, but is also very shy. The chameleon is also common and in its shape this creature resembles a turtle somewhat. It is about the size of a twelve-year old child's hand. It does not run fast, and then only a short distance of five or six steps. Consequently, it is not difficult to catch one by hand. Its skin is marked by several pretty colors and on its head it has a small horn that is supposed to distinguish it from the African chameleon. As concerns the changing of its color, I believe that I have observed it, but it was so insignificant that it could have been in my imagination. We have rarely seen the squirrel that does so much damage to corn. On the other hand, there is no lack of *blackbirds*, a species of thrush with a glossy, black tail that resembles a chicken's tail. There are several types of them and they like to congregate in the vicinity of our homes. They customarily sit around on fences and on the top of fence posts and stretch their necks and their sharp bills straight up in the air. Their body shape grows gradually heavier from their bills down to their tail feathers, and they remain in this [aforementioned] position without moving for a long time, resembling the iron point of a spear. They are about the size of a magpie.[13]

This bird produces the strangest and most contradictory sounds. Often when I was lying in my hut early in the morning I heard a noise that resem-

---

[13] Ludecus's source for the word *lacerta* is unknown, but it is the Latin word for lizard. *Lacerta* is also the name of a constellation in the Milky Way between Cygnus and Andromeda.

The turtle-shaped lizard with a horn on its head was probably one of several species of horned lizards. However, the description Ludecus provides offers little help in definitively determining its identity. Of the 120 or so African species of chameleon, most have some type of horn. See R. D. Bartlett and Patricia P. Bartlett, *Chameleons. Everything about Selection, Care, Nutrition, Diseases, Breeding, and Behavior* (Happauge, NY: Barron's Educational Series, Inc., 1995), 6, 46, 53, 58, 67, 76.

The bird described by Ludecus was probably the "common grackle." Its "song" has been described as "a split rasping sound that is both husky and squeaky." Roger Tory Peterson, *A Field Guide to the Birds of Texas and Adjacent States* (Boston: Houghton Mifflin Co., 1963), 234 (quotation).

bled the splashing of water. I assumed it was coming from the fountain that had been dug near my hut. I investigated it, but found no dripping water there at all. After I had been deceived several times, I finally learned that it was these birds that were sitting in the trees behind my hut. As quiet and as pleasant as that sound is, these birds scream in flight so noisily that one thinks one is hearing a machine that is screeching and rattling as if it had not been greased for a year. At other times it makes a sound as if a piece of wood was breaking, and then other times they sing like a thrush. They also do a lot of damage to the young corn.

Another inhabitant of this area, and a pleasant one, is the hummingbird. A pair of these cute creatures has begun nesting in the little patch of woods on my *lot*. The nest hangs from the branch of a little dead oak tree, and when one of them flies by, one thinks that one is seeing a bumblebee or a moth. It moves its wings with incredible speed. I have seen only one species here and it is probably one of the largest types. Its plumage is not very pretty. Brazil is the home of the smaller and prettier ones. Monkeys are not to be found here either, nor any parrots. The wild turkeys that in our camp we used to hear calling every morning are almost completely gone. They seem to be native to Mexico, for they were here already at the time of Cortéz who called them *gallinas* [chickens]. As the [human] population increased in the southern provinces, the turkeys migrated to the north. The *turkey buzzard* is extremely common here, but it stays only in populated areas where it consumes carrion. Several types of lark are found in these regions also, and they are different from the European ones in that they light on small trees and only sing there, and not in flight. Their song is not as pretty either. Overall, birds as a species are in these upper reaches of the country very rare, which is not surprising since it is almost completely devoid of forests. As far as fish are concerned, I have seen only one small species in Las Moras Creek. One finds also crabs there in great numbers, of course, but they are also small.

Now I must close in order to go find my horses. It is a job that one must do over and over again, and incidentally, it is a very onerous chore and time consuming. Tracking the horses is almost the only way of finding them, and it requires first of all a lot of practice, but I am gradually getting the hang of it. My next letter will probably be dated at San Fernando.

[Attempt to Restrain the Colonists. Dispute between Rasbon and Mr. Hartman. The German Cook's Refusal to Continue Cooking. No News from Addicks. Arrival of Several Lipans. Description of the Indians.]
San Fernando de Rosas, June 25, 1834

So, once again I am on the move, a homeless rambler who was flung off course by a strong wind in a storm and who now with calm weather is abandoning the unproductive land in order to pursue once more the goal I had previously set. How strange are often the turns of one's fate! It has been twelve months since I sat calmly with friends and relatives in Germany. I had plenty of everything then and yet I was dissatisfied. Now I am in the interior of Mexico, five hundred to six hundred miles from the coast, alone and without a cent of money. Often I have only corn to eat, at other times just some meat. Now I am forced to get down to the coast with my wagon in the hot summer, traveling through an arid desert over inaccessible roads and exposed to wild Indians and predatory Mexican robbers—and yet I am content. I am not the least bit worried about what my fate will be in the future. Consequently I do not want to waste any more words about it. Instead, I will now occupy myself, or actually you, with things past.

My business transactions allow me enough time to continue my reports, for you see I have opened a *store* here where all of the firearms and other things I had brought from Europe, etc. are displayed for sale in order for me to obtain through the sale of some of them as much money [as I need] to cover my expenses. The whole world, including the people in it, seems to be going around and around in a circle. I have gone from being a businessman to a man of private means to *squire* to a drover of oxen to landowner to day laborer and from that back to businessman. So, I have rotated once successfully on my own axis, and in doing so I have certainly gained in the turnabout.

Earlier, I used to sell a hundred bales of wool for my employer and I had no real interest in doing it. Now I sell a pair of wool stockings and I gain some money from the sale. Earlier, I sold new wine as old, and now I am selling old pocket handkerchiefs as new neckerchiefs. On one is [the image of] Paganini and on the other is General [Josef Baron] Chlopicki.[1] I tell my Mexican customers that the first one is the man who with his music makes people believe that heaven is a double bass and that the pope is in Rome.

---

[1] General Josef Baron von Chlopicki (1771–1845) was a Polish general who, after the outbreak of revolt against Russia in 1830–1831, took command of Polish troops because he lacked confidence in the leadership's ability to succeed. On December 5, 1831, he appointed himself dictator of Poland. Brockhaus. *Enzyklopädie*, IV, 515.

But I tell them that the other man is General Santa Anna and they take my word for it. While I used to lie to a customer in Europe and tell him that Polish wool was as good as Silesian wool, and he had the impertinence not to want to believe me, that same scoundrel had once sold charred clay as [roasted] chicory. Business people are an inventive clan, and I love thieves who do not let themselves be caught. On the other hand, five minutes ago I threw a stupid Mexican boy out of my second-hand shop. Because I have trousers, vests, and jackets on display here, he thought I was a tailor and wanted to have a pair of trousers cut to measure. What stupidity to think that I, a man wearing the mustache of a militiaman and hence the mustache of a hero, am a tailor! It is time that I leave this country, but first I am going to hurry back to Dolores.

The intrigues and the chicanery [in Dolores] were increasing with every passing minute and at the same time everyone's irritability was also on the rise. When they [Beales's subordinates] saw that nothing could be achieved by the devious course they had embarked upon earlier, they began to use other means and promised to double, even to triple everyone's wages. But that accomplished nothing. On the one hand they had made so many promises that they could not keep, and on the other hand they were careless enough to show how two-faced they were and were talking in several languages. While they were telling me that they could not approve even a half day's wage for the Germans' work and that they did not care a bit whether the Germans left or stayed, they were trying in every way possible to persuade the Germans to stay. They made promises on top of promises, but the colonists were smart enough to see that when my departure eliminated the path of retreat, they [Beales's subordinates] would suddenly be playing a different tune. Consequently, the colonists did not fall for any of the promises because I was the only one through whom they could come to some understanding with the *entrepreneurs*.

During this time there was again a dispute that gave cause for a formal complaint. The parties as well as all the inhabitants of the *villa* assembled in the hut of [Mr. Egerton,] the [acting] *alcalde*. I had been chosen by [Mr.] Rasbon as *hombre bueno* [arbiter]. Mr. Power, who had [at first] refused to accept that position on behalf of the other party [to the complaint], the master carpenter and builder, then accepted it in order to oppose me. The matter was as follows: Mr. Hartman, a master carpenter and builder, had hired workers in New York in order to use them to fulfill contracts he was going to take on to build houses. He had found Rasbon to be willing to go, but unwilling to enter into a contractual agreement to work. On the contrary, the latter had declared that it would depend upon the circumstances here whether he would work or not. Once they were in Dolores, Hartman concluded a contract for building a house and offered Rasbon a contract in which he would agree to work for a year. They agreed upon a salary, of course, but Rasbon still refused to sign the contract because he had already earlier declared a desire to work, but he would not commit to a period of time. He appears to have indicated this [unwillingness] only by shaking his head when the contract was offered to him. Hartman maintained that as a result he had taken Rasbon's behavior to mean that he was agreeing to it. A witness who held the same opinion, had left before the conversation [between the two men] ended. Hartman's brother maintained that he had taken no notice of the matter.

Rasbon had worked for one and a half months, and then he had quit working. Hartman had then refused to settle up with him and pay him his wages. Egerton and Power made every effort to smooth over the whole matter so that Rasbon, who had decided to go down the river in a *flatboat* with several others, would stay. But Rasbon would not change his mind. Hartman, on the other hand, who had concluded a contract with Beales and had nowhere else to go, had declared his intention to remain here.

Egerton, who wanted to gain some time, declared that the matter was so questionable and yet so important that he thought it was necessary to postpone a decision for twelve hours. I opposed this view by explaining that since there was no contract and there were no witnesses [to an agreement], and since Hartman had not been able to fulfill his own obligation to pay monthly wages, he had lost the right to insist upon [Rasbon] fulfilling a contract, the existence of which he could not even prove. But Egerton invoked his authority as *alcalde* and the deliberations were ended.

Obviously everyone saw in this that Hartman was going to be supported against Rasbon and the irritable mood of most of the *settlers* caused me to fear an outburst. I remained behind, therefore, in order to tell Egerton and Power [of my concern]. My good intentions, however, were misunderstood. Egerton believed that I wanted to intimidate him in order to gain some influence over his decision in the matter. He declared his intention of not deviating an inch from the letter of the law, no matter what people were planning to do to him. While I was explaining to him that he was misunderstanding me, the uproar erupted in front of the hut. Two *settlers*, Wilson and Wykop, confronted Hartman, calling him an infamous liar and declaring that with threats Hartman had prevailed upon his brother to tell a falsehood. It had in reality been like this: Three witnesses had been there outside of Hartman's hut and had overheard the conversation inside. Hartman's brother had not denied this, but it was not mentioned in order not to alienate the two brothers from each other, because a different outcome of the dispute had been expected. I thought I was seeing a fistfight in preparation, but the master builder seemed to have a fear of the powerful fists of his opponent, [Mr.] Wilson, and was in retreat. Egerton wanted to get them apart, but he was dismissed rather rudely and warned not to interfere.

So, the Sunday came when we were expecting news from San Fernando about what the last mail delivery from Matamoros had brought. At breakfast I commented about what we had been futilely waiting for, saying that if no news came from Addicks, then I would be leaving in two days. Mr. Plunkett directed a crafty question at me, asking how I intended to cross the river which had recently risen several feet. I answered that Mr. Allen, the carpenter, would take us across. Then he replied that at this time the boat would hardly be at Mr. Allen's disposal, pointing out that Mr. Power, who was paying for the construction of the boat, would deny us the use of it. One can see from this [remark] the means that one was willing to employ to keep us here. I took pleasure, therefore, in being able to answer him that he should not worry about that since Mr. Allen had in any case already finished building a large ferry and we would not need Mr. Power's boat. [I went on to say], however, that I would take the boat if I needed it, whether it was placed at our disposal or not. This remark astonished Mr. Plunkett quite a bit. Mr. Allen had come to Dolores several times regarding the delivery of the boat, but he was not willing to deliver it until its price had been paid. He was familiar with the mood of the *settlers* too and had built the ferry as a speculative venture of his own for bringing a number of the *settlers* for a fee down to Matamoros.

In the meantime we were still waiting in vain for our breakfast. I knew very well that it would not come, because the time period that the Germans had been obligated to work had expired the day before. Sometime earlier I had already notified Mr. Power, the maitre d', that Marie, our cook, did not want to cook for us any longer than she was required to do. He had taken no notice of my words, although I had repeated them to him just a few days ago. After he had made a few futile attempts at proving to me that the cook was still obligated to continue her service, I demonstrated to him the opposite. Then he ran around to all the women trying to find someone to cook. But no one wanted to agree to do it. Finally, around noon Mrs. Horn allowed herself to be persuaded to do it, but by evening Mr. Power was in the same predicament again. Her husband, who had often condoned the complaisant spirit of his wife, was angry that he had been forbidden to use a cart he had made for transporting his belongings out of the colony, belongings that had been made out of wood that did not belong to him. [In turn], he forbade his wife to repay this treatment with her cooperation. So, Mr. Power was forced to accept a fat, dirty Irish woman, Mrs. Emeline, as cook. She had cooked before for the most lowly laborers, and even they had dismissed her because of her filthy habits. But I have a very weak stomach, so I left my old dining spot and started taking my meals with the Germans.

Just before sunset a rider galloped into town. It was the carpenter Allen from San Fernando who had left town right after the mail from Matamoros had arrived, bringing no news at all from Addicks. Immediately I called Tallör and we began hurrying to get the wagon in order.

This news crushed the last hopes of those with an interest in the colony. They held a long meeting in which the decision was made that they would all leave the colony with bag and baggage. They would take everything to San Fernando de Rosas and await the arrival of the money there. Then they would return to Dolores with an escort of fifty soldiers which the general in Matamoros had promised to Dr. Beales when he was passing through there [on his way to New York]. This was reported to the colonists the next morning, and by that evening the most superfluous goods were supposed to be brought down to the river on all the wagons. This decision was cheerfully received by all the *settlers*, and immediately everyone began packing. I lent Egerton my wagon and oxen and that evening the first transport left, accompanied by Mr. Power.

The new cook had not been able to stimulate the men's appetite. They turned to me to use my influence with the Germans to hire another *cocinera* for them. So, I persuaded the former cook to perform those duties for a few days and to do it even without taking payment for it. The men were happy about this news, but the happiness did not last long. I had promised to advance the freighting fee to two German family heads which they had to pay to have their baggage taken to San Fernando. But they were of the opinion that since the colony's owners had at their expense brought the colonists here, who now had to leave, it was also the owners' duty to bring them at least to another place where there would be some personal security for them. Probably, in order to save me some expense, they had gone to Egerton with the question: What was to become of them now? But he had answered them that he did not want anything at all to do with the Germans. The cook heard this and the next minute she left the kitchen. Around noon people were again waiting for something to eat when they learned to their hungry astonishment that the cook had quit again and there was nothing cooked. Again they came looking for me, and I inquired about the cause, and then I went back to them with the answer: Since Mr. Egerton wanted nothing to do with the Germans, the German cook saw no reason to force her company on him. Then there was some talk [from Egerton] about necessity and the law, and I asked with curiosity which law he wanted to apply to someone who had offered to work out of the kindness of her heart for no pay, and who had done so without setting a time limit on her duties. Somewhat worked up by now, I told him that I could only approve of the lady's behavior, but I found his behavior reprehensible. I then wished him and the other men there a good appetite and went away laughing.

During all this we continued to play *whist* or chess every evening on friendly terms and joked about our not very funny situation, as we stimulated our sense of humor as always with the clear water that we drink.

Tuesday and Wednesday passed with the settling of accounts, packing, etc., when around noon of that last day these chores were interrupted in an interesting way. I was standing at the entrance to the enclosure [around the settlement] engaged in a conversation with several people when Luna, a Mexican guard, called out, *los Comanchos, los Comanchos!* I rushed out into the open and saw several Indians with some extra horses just coming around the corner [of the fence] and calmly approaching us. Luna and I went to meet them when I saw that it was Lipans. They extended their hands to us from atop their mounts and said in broken Spanish that they were our friends. It was the chief and his friend. Gradually, the others came along too, about twenty of them, with a hundred horses. They were mostly of tall, handsome stature, all of them naked, and armed with long spears, bows and arrows, and a round shield about three and a half feet in diameter, covered with buffalo hide and padded to catch enemy arrows. They had also tomahawks and knives. Two were armed with poor firearms. They set up their camp next to the camp of the Mexicans who immediately did everything they could to receive the visitors as hospitably as possible.

While the older Indians lay down in the shade of the trees, the younger ones caught the horses and hobbled them. They were actively assisted in this work by the Mexicans. When this was done, they came back to camp with the horse meat they had brought with them and hung it up to dry in the sun. This is almost their sole form of nourishment. Then the Mexicans gave them the present of a goat which they immediately slaughtered. It was done in a way that I had never seen before: A knife was thrust into the animal's heart and after withdrawing the knife, it was then pressed over the wound, which killed the animal in the blink of an eye and without more than three or four drops of blood being shed—and now one might still say that these sons of the prairie are bloodthirsty. Nevertheless, the Mexicans do not trust them, and all of the friendly gestures that they make to the Indians are calculated to prevent them from practicing their not so bloodthirsty skills on them. [I do not think that] they are to be trusted, for opportunity makes the thief!

Soon the Indians had scattered to all the huts where they collected food items and examined the things that were new to them. Weapons especially attract their attention. My shotguns, rifles, and pistols soon had the whole brown mob gathered inside and around my hut. Everything there was touched and handled. My watch, my shirt buttons with miniature images of German lovelies, a purse covered with pearls, and other such things seemed to amuse them quite a bit. I was wishing that I owned a full set of their weapons, but I could not persuade anyone to trade with me. They needed them themselves.

Their bows are small, about four feet long and are carried in a leather sheath. On the other hand, their lances must probably be from twelve to fifteen feet in length and they have the blade of a sword about one and a half to two feet long on the tip. The shaft is made of an extremely hard but very light and flexible wood, and it is trimmed with feathers.

In the whole group were two Indians who stood out from the rest. One of them was a man about fifty years old and about five feet five or six inches tall. His build and facial features were quite distinctive in their elegance from those of the others, and his light gray hair fell in long, loose curls over his brown shoulders. His refined manner and adroit behavior suggested that he was the chief of the tribe, while his head and face were more reminiscent of the image of a priest, and yet he was neither. On the other hand, he had always enjoyed a certain esteem among his people, and when [Agustín] Iturbide became emperor, he was sent as his tribe's emissary to Mexico City, since he was fairly fluent in the Spanish language.[2] He remained there for a longer period of time and received a great deal of attention there. He was finally dismissed [and sent home] with the [honorific] title of captain. He presented a pretty foal to the German, [Herr] Schwartz, who had extended to him the hospitality of his hut. He liked to walk around arm in arm with us and tell us about his stay in the [Mexican] capital.

The other Indian, who had a tall, powerful build, was different from all the others in every respect. He was a Comanche who had been taken captive as a boy and has become so thoroughly a member of his former tribe's enemy tribe, the Lipans, that he fights his own people to the death. And yet he still wore the attire of his people, possibly in order to serve as a spy. A braid of plaited horsehair was hanging from his head all the way down to his knees. The weight of it must have been very cumbersome. He also allowed the hair on his upper lip to grow. The rest of his face was kept entirely free of hair by the usual method of plucking the hairs out. On his feet and legs halfway up the thigh he wore a type of leggings made from heavy leather. The seam ran down along the outside of the leg and was trimmed with a stripe made from the hair of a horse's mane. These leggings must have been

---

[2] [Agustín] Iturbide was emperor of Mexico from May 1822 to March 1823. On January 4, 1823, he signed the first permit for the settlement of Anglo-Americans in Stephen F. Austin's colony in Texas. Carolyn Hyman, "Iturbide, Agustín de," *New Handbook of Texas*, ed. Ron Tyler et al., III, 880–881.

heavy and certainly very uncomfortable to wear. His physiognomy also did not resemble at all that of the other Indians.

In order to show the Indians the superiority of our weapons, we practiced some target shooting with them. While we never missed, they did not hit the target a single time with their carbines. As a joke, I offered to trade my rifle to them, but I was surprised to receive no better offer than a horse worth only about eight to ten pesos. To them a firearm seems to be just a firearm. They do not recognize any differences in quality and they seemed to believe that our skill in shooting and not our weapons had given us the advantage.

Their language consists of low guttural sounds articulated with the mouth half open. These sounds resemble somewhat the sounds uttered by a mute person.

They spent the rest of that evening stretched out on their animal hides humming their monotonous song until they fell asleep. The next morning at about ten o'clock our wagons came back and around noon the Lipans left. I would have liked to trade with them for a few horses if it would not have been so difficult to take them with me on such a long journey. Two foals about a year and a half to two years old and with exceptionally beautiful markings were offered to me for two or three pesos. In Germany they would have certainly been worth twenty to thirty *Louis d'or*.[3] In their herd were also many horses and mules that had been stolen. One could see this from the marks burned into their hides and which the Indians had tried to make unrecognizable. In general one must be careful [here] when purchasing livestock and one should trade only with people whom one knows, for if the livestock has been stolen by the vendor, and the former owner happens to spot them, then he can simply reclaim his property. The purchaser of the livestock has no recourse than to seek recovery of damages from the person who sold it to him. As one can imagine, this can be very difficult, and with the Indians impossible. Consequently, one customarily issues here a bill of sale that goes with the horse from one owner to the next.

---

[3] The Louis d'or was a French gold coin that was first struck in 1640 and was issued until the Revolution in 1789. It was also the name of the 20-franc gold piece issued after the Revolution. *Webster's New Collegiate Dictionary*. (Springfield, M.A.: G. and C. Merriam Co., 1979), 675.

Sixteenth Letter
Withdrawal of All the Colonists. Memorial. Passage Across the Rio Grande. Reception in San Fernando. A Festive Ball. The Inhabitants' Mode of Life. Departure for the Mexican Coast. Arrival in Laredo. A Difficult Way to Revilla. Mode of Life There. Acquaintance with a Priest and Renter of Mules. A Remarkable Declaration of Love. Entertainment of the Inhabitants.

San Fernando

I am going to continue to report on how our departure [from the colony] was conducted. By nine o'clock in the evening everything was all loaded up, and the oxen, which were as chubby and fat as quail for having done little or no work in three months, were hitched to the wagons. Everybody had left the town. I was standing there like Scipio on the ruins of Carthage and, without shedding a single tear, I looked out without pity at the forsaken heroic city. Mere prose cannot describe my emotions then. Verses, divine verses, came pouring forth as they did from the Maid of Orleans. Inspired by divine powers, I, the youth of New Orleans, was impelled to sing my swan song and with my breath I uttered the following words. All around me nature heaved wistfully a moribund sigh and dictated a farewell letter to life [there]:[1]

DEPARTURE FROM VILLA DE DOLORES

Farewell, you huts, you miserable holes,
You half withered trees, farewell!
Eduardo will no longer amble among you,
Eduardo happily bids you farewell.
You meadows that I burned, you yellow, not green, corn,
That I planted and which so quickly withered.
Farewell! You snakes and you scorpions,
Tarantulas, lizards, ticks, mosquitos,

[1] At the time Ludecus left Dolores, a few families and several unmarried men remained in San Fernando waiting for the return of Addicks and Beales. Among those who remained were Mr. and Mrs. Harris and Mr. and Mrs. Horn (and their two children). Early in 1836, after the colonists had reoccupied the colony (i.e., Dolores), they were attacked by Comanches. Carl Coke Rister has reprinted Sarah Ann Horn's narrative of captivity among the Comanches, her ransom by traders in New Mexico, and her return via the Santa Fé Trail—see Rister, *Comanche Bondage*, 89, 106–187.

Publius Cornelius Scipio (ca. 185–129 B.C.) was a Roman general who destroyed Carthage. As Ludecus stands on the abandoned remains of Dolores, he is reminded of Scipio. No description of Scipio standing on the ruins of Carthage could be found.

You prickly cactus, you thorn bushes.
Joyfully I now go down to the sea,
Eduardo goes away never to return.

You scenes of my eager craving,
You empty pots of repulsive stewed fruit;
Rabbits, play merrily again your happy games
In the brush that we often wandered through.
You buffalo may safely graze again
There, where the desert almost let us die of thirst;
I ventured out on you, savannas, with great joy,
And now with greater joy still, I am leaving here.

Farewell, Ludecus Street, you houseless street,
Probably never will a mansion be glimpsed in you,
If an Indian with his copper-red nose
Does not erect his wigwam of dry branches there.
Now I must travel again into the prairie.
I must pull myself away by my own hair.
Farewell, Dolores, for now at Don Lodrigo's★ command
The coach whip cracks and his oxen roar.

★ The Mexicans, who could never remember my name, called me Don Lodrigo.

[*Author's Note*—Eduard Ludecus]

While I hoarsely recited this jeremiad, my wagon, hitched to four oxen, drove away. On it, besides my own baggage, were Tallör's baggage, a few trunks belonging to the Germans, another one belonging to the Negro Henry, and those of a Scottish family, because Egerton had refused to transport their belongings. Tallör, who had had a rash on his foot for four weeks and was not able to walk, was riding on the wagon. I had given my horse to the German girl and we were going to take turns riding on it. I was riding behind her so that I could do my job as drover.

We had gone hardly a thousand paces when we heard someone behind us calling out, "*Stop, stop!*" Mr. Egerton came galloping up to us then and said that his small carriage had been left behind, that it was supposed to have been hooked behind another wagon, but it had already left. Then he demanded that some men pull the carriage up [to our wagon], but none of the formerly subservient subjects made a move to lend a hand. Their response to him was a friendly "*Go to hell!*," and Egerton was forced to have one of his own wagons drive back to fetch the abandoned carriage. This was the consequence of the behavior of these gentlemen toward the colonists. Silently the procession soon got underway again. A good many of these travelers, especially the families, were in the most dire predicament. Without money or anything of value, isolated in an impoverished, savage country, and without knowing the language, they found themselves faced with two choices: try to return [to civilization], with all manner of attendant sacrifice, or try to live among the natives. Everyone was lost in his own thoughts. About one o'clock I stopped at a nice grassy spot where Wilson had already unhitched his oxen, while the others continued on. Before sunup we got underway again and then at a place where the others had stopped we halted also for a short rest. In hopes of crossing the river the same day, we went too far too fast and it became so hot that I had to stop every quarter hour in order not to push my oxen to exhaustion. The water in my glass bottles that had been out in the sun for a while was hot enough for making tea. Finally, about three o'clock we reached the river valley where there were some tall mesquite trees growing. I did not dare go any further and we unhitched the oxen.

Some people on foot and some riders had hurried on ahead to quench their thirst. Lying [in my wagon] half asleep, I heard the sound of a horse's hooves approaching. I sat upright and saw a Scotsman racing back from the river at full gallop and as he chased past me, he called out that the Comanches were close on his heels. To my question about the whereabouts of Mr. Pepin who had gone on foot with him, he gave no reply. I ran to my horse in order to rush to the aid of the others when I saw the alleged Comanche already approaching me. It was a Mexican from San Fernando who was bringing nothing less than the news that Addicks had finally arrived there with the money.

So, we had been waiting six weeks for his arrival, only to leave our homes twenty-four hours too early. Nevertheless, we continued on our way and soon we found a good spot on the river for crossing. It was somewhat upstream from the place where we had crossed before. It was too late to attempt a crossing that day, so we made camp nearby on the high bank of the river where we could see on the opposite bank Mr. Power's tent and the baggage that had been sent ahead. We found there also the remains of a large Indian encampment where probably several hundred men had camped. After several hours Mr. Egerton came along also and with him the *gros d'armée* [i.e., most of the Mexican guard]. From then on my wagon was the headquarters of the Germans.

I had just stretched out on my buffalo hide under a magnificent starry sky when Mr. Egerton and Mr. Plunkett came to me to notify me that Mr. Beales had sent the money from my bank draft on [a bank in] New York. At the same time they proposed that I go back. But that was not in my plans. Of course, it had been my wish earlier to wait until a road had been cut from Dolores to the road from [San Antonio de] Bexar that passes through Presidio de Rio Grande. I wanted to go by this route to visit the Austin colonies which are reported to be enjoying great prosperity. But I was already underway now and if I went back, then the Germans would have to turn around too, but I had promised them and the others whose baggage was in my wagon to help them with all my power to get away. Those two men knew that very well too. I told them about my promises and that I had decided to go first to San Fernando in order to make further plans there. The others [with me] were not interested in their proposals either.

The night did not pass very quietly. The young bears that had spent the last twenty-four hours in the wagon, were galloping all around trying to catch up on the activity they had missed. They were racing around over me so that I was forced to whack them both soundly with the rod I use to drive the oxen and that helped some. *Sally Brown*, the female bear, had often created havoc in our camp. Four days earlier she had gotten off her chain and had entered Mr. Egerton's hut through the window opening. Among other things, she had spilled the contents of the inkwell over his papers and had broken a porcelain pitcher and a gold watch. Her worthy brother had once broken into my hut, but I came in just in time to put an end to his activities. Their antics, however, had entertained us for many a boring hour.

The next morning we hurried about unloading our wagons. We carried everything down the forty-foot high riverbank and then it was placed aboard the ferry. The Rio Grande had always behaved with hostility toward me, and this time too it dealt spitefully with me. As soon as the boat was loaded with my wagon and horses, the baggage and the people, it pushed out into the river, but we had no sooner gotten out into the current than the boat began tilting to one side, taking on water, and was threatening to sink. The women were screaming terribly, and I rushed to the horses to force them overboard, when the boat righted itself and we reached the other side safely. But this was only a prelude. After returning to the other bank, Wilson and I tried to drive our oxen through the river. But three or four hours of trying yielded no success. As soon as the oxen's feet lost contact with the river bottom and reached the strong current, they turned around and nothing we did was able to keep them from turning back. Luna and I swam after them several times, grabbed them by the horns, and almost beat their skulls in trying to keep them going in the right direction, but it was all for nothing. We had to give up in order to make another attempt later in the company of the entire herd and the *cavalcade* of about thirty horses. Together with the Mexicans then we drove the oxen safely to a different spot on the other side. Unfortunately, some horses were induced to go back again by a few mares that had remained behind with their foals. Several attempts that we made later to bring them over were equally unsuccessful. The current swept me away several times and I was forced to swim back. Then I jumped on my horse and borrowed a *cabestro*, which I used as reins. I wanted to repay the three mounted Mexicans for the favor they had done for me earlier. We were all swimming in the middle of the river and driving the herd in front of us when the horse of one Mexican was allowed to turn back. I called out to him, but he paid no attention to it. I expected to see all the lead animals turn around. Then I tried to turn back, but my horse wanted to follow the herd. The current was sweeping us both away, so I let go of the horse and was struck by him on the head. I ended up under him then, so I dived down deeper, and when I came up again, I discovered that both of us had unfortunately been swept along at the same speed. For several seconds I stayed at the same spot treading water and after that little *intermezzo*, when I came up, I was delighted to see the light of day again. Since I was wearing boots and spurs, I looked around for the shortest way to the bank (it was the side I had just come from). I had every reason to get myself on solid ground as quickly as possible, so I steered a course straight for the bank. But I had gone hardly halfway when I spotted right there ahead of me a pirate, the head and back of an alligator (not to be confused with an Egyptian crocodile) protruding above the water. In order not to get within range of his gun battery, that is, the two rows of beautiful ivory teeth, I changed my course to go further downstream. So, I raised all my sails and ran up on the beach a few hundred paces below the landing. My foundering had been witnessed by the Mexicans on the distant bank and by the Americans on the nearby bank. They had given me up for lost, but when they saw the wreck standing safely on the bank, there went up a loud "Hooray!" For the moment I did not thank them, for I was out of the very thing that I needed most—breath. As soon as I had caught my breath somewhat, I walked back with some others to the crossing spot.

In order to give you an idea of the force of the current in the Rio Grande, I want to note here that while Luna, the Mexican, was swimming across, a new cotton shirt that he was wearing was torn into two pieces. The sun was hot and shining very brightly. There was no shade anywhere. There was nothing for us to do but go sit in the water. After an hour the ferry finally returned. We got on board to go back to the left [south] bank. The wagons were loaded aboard the ferry and we arrived at Morales, the usual landing, under a brightly shining moon. I had to pay no less than ten pesos to have my wagon and the Germans' cart ferried across.

Very early the next morning Wilson, the Germans, and I hurried on our way, but at ten o'clock the heat forced us to take shelter under some trees. The little water that we had was soon gone and we had to fill our kegs in the San Rodrigo [Creek] that was an hour away. In the cool [of the night] we continued on our way and at two o'clock in the morning we reached the San Juan River. We stayed there until the following afternoon and then we made a new route through the somewhat swollen river. Around midnight we reached the outskirts of the town [San Fernando], and in order to allow the animals to graze the rest of the night, we called a halt there. The next morning I hurried on horseback to San Fernando to find some quarters for myself. I was unable to find anything suitable, so I accepted the repeated invitation of my friend, the postmaster Don Louisiano de Garson, to stay at his house. He gave me a room facing the street and soon I was all settled in. In the meantime, the Germans had accepted the offer of the Mexican wagoner to take quarters in his house. From all over they had received offers. One person wanted to take them into his house; another one offered them for free a dwelling and some land to live on for several years. A third person delivered food to them *gratis*. They have been staying until now in the quarters that were first offered to them, but they are uncertain as to how they can manage the rest of the journey with me. Meanwhile their quarters are being besieged by a crowd of the curious. The first serenades of the evening were performed for them, even after the *fandango* was over. Then they all laid down to sleep in the street, the common bedroom in the summer, in order to keep the visitors company at night too. I am just hoping that all this courtesy and hospitality will not end when their curiosity is satisfied.

To my astonishment I heard yesterday from Egerton that when Addicks arrived, he had brought along instead of the anticipated sum of five thousand pesos, only two thousand, and that it would be impossible therefore to give me the sum I was expecting. [Here is] proof of how poorly Mr. Beales had arranged his financial matters, and the colonists are now in the same situation as before: the amount of money does not suffice now to cover the debts that had been made. I am still not quite clear about the cause for Addick's delay, but I know this much, namely that the reason they told me is not the true one. Young Addicks committed the unpardonable error of not saying a single word either to explain what delayed his return. But after his departure [from here] for New York, Mr. Beales committed the error of utilizing for such business a young person who had no knowledge or experience for it. Now he must make serious amends for the consequences [of his error].

I had gone back to my quarters with empty pockets, but filled with good cheer, and I was hurrying to finish my *toilette*. Captain Gallon, the troop commander here, had invited me to a *fandango*. My host took me to the captain's house about eight o'clock after we had first eaten something at home. I had given him one of my old velvet vests, and he was very happy in it. I was wearing boots, white trousers, a silk vest, and a Nanking evening jacket. Thus, from my attire, I could make claim to the rank of a first-rate gentleman.

We first entered a vestibule of the house and from there we went into the main hall. It was an oblong room, furnished all around with benches, and on them some of the *señoritas* were seated, while others were sitting all around on the firm earthen floor and were using the benches as backrests. I had myself introduced to the host. I thanked him for the invitation and expressed my joy at receiving it. So much ceremony seemed to be something new and somewhat embarrassing to him. He tried to respond, but his book of compliments left him in the lurch. I behaved the way certain big shots in my fatherland are wont to do. I did not wait for a reply and moved on.

People danced for a few hours in the same manner as I described it earlier in La Bahía. A violin and a guitar were playing very sleepy music. Soon the heat became unbearable for me and I was feeling a terrible thirst. I looked all around, but I could not discover anywhere any arrangements suggesting that some consideration would be given to our stomachs. Gradually I was becoming worried about this and just when my distress was at its greatest, I spied a plate on which there were four glasses. To be sure, they were intended for the ladies who took turns drinking out of them (brandy and water), but I found hope there that someone would sooner or later remember the thirsty gender also. I had not been mistaken, for soon afterward all of the *cavalleros* were led into an adjoining room where some kind of liqueur was being served on a table with some baked goods. This very hungry and thirsty pack formed a semicircle [around the refreshments], but the men did not at first attack the game being offered to them. The order to eat and to drink was repeated several times, but no one wanted to be the first. With words and elbows everyone was urging his neighbor to dig in, but if one person was pushed forward out of the zone of modesty, he did an about-face and took up a position in the back row. Weary of suffering the tortures of Tantalus any longer, I finally led the way myself and was just about to step into the breach, when another volunteer, denying me my fame, rushed forward and seized the fortress. [2]

Then without any show of timidity everyone helped himself, and my host, who was acting as a sort of *maître de plaisir*, was soon in such a mood that he was throwing glasses to the floor like so many pebbles. After a brief intermission the dancing continued, and in order to have danced one time in Mexico, I finally accepted the invitation to dance one round of the *fandango*. When it was my turn, I took my place and found my *vis à vis* to be the ugliest skeleton that may have once come to the Brocken mountain on a Walpurgis Night. [3] The dance allows one complete freedom to approach his

---

[2] Tantalus, a Greek mythological figure, was condemned to stand in a pool of water with fruit hanging before his eyes. When he tried to eat or drink, the food or water disappeared. Hornblower and Spawforth (eds.), *Oxford Classical Dictionary*, 1473.

[3] Brocken Mountain is the highest mountain in the Harz region of Germany. Under its alternate name, "Blocksberg," it was reputedly the scene of "Walpurgisnacht," a legendary witches' Sabbath that occurred each night of April 30 to May 1. The legend appears in Goethe's *Faust*, Part 1. Garner and Garner (eds.), *Oxford Companion*, 109–110.

compañera or to elude her. The whole time I found myself on the run, hoping in vain for another to relieve me, but my signals were going unheeded. Finally, with one *entrechat* [leap], I fled the scene like a solo dancer. The beauty I had left behind did not lose her composure at all, but continued to dance on until a new *compañero* decided to continue the dance in my place, and finally she sank perspiring and panting onto a seat.

Minute by minute the merriment of the party increased. Soon a new *fandango* was begun, but almost immediately it was interrupted by Don Louisiano clapping his hands. Then there appeared a tall figure dressed in black which approached the lady and delivered a speech to her.[4] This ceremony was repeated with each change of the female partner. My little knowledge of Spanish enabled me to understand only parts of the speech. For the most part, it was a declaration of love and the person giving the speech was a priest (*padre*). Each time, when the speech was concluded, depending upon the degree of its appeal [to those present], it was greeted with a shout of "*bravo*." His colleague tried his luck, but he got stuck, and withdrew laughing and to the laughter of others. A third man tried his luck too and had more success than his predecessor and he received a "*bravo*" too. I was not familiar with his words, but their meaning must have been funny because as my host was clapping his hands, he was sliding around in a circle on his knees. I find confirmation here of everything that I reported earlier from La Bahía about priests in this country. I do not believe that they will apply to the pope for a lifting of the celibacy rule, as long as he cannot prevent them from living in common-law marriages.

As I was leaving, the captain bade farewell to me very courteously and assured me that if he could ever do anything for me, it would be his pleasure to accede to my wishes. My host wanted to drink the drink the cup [of pleasure] dry, so he stayed behind. For some reason unknown to me, his wife had stayed home. She is one of the most attractive women that I have seen so far in Texas. The two of them have also a small, very cute, two-year old girl, their only child in a ten-year marriage. When we eat, she does not sit at the table with us, but squats nearby on an animal hide with a servant girl and serves the meal. This is said to be the custom throughout Mexico. On the other hand, the Mexican woman is treated by her husband in the most courteous manner. Rarely or never will a man permit himself a display of rudeness toward the other sex, and he will spend his last *real* to satisfy the wishes of his spouse.

While a man's wife goes about in silk stockings, they often suffer want of the most basic things. For example, in the house of my host there is only one

---

[4] Ludecus seems mystified by the appearance of the dark figure and the reaction of the other guests to its speeches to the ladies.

knife and the wooden handle is broken off of that one. The meat is skewered in small pieces onto an iron or metal spit and set at an angle over the fire the way we used to do out on a hunt. Spanish pepper plays a large role in their culinary art, and they eat everything also with a lot of fat. Coffee, rice, and tea are luxury items which even the wealthy see only rarely on their tables. However, I am referring only to these regions here, the poorest, worst, and wildest of all regions of the Mexican nation that are populated by whites. The Mexican woman nurses her child for a very long time. Our little *muchachita* sits sometimes next to her mother on an animal hide and fetches some meat for herself. Often her mother sits or squats in the doorway [of the house] while her naked child stands next to her and drinks at one of her mother's breasts.

These people live extremely happy lives. They have few needs or none at all. The work of planting the corn and sugar cane is done in a short time, and their herds, which they bother about only when they slaughter an animal or want to brand it or notch [the ears of] a maturing calf or goat, give them plenty of meat. Dances, horseback riding, and gambling fill the time that their life of extreme leisure affords them. Every evening at twilight the young people, all of them dressed in clean white clothes, assemble under the [pecan] nut trees and mulberry trees at the dance plaza and then they dance to the music of a guitar, a violin, or probably only the voice of a singer. It often lasts until late into the night, even until the next morning. Moreover, everyone conducts himself with a great deal of civility, and I have never seen any bickering, let alone any fighting among the dancers. But if a quarrel does occur, their hot tempers cool quickly. The exchange of words ends and one stab with a knife causes one opponent or another to become more inclined to yield.

Horseback riding is one of their chief pleasures. Everything is done on horseback. Yes, even public assemblies are attended sitting in a saddle. With their great love of horses, horse races are very common here, but they run the horses only for very short distances (approximately 200 feet). Usually, every spectator has a wager on the race, which spells the ruin of one person or another. As I have mentioned before, games of chance are their chief passion. Facing my host's residence is a house where people assemble every day, and early in the morning, when I get up, I often see the same people who had come the evening before. Even the church services cannot interrupt their gambling, although several of them are probably hurrying to Mass to ask God perhaps for a little more luck. But then they hurry back. This inclination to gamble can be easily explained when one considers that in view of the few needs that these people have, they do not know how to make good use of their money and they do not know any better way to spend their time. They are said to be very honest in paying their gambling debts, and since cash is extremely rare here, they commonly pay with oxen, horses, etc.

I have to break off now, because yesterday's ball did not do my health much good. I feel a great fatigue in all my limbs and I am exhausted. As soon as I have taken in as much money as I think I need to get to Matamoros, I will get underway.

July 10, 1834

Unfortunately, my stay here has been extended until now, but I hope to be able to get underway tomorrow. I had hardly concluded my last letter when my indisposition became so severe that I had to go to bed. Then I developed a case of diarrhea, which grew worse from day to day. I thought that the water was to blame, so I drank milk, but that made it only worse. I could not eat anything at all. In the meantime I was suffering even more from thirst. There was a physician in town, an American. Although I did not have much confidence in the sons of Aesculapius in this country, I staggered to him seeking his help.[5] He gave me some medicine which contained opium and some pills with the same drug. But it did not have the slightest effect. On the contrary, my condition became more and more serious. I could no longer walk without the assistance of others. Then I was given an emetic which completely overwhelmed me. The next day I had to remove the mustard plaster which I had endured for four hours, but it was hurting me a lot and keeping me from sleeping. I had become so weak that I could no longer speak distinctly. The only thing that I could eat was chicken soup with rice, but I could not bear the thirst. Then, when I learned that during this time [of the year] several inhabitants of the town had died of this ailment, I abandoned all hope of a recovery. In order to drink my fill of water at least one last time, I sent Tallör to a spring that was said to have good water. To the horror of everyone present, I drank as much as my stomach could hold, and then I fell back on my bed to await my fate.

The unexpected result was about two hours of sleep which I had been trying unsuccessfully to get for days. Afterwards I felt strong enough to get up, so I walked a few hundred paces to the doctor's apartment. He was in no small measure surprised to see me in such a different condition, and he was even more surprised when I told him what had brought it about. Since that hour my condition has improved some, but only a little. My weakened condition allows me to walk or ride only short distances, but nevertheless I am

---

[5] Aesculapius was the Roman god of healing. Hornblower and Spawforth (eds.), *Oxford Classical Dictionary*, 29.

determined to go on, because I have abandoned hope of recovering my health here. I will try to regain it on the journey [ahead].

People are predicting that I will not reach Laredo, but it is all the same to me. Wherever one dies, the result is the same. If my condition should grow worse, I will add a few more words to this page, no matter where I am. I will send all of you an eternal farewell and make all arrangements so that my words will be sent to those to whom they matter. But I must close now, for I am not capable of any more mental or physical effort.

Revilla, July 29, 1834

It is with delight that I report to those who will be happy to hear—the others are completely at liberty not to do so—that I have arrived here safely and my expectations of regaining my health on the journey have been for the most part fulfilled. To be sure, I have not yet completely recovered, but I do not doubt that with the better foods that are available here, especially the wheat bread, that the remaining symptoms of my illness will soon disappear. I have never been in doubt about the causes of my illness: the hardships on my travels and on hunting trips. Sleeping on the damp ground, often in the rain, the inferior, un-nourishing foods, and the heat that we are still not accustomed to must have had a deleterious effect on my constitution, especially on my already sensitive stomach. An additional complication may have been that on the day we crossed the Rio Grande I had to exert myself beyond my physical limits. I swallowed too much water also, and then I failed to change my clothes as I was often unable to do on hunting trips due to a lack of fresh clothes. I was forced to let my wet clothes dry [on my body]. I slept in them, and after a hot day, I spent an unusually cool night under the stars, as the dew was falling, without a blanket over me.

I am not exactly in the most pleasant situation here. Rather, as they say in my dear German fatherland, I am in the soup. To be sure, I dragged myself here under unspeakable difficulties, and I really do not know how I am going to continue on. So far, all of my attempts to do so have been futile, but I shall continue on, chiefly because I have to! But I want to pick up my narrative again where my life seemed to be hanging in the balance, and to do so, I will return to San Fernando.

During my last days there I was busy getting my affairs in order. I settled up with Mr. Egerton. He acted as though he were somewhat interested [in my welfare] and he got a little more money [from me]. Then I fetched from the physician some medicine which was supposed to stimulate my appetite on the journey when I had had nothing to eat. I paid him the thirty *pesos* he demanded and expressed my surprise that he could absorb so much silver at one time. Then I hurried home to pack.

Doctor Long, which is the name of the man with the deep pockets, is one of those people who have come to Mexico to get rich at a galloping pace.[6] He is a seeker of mining wealth, but it is said that good fortune has not been kind to him and that he has put more silver into the mines than he has taken out. During my first visit in San Fernando he was on an expedition to the abandoned mines to the west and, as he told me, he wanted to go to Saltillo★ in a month in order to open a mine there. He still owes me an answer to my question about how deeply he was planning to bury my thirty pesos.

★ Saltillo, a city on the border between Coahuila and [Nuevo] Leon, lies in a sterile plain. Travelers there suffer from the lack of water.

[*Author's Note*—Eduard Ludecus]

On July 11, at eight o'clock in the evening, everybody was standing in front of my door finally ready to get underway. I bade a very emotional farewell to my hostess. I regretted only that my meager knowledge of Spanish did not permit me to describe my gratefulness to her as I felt it, and really, I had every reason to be grateful. I had been cared for with a dedication that a son can expect only from his parents. Anything that I wished for was acquired if it was within the realm of possibility. My good hostess did not allow anyone else to give me my medicine and she interrupted her *siesta* every day when the time for it approached. Don Louisiano [de Garson] had left here five days earlier when business called him away to Monclova.★ When he left, I gave him a few presents from my wardrobe as a farewell gesture which made him very happy. I left a few souvenir gifts also for my nurse and hostess. A pair of embroidered house slippers and a flask of *eau de cologne* seemed to please her a great deal.

★Monclova is a military post and the capital of Coahuila.

[*Author's Note*—Eduard Ludecus]

The following people set out with me on the road: a Scottish family, a man, his wife and child, the Negro Henry, and an American shoemaker whose baggage I had taken along on my wagon. There was also the German Dippelhöfer with his wife and two sisters. For them I had borrowed the infamous cart from Schwartz who had stayed behind at the [Rio Grande] River and together with several carpenters he had built a boat.[7] They had left Morales under sail a few days before us. It was impossible for me to take

[6] Doctor Long could not be identified.

[7] Schwartz was more optimistic than Ludecus (and most others in the party) that the Rio Grande could be successfully navigated.

the other two German families with me because I was not able to make any arrangements to bring along their baggage. Settled there in houses and on land that had been given to them to use for several years, they preferred to remain there until they would receive news from me about the kind of prospects that would be available to them when they came down to Matamoros.

When everyone was all assembled, I gave the signal for departure. I climbed on my horse and bade farewell to the other men. But I was hardly out of town when my weakened condition forced me to dismount and lie down in the wagon. We had a splendid road and in a short while we passed the town of Morillos. About two o'clock we stopped near another town, called San Juan. At dawn [the next day] we continued on and about noon we reached a third town, Begates by name. Like San Fernando, these three towns irrigate their fields by means of ditches. The heat forced us to stop. I did not want to do so because the people in San Fernando had nothing good to say about the inhabitants [of Begates]. I made inquiries in the town as much as I could about the road ahead. Laredo was six or seven days of travel ahead, [they said,] and the watering holes, often some distance away from the road, are difficult to find. I did not want to risk going on without a guide and I would probably have to entrust my safety to the best man who accepted my offer first. Soon I found one, but later he demanded that I should pay him his money in advance. This roguish trick was just too blatant for me to be able to ignore it, however, and I asked him if he thought that I was fool enough to pay him in advance, just so he would run off after the first day's travel and leave me in the lurch. In response, he did not make the slightest effort to disabuse me of my suspicion. Instead, he only laughed and insisted on his demand. At that point I broke off negotiations with him.

Several others refused my offer because of their fear of Indians until I increased the pay. Then I reached an agreement with another man, an older man. Although the opportunity to earn six *reales* a day in addition to meals may be rare here, it was still difficult to get a guide. The cause seemed to be the fear of Indians who just recently had committed several murders in the vicinity. In the meantime, it had become late in the evening. Consequently, I abandoned the idea of going any further that day. Instead, we made preparations to get underway very early the next day. I sent for the animals that we had driven out into the prairie, but after a few hours I saw one searcher after another come back without having found them.

I soon realized what was going on, namely that someone had driven off the oxen in order to earn money [finding them]. One Mexican who had been hanging around our camp the whole time seemed to me to be the one who had organized the scheme. There was, therefore, nothing else to do but to promise him two *pesos* finder's fee, and in a short time all our oxen and horses were back. Then we got underway and about noon we reached an abandoned *rancho*, but we had to continue on our way since there was no water to be found there. Trouble with Indians had forced the owners to move back to town. What we missed there, however, we soon found at another place. A short distance to the left of the road was a small pond at the edge of some brush. We stopped and our animals enjoyed the beautiful grass there. Due to a lack of grazing for them they had been fasting almost the whole time since we left San Fernando. At sunset we continued on our journey, but at midnight we had to call a halt in the middle of a burning prairie because the pin in the turnbar of my wagon had broken and had to be replaced by another one. In New York I had had the foresight to purchase a lot of used iron hardware and especially such things as one needs for a wagon. That day the iron hardware came in handy.

We hung a lantern up on a burning tree and went to work. No matter how much we hurried, the work was taking so much time that I decided to set up our camp for the night right on this field of ashes. There was nothing left for the animals to do but either race after the fire to get some grass before it burned or to merely wipe their mouths and lay down in the ashes to rest. They preferred the latter. Around noon the next day we came to another watering hole and we stopped in order to avoid traveling in the blazing sun. The prairie there had a dense population of rabbits and as weak as I was, I still could not resist the desire to eat some fresh meat. So, I took my firearm and hobbled off to hunt. Hardly a half hour later I delivered four rabbits to our field kitchen. Mexican rabbits are not as large as German rabbits, but they are a much prettier color. We had not been there very long before we were suddenly surrounded by a large herd of goats. A distinguished and handsome man, about thirty years old, was following them. He was dressed in buckskin and was carrying over his shoulder a *calabaza*, a *cabestro*, a *frazada*, and a sack in which he was carrying corn. He had rested his firearm against a tree. He approached us with a noble demeanor and offered his hand. In good faith I grasped the hand of this son of the prairie and shook it. After a brief conversation, he took his leave with the courtesy typical of Mexicans and walked away like a king into the wide prairie, driving his numerous companions ahead of him. This man has no other bed than the earth and no other tent than the sky. Winter or summer, it makes no difference to him. If he gets thirsty, then he milks one of his goats, and if he gets hungry, then he slaughters her young kid. If he needs corn, then he goes into a town and trades from his abundance for some. He frightens the Indians by his formidable behavior. So, he has no worries and has the most freedom of any man on earth.

As usual, we continued our march as the sun was going down. Soon we found ourselves on a stony path that with its rough bumps was very hard on my fully packed wagon. We had traveled hardly two hours when our guide called a halt. When I inquired whether there was water there and why he wanted to stop so soon, he gave a negative answer to my first question and did not answer my second question at all. When I ordered him to continue on, he told me that it was dangerous to travel at night there and that the area was notorious because of robbers who had committed a lot of murders there. This statement seemed to me very doubtful, because I could not believe that people would lie in wait there for months just so they could ambush a Mexican and murder him for his few possessions. It seemed to me more likely that he was up to no good himself. I recalled that as we were leaving Begates the morning [before], several riders whose faces were not exactly models of honesty had ridden down the road ahead of us. Perhaps this place had been agreed upon as the *rendezvous* spot. Coincidentally, the place where we were seemed well suited for someone to be able to carry out an attack in safety. This persuaded me even more to go on and I forced the guide, in spite of his resistance, to saddle his horse. So, on we went until midnight, our firearms resting in our arms, when we came upon a good watering hole. This amazed me quite a bit. Earlier, in response to my demand that we travel to the next watering hole, the guide had said that it was too far and could not be reached in one night, and yet we found it so near. This new untruth did not diminish my suspicions. I decided not to remain there either. I let the animals drink and then I had them hitched up again, but then we discovered that the swing bar on the wagon was split. We could not risk traveling on without repairing it.

Immediately we went to work and in a short while we had made a makeshift repair. In our guidebook it seemed to be written: To this spot and no further! We were ready to leave, but then [we discovered that] my horses were missing. Contrary to their customary behavior, they had gone off wearing saddles and bridles, and every effort to find them was fruitless. I had to stay there in order not to leave them behind. I had not kept my eyes on the guide during our work, and he had disappeared too. But earlier I had taken charge of his shotgun with the excuse that it seemed to be threatening rain and in order to protect it from the moisture, I had placed it in the wagon. This new obstacle [to our progress] did not seem to be accidental and I kept a sharp watch. But the night passed quietly. The next morning, first the Mexican, and then the horses reappeared. The circumstances of their return made it all too clear to me that the horses had been tied somewhere all night. It became clearer to me also that the Mexican had something more up his sleeve. During the night this fellow had probably looked for his accomplices or had intended to look for them because they may have missed our camp. I would have been happy to dismiss him from service and send him home, but without knowing the location of watering holes, I had no other choice than to run the risk of perishing perhaps for lack of water, or of being robbed or perhaps killed. I preferred to run the latter risk.

The next day's travel led us at first across some splendidly fertile land. The *nopal* [cactus] and the mesquite trees were unusually tall. The former were laden with fruit so full of juice—juice that can serve in place of a beverage and that even has a fine flavorful taste. Consequently, I could not resist the temptation and I probably ate more of them than was good for me in my condition. [It is said] that extremes meet somewhere, and I found that confirmed here also. Adjoining this region was the most complete desert. We were dragging ourselves through it in a blazing heat until three o'clock in the afternoon. Then, when it was high time [to find relief], we found a watering hole surrounded by trees, and there was also some good grass for our animals.

More and more my wagon had begun to cause me worry. The sun had dried out the wood in the wheels so badly that cracks had developed in it. The iron rims and the mountings were working loose, while the fellies and the spokes were all beginning to grow loose too. We did what we could. We removed the wheel that was in the worst condition and left it overnight in the water. I decided to apply the procedure to myself too. I thought that a bath would give me strength, and I was not mistaken in my expectations. With a good appetite I ate some of the lamb that we had slaughtered. Toward evening I began to feel very sick and it soon became so bad that I had to vomit several times in rapid succession. But the next day I felt better again, except that I was weaker than before. That day we traveled through a fertile region covered by beautiful *nopal* [cactus]. At one glance one could see millions of their large ripe fruits. I have noticed that the blackish brown ones are juicier and better tasting than the bluish brown ones.

We spent the noon hours again in the shade of trees because a deep ravine prevented us from traveling on. We could not try to drive down into it by night, so I had called a halt. Far and wide there was not a blade of grass nor other trees in sight. We even had trouble finding the wood we needed for cooking. The next morning revealed that with proper caution it was not going to be so difficult to get beyond this bad defile. We unloaded the wagons and lowered them down with ropes. Then we brought the baggage down and soon we were ready to clamber up the opposite incline. On this day the heat was even more unbearable because the road led the whole time among mesquite trees that blocked the breeze. Our oxen were running off constantly to the left or the right, trying to find protection in the bushes from the burning rays of the sun. They seemed to be in general very sensitive to the sun, even more so than the horses which only rarely look for shade. For a long time we were hoping in vain to find a watering hole.

Finally we saw some cows on the prairie and [we knew that] where they were, there must also be some water in the vicinity. Soon we found it. About ten o'clock that evening we reached a *rancho* situated on the upper bank of the Rio Grande. It consisted of one large log cabin and several small huts in addition to a large pen for the cows that were to be milked. The *ranchero* or owner was reclining with his wife and all of the workers and servant women under the overhanging roof of the house. The noise we had made awakened them and soon they were all around us filled with curiosity. Immediately we rushed to their vessels of water. As sandy as the water of the Rio Grande is, it does nevertheless have a good taste. We felt very lucky to have for once something to drink other than the disgusting, warm, slimy, and often stinking water from the pools [at the watering holes].

We had just set up camp, meaning everyone had thrown his animal hide or his blanket upon the ground, when a woman appeared. This was in itself nothing remarkable, but this woman was so fat that everyone who saw her had to pity her. She had walked hardly twenty paces from the house to our wagon and she was already out of breath. She was only able to whisper these words that were barely audible, "*Adonde está el capitán?*" (Where is the leader?) When someone pointed to me, two servant girls stepped forward who had been modestly concealed on the *lee* side of their mistress. They handed me five or six beautiful *sandías* and *melónas* as gifts from the fat Baucis.[8] I accepted them with thanks and asked for permission to share them with my companions, for my ailing condition prevented me from enjoying them. She inquired immediately about my illness. When I explained to her my condition, she handed me a *sandía* (watermelon) and insisted that I could boldly partake of it. Adam then accepted the seductive apple from the hands of the fat Eve and ate, and later he did not suffer any ill consequences from it. I learned there too that the two flatboats with some of our *settlers* had passed that place two days earlier.

The next morning brought the opportunity to buy some milk from our hostess, but for me it was forbidden food. Our route led us the first day through a large plain interrupted alternately by patches of sand and then fertile soil. We were suffering badly from the heat and finally our oxen could not be driven any further. Several tall mesquite trees lent our campsite meager shade, but there was no prospect of water which we needed badly. My little water keg that I filled every morning was empty already by noon because all of us travelers were dependent on it. This had caused us several times to suffer agonizing thirst, but on the other hand it had the beneficial

---

[8] In Greek mythology, Baucis and her husband, Philemon, were an elderly peasant couple who provided food and drink to Zeus. They were handsomely rewarded for their kindness. Hornblower and Spawforth (eds.), *Oxford Classical Dictionary*, 236– 237.

effect that we did not feel hunger so acutely. Another consequence also was that nothing could be cooked in water. The Rio Grande could not be very far away [we thought], and so the attempt was made to fetch some water from there. A few men went down on horseback and returned in fact two hours later with a full keg. When they arrived at the river, they saw a band of Indians who had crossed the river a mile upstream.

As soon as the heat began to abate, we got underway again and about eleven o'clock we made camp on a forlorn knoll. We, people and animals alike, were having a day of fasting. We had no water in which to cook our dried meat and all around us there was no grazing for the animals. On the other hand we had the pleasure of hearing a drum beating during the night. We assumed therefore that we must be very near to Laredo. We arrived there the next morning.

The town is situated actually on the left bank of the river. The ten or twelve shabby huts on this side maintain a connection with the other side by way of a canoe, in which I immediately hurried to the other side in order to buy some fresh meat. I met there the carpenter, [Mr.] Allen, who had brought his boat safely down the river and sold it. The others had continued on their course to Matamoros. He was very surprised to see me still alive. When I asked him how he and the others had fared on their journey, he told me that as they had passed the twelve-foot high falls near Presidio [de Rio Grande], that they had almost perished. The water had also washed a number of their light implements overboard. Because of the rocks there that spot is extraordinarily difficult to pass and impossible for steamboats.

I found the town of Laredo in a better condition than I had expected. The houses are built for the most part of stone and in its way it has an appearance of wealth. To my delight I found there a type of pastry prepared from wheat flour or oatmeal with a trimming of sugar, and some wine made from domestic grapes. In taste it resembles Malaga wine. As expensive as everything was, I bought some in hopes that it would repair my health. I was able to obtain also some rice and coffee there. Loaded down with my treasures, I hurried back, but I was just barely able to reach the riverbank. In spite of resting several times along the way, the walk had exhausted me terribly.

I had received very unfavorable reports about the road to Revilla. It was described as extremely difficult for wagons. I would have liked to have the tires removed from the wheels on my wagon and reduced in size if there had been a blacksmith there who understood the task. Besides, it was very complicated to get the wheels across the river. I hoped with a little care and the planned repairs to be able to plod along as far as Revilla.

My guide from Begates had offered to go with me [to Revilla]. My attempts to hire another guide [in Laredo] were fruitless, because the two men there who offered to serve as guides had the appearance of such *com-*

plete rogues, that although I had never studied Gall's craniology, I thought that I was justified in turning them away.[9] My old guide's behavior had been very ambiguous, of course, but he had not absconded with my livestock. I was hoping, therefore, that since he could not easily find any accomplices because he probably had no connections here, I was not risking more with him than with anyone else. So, I kept him.

But as the evening approached, my Mexican [guide] kept me waiting in vain for him. In the expectation, therefore, that he would follow after us, I had the oxen brought in and I left. The others, who had decided to trade their few possessions for horses, intended to follow me the next day.

I had been careful about getting directions and people had told me that there was only one road to Revilla. Nevertheless, after a half hour [on the road] we came to a fork. Since I was reclining in the wagon, Tallör drew my attention to it and asked which way he should go. I told him to take the road to the left since, as he had insisted, it was the more traveled one and because it was supposed to follow along the river which was on our left. Nevertheless, two hours later we found that the road was diminishing more and more until it ended in a deep ravine. I dragged myself out of the wagon, mounted my horse, investigated the ravine, and found that it was difficult to cross.

We had to turn around. We started down another road and were forced by nightfall to call a halt. During all this Tallör behaved so rudely that it was not possible for me to ignore it as I had done so often before. I told him off, but he became even surlier. Irritable already because of my illness, I became angry and had a mind to teach him some respect with my saber, but I regained my composure and told him that if he took such liberties with me again, then I was going to take his baggage out of my wagon. Then he could travel on his own, which he seemed to be wanting to do. His answer was that I could do as I pleased. It was fine with him.

At my expense I had brought this person with me from Germany. His situation was like that of others who had to work six months for their master. His good traits such as honesty, loyalty, and industry had prompted me [in the past] to readily overlook his faults such as conceit (he was in his opinion the only one who understood something), quarrelsomeness, and boundless obstinacy. I had treated him more like my brother than my subordinate, but this usually makes people cruel. They think that they are indispensable and that someone is treating them well for selfish reasons only in order to put them under some obligation. He was completely free to work when it pleased him. Often when others had to work in the heat, he was sleeping or

---

[9] Craniology, the study of the human skull, was founded by [Franz Joseph] Gall (1758–1828), a physician in Vienna and later in Pforzheim, Germany. Brockhaus, *Die Enzyklopädie*, VIII, 117.

he went out with my shotgun to shoot some rabbits. It was completely with my consent that he did this. His stubbornness and strangely conceited behavior had already earned him the ridicule of other people on our journey here, and later his ill-mannered and unaccommodating behavior toward everybody, especially toward the [other] Germans, had forced me to call him to account several times. Once he had behaved the same way toward my hostess in San Fernando who came to me later and asked me to have the Germans cook for me in the future. I soon got wind of what was going on and it took a lot of effort on my part to restore our good relationship. That same morning the Germans, who every day were doing him favors, complained to me about his rudeness. I then pointed out to him very calmly his [rude] behavior, but he merely replied curtly that he had not been rude. I went on to say to him that it had already become a habit with him and that he did not even know it. I had often observed it myself, but I had kept quiet about it because I do not like quarreling. I warned him and added that it would only hurt him in the future.

The next morning our fellow travelers who had remained behind [at Laredo] were quite astonished to see my wagon back at the same location where they had seen it leave the evening before. By morning I had also gotten over the whole incident with Tallör and it was no longer on my mind. I was therefore all the more surprised when he came to me and with a prideful attitude asked if it was agreeable with me if he unloaded his things then. I looked at him to see if he was serious, gave my consent to his request, and went immediately to work.

As he was unloading his baggage, which was done very quickly, he became very downcast. His actions were becoming completely clear to me. Believing that it was impossible for me with my illness to get along without him, he had wanted to get on his high horse with me. But now, when he realized that I was going to let him go it alone, he was in quite a predicament. With no knowledge of either the Spanish or the English language in such a savage land, he had baggage that he did not want to leave behind but very little money! What else could his plan be than to humiliate me? The Germans had warned him about this possibility and predicted that he would be wrong to underestimate me. But he had not listened to them and now he was suffering the consequences. [In the past] he had been forced to abandon just as quickly several [other] foolish plans that he had concocted.

In the meantime, I had myself ferried over to Laredo to look for an American with whom I had spoken the day before in order to hire him in Tallör's place. He was not at home and I had to return without having completing my errand. Then I heard about a new misfortune. My Mexican [guide] had finally made his appearance in order to bring the unpleasant news that an ox belonging to Dippelhöfer was sick. We got there just in time to see the patient die. That day we had to postpone traveling on. The hide was removed from the deceased and taken away. A half hour later someone came back in order to get the tallow for greasing wagons and found only a small part of the animal left. The Mexicans had already carried off the rest. They do not seem to make any great distinctions between a slaughtered animal and one that just dies. Another ox would have to be purchased, but Dippelhöfer had no real desire to do so. It took a long time to come to some decision and finally the matter was worked out in such a way that I gave Tallör the cart for which he would have to buy some oxen. Moreover, I took the Germans' baggage on my wagon, and Dippelhöfer took Tallör's place with me. So, Tallör was traveling now as his own boss, but also at his own expense, and this latter fact, given his great parsimony, appears to have diluted somewhat his joy. The next morning the Americans and the British departed. In the canoe I crossed over to the town to buy provisions. I saw Tallör and Dippelhöfer there who, without knowing a word of Spanish, were trying to buy some oxen. The stubbornness of the former would not permit him to ask me to arrange the purchase for him. When I was asked by the latter, however, I took charge in order not to have to leave the other man behind also which probably would have resulted in the loss of the cart, etc. I did not want that to happen since he had left San Fernando with me. I did not want it said that I had refused my help to a man who had come with me from Europe and that I then left him behind helpless.

It was more difficult to find what we wanted than I had thought. To be sure, everyone wanted to sell some oxen, but they were all so far away that we could not have them by evening when we wanted to get underway. Finally, I went to the *alcalde*, a tall handsome man who greeted me quite cordially, but his cattle were also on a very distant *rancho*. But then he took his hat and cane and walked with us to another house where we struck a deal. The oxen that were being offered for sale were on a *rancho* that was to be sure two *leguas* distant, but they could be delivered by evening. Tallör, who was too proud to ask me for one of my horses, went there on foot to look at the oxen and to negotiate.

I thanked the *alcalde* for his kindness and went back to buy a few melons. When I reached the riverbank, I saw that the canoe was at the opposite bank and I had to wait. Then a young Mexican girl came out of a hut that was on the high bluff of the river. She was about fifteen years old with a youthful slender build. Her clothes, although clean, indicated that she belonged to the lower class. She had on a fine white shirt that hung far down from her shoulders and a cotton dress that because of the heat was loosely fastened. Neither shoes nor sandals protected her small feet from the burning sand. Her facial features were, however, more beautiful than any I have seen in this country before, hardly in any civilized country. Her luxurious raven hair, her smooth forehead with beautiful eyebrows, her eyes like milk and coals, her beautiful nose, and her delicately shaped mouth, all were framed by a beautiful oval face, and would please even the most severe critic. But the egoistic European would find something missing in this beautiful Mexican girl. There was no subtle rose aurora shimmering in her cheeks. There was only the burning sun of midday glowing in them. Her complexion was not the milk and red blood of my beautiful female compatriots. The pale brown, somewhat yellowish skin color made her whole appearance more interesting to me than alluring.

We looked at each other filled with curiosity. I approached her, hoping that she would invite me into her hut since I was exposed to the blazing sun and, I confess, so that I could get a better look at this beautiful resident of the riverbank. I was not mistaken either. She did invite me to enjoy the shade of her hut. I did not wait for her to repeat her offer. I found her sister there who was married and cordially bade me welcome. A conversation ensued which, of course, on my part could be carried on only very haltingly. After the woman had asked me some questions at length, I turned to her beautiful sister to draw her into the conversation more. She came from [San Antonio de] Bexar and had followed her sister here when she married someone here. The hut, which was constructed of slender tree trunks, was also their winter home. The wind blew the fine sand from the riverbank right through the walls. To me this seemed to be proof that these people were very poor. Until then I had still imagined the opposite about them. Beauty, amiability, and wealth always seem inseparable to the imagination of the spoiled Europeans.

The girl asked me if I was ill, for my appearance and my unsteady gait must have betrayed me. To my affirmative answer, I asked whether I was going to die, to which she gave a negative answer. The beautiful Spanish language never sounded more pleasant to me than when it was coming from the mouth of this charming Sophia. Her Sargines had learned really more from her in a half hour than in a whole day from her mostly ugly female compatriots. In the meantime, the canoe had returned. I started to go, and despite my protests, she took the melons from me and accompanied me down to the riverbank. Thanking her, I bade farewell to her, and I would have liked to leave something with her as a souvenir of the ailing stranger, but I could not find anything suitable. Certainly money would have been refused. From the middle of the river I saw the beautiful girl still standing on the riverbank, and in my imagination I could picture her plunging like a naiad into the waves of the wild river.

At Laredo the current of the Rio Grande is extraordinarily rapid. I have never seen a river like this before, and it is unpleasant to remain here on the riverbank.[10] Especially at midday strong winds are constantly blowing sand about so that one is unable to breathe or to open one's eyes. I was extremely happy that Tallör finally returned at nine o'clock that evening with a pair of oxen and we left immediately.

Laredo must have about 250 houses with 1,200 inhabitants. Most of them make a living from raising livestock, which they do on their *ranchos*. They raise chiefly horses and mules, which are cheap here. One can have one's choice from among hundreds of mares for eight pesos. Geldings cost twice as much. Mules cost easily four times as much. A pair of good experienced oxen cost from twenty to twenty-four pesos, and a cow six to eight pesos. The people have an abundance of goats. Sheep are rarer; more of them are raised in the mountains southwest of the town. [The people in] the town do some shipping and some smuggling trade with the colonies to the northeast that are inhabited by the Americans. I have seen a lot of grapes, pomegranates, and melons coming from the south. Everything is transported on the backs of mules since the roads are hardly practicable for carts. In their taste the pomegranates do not match their appearance, but on the other hand I have found the grapes to be extremely tasty.

Following the road to Revilla, this time by going to the right instead of to the left, we covered a good distance by two o'clock. But then it began to get bad and we stopped. But the sunrise found us on our way again and the difficulty of going forward was increasing every minute. For the most part, the road was completely impassable and we had to leave it in order to make a new one over the prairie and through the bushes and thorns. But this required some preliminary scouting. Our guide, who had had the task of conducting these investigations, had brought us several times into the most difficult situations by failing to do his job. All of my commands had not been able to motivate him to greater activity, so there was nothing left for me to do but to get on a horse myself and take over this duty. The constant bouncing up and down as my horse galloped along exhausted me, however, only too quickly and forced me to lie down in the wagon from time to time. Often after a few minutes we came to another bad place which forced me to get out again. So, we dragged ourselves along until two o'clock when the heat became unbearable and the oxen did not want to go on.

I had sent the Mexican [guide] out ahead to look for water, but he did not come back. So, I rode out ahead too, but I did not find him. I did notice, however, a number of well-worn cattle paths that went off to the left and

---

[10] In March, when the colonists first saw the Rio Grande, Ludecus remarked that the river could be forded during most of the year at most sites. Ludecus, *Reise*, 160. Hence, his surprise that the river was so swift at Laredo.

soon I found some cows. I no longer had any doubts that there was water to be found in that direction. When I came back to the wagon, I found our guide who suspected that the Rio Grande must be nearby. Tallör remained behind to guard the wagons and the women, while the rest of us drove our livestock along the path which after an hour really did bring us to the Rio Grande. There the people and animals alike slaked their thirst with the dirty water of the river. We filled all of our containers and had just started back when to our considerable delight a thunderstorm came up that cooled the air down a little. The intense shower, the first rain [we had seen] in six or seven weeks, forced us to seek shelter in a hut that was standing on the river-bank. It belonged either to a cattle hand or to the manager of the *rancho*. That is where I found myself when I was compelled to lie down a while, partly from exhaustion and partly from a chill because the rain had wet my clothes through to the skin. It had affected my weakened constitution very severely. After a half hour we left the hut. Those who had remained behind with some apprehension were delighted by our return.

I will touch on the ensuing days of our journey only briefly: The difficulties of continuing on increased with every hour, and the road became worse and worse. We suffered often from the most awful lack of water and there was no grazing to be found anywhere for the poor animals. The prairie was as barren as a highway. Also, the gullies that appeared to have been created by earthquakes became more numerous and were being continually enlarged by rainstorms. They often obstruct the road so completely that even mules can cross them only with difficulty. It is a miracle for a cart to pass there and my wagon certainly was the first one even to be seen there. Rainwater collects in these gullies, of course, but now in the hot season of the year they are usually dry. These gullies are found in the valleys because the region between here and Laredo is generally hilly. In one of the more dangerous ones which formed a large hollow, we found that the road led across an enormous rock as flat as a table and broken up here and there by large cracks. The steep slope had forced us to unload the wagon and lower it down inch by inch. This was going on right in the worst heat of the sun. Fortunately, there was water nearby. On the left side [of the pond] it was salty and bitter, but on the right side it was at least drinkable. I tried to take a bath in it, but I had hardly gone a few steps into the water when thousands of the inhabitants of the small pond pounced on me and forced me to retreat. They were little fish that did not injure me, but their nips and tugs at fifty different spots on my skin were unbearable. The women had the same experience. When they put their hands into the water to wash, they were attacked the same way.

Labors such as these occurred frequently: the oxen were unhitched, the wagon was unloaded, and everything had to be carried by hand, and because of the water [shortage] we were several times in the greatest distress. Halfway along the way [to Revilla] we camped at a river that flowed from the west and emptied into the Rio Grande, but I did not find it on my map and was not able to learn the river's name. At the point where we crossed it, it was hardly a foot deep and the riverbed was stone. In spite of taking precautions, my wagon turned over three times, fortunately without breaking anything on it. But it caused us a lot of hard work. Because of the bad road, it was impossible to travel fast by night in the heat. Another difficulty about traveling in this country is that the guides cannot estimate distance by hours, for they do not have any clocks, nor by miles. They can answer the question [about distance] only with *lejos* (far) or *cerca* (near). Of course, that is so indefinite that no calculations can be made at all and as a result I often suffered the most severe need for water.

So, on the afternoon of the twenty-fifth [of July], we arrived in the vicinity of Revilla without having found a drop of water in the last twenty-four hours. The road, which led over jagged rocks, had lowered very much my hopes of reaching the town with my wagon. All of our banding, nailing, and fastening with wedges was not helping any more. A few minutes later the rear right wheel broke apart and that completely wrecked our ship. For some time I had had the white houses of Revilla in sight and was of a mind to ride on ahead to get some water because we were almost dying of thirst. A Mexican who came riding by gave me the *present* of a half of a watermelon, but what could that do for six people? But he did not have any water with him. Without any delay I sprang into my saddle, took the [water] keg, and raced away at a gallop toward the town.

I had not taken the time to see after my appearance and my outfit was of a very bizarre sort. I was wearing a straw hat, and parts of the hat's black silk lining were flying loose in the breeze. I was wearing neither a vest nor a jacket, and my trousers and boots were ripped and torn. I had a long stiff beard, long sideburns, and a large mustache, and I was burned as brown as a sweet chestnut. With a long, sour face, and carrying my little keg under my arm like a schoolbook, I bore no resemblance to the young stylish gentleman of the year before. That man was in despair if he had forgotten his kid gloves, and had to allow himself to be seen by the elegant people on the rampart promenade in B[raunschweig] wearing the washable leather gloves which he had fortunately found in his pocket. But necessity is the mother of invention.

I felt very happy to be once more among people and houses, and to have the prospect of quenching my thirst. At full gallop, my horse raced with me into the first house. A successful parrying move that no Mameluke would have to be ashamed of kept me from running over the *señorita* who was standing right in my path. She was quite astonished by the scarecrow [on the horse] and tried to run away. However, I held onto her and asked her with the most urgent modesty in my voice for water. The Mexicans who live in this region are not accustomed to hearing foreign tongues. I pronounced the word *agua* the way the late assistant deputy headmaster and the frogs in the *Schwanensee* had taught me.[11] Instead of that I should have dragged out the word as in a Berlin dialect which would have made it sound like *ahua*. She stared at me impertinently with her black eyes, burst out laughing, and ran through the door into the adjoining room. I trotted bravely after her and found the whole family, at least ten or twelve people, lying like so many pigs around a trough full of cut watermelons which they were devouring.

The appearance of their fleeing daughter and her strange pursuer brought the whole crowd to their feet. Instantly I was surrounded and for the second time I brought forth my request. My mouth had begun to water at the sight of the watermelons and this was the reason that my pronunciation became clearer. The people understood me and brought what I was asking for. But then I had to fend off a barrage of questions. I evaded them with the explanation that my wagon had broken down and that I had hurried ahead to bring water back to those who had remained behind and who were about to die of thirst. They asked me whether there were women among the others and my affirmative answer sent everyone scurrying. Everyone was curious to see the Americans. The old lady asked whether there were some old people, and the young ones asked if there were some young people there. To satisfy them all, I said over and over, "*Sí, Sí!*" Everything was done to bring my people here as quickly as possible and then to get me to hurry. I gave the youngest son some money and he hurried off to get some meat for me. Another son filled my keg with water, and a third person sent for the carpenter, an American. I wanted to talk with him about my wagon, and then while everything was being rounded up, I rode my horse down to the Rio Salado (salty river) to let him drink. The people had given me something to take with me to eat, and I purchased also some bread from them. The fact that I had some money seemed to make an even better impression. When I returned to the house, I found the American there. He promised to repair the wagon [later], but unfortunately he had the black fever (*fiebre negra*).

Everything was ready. The son-in-law, the husband of the young woman to whom I had made my bizarre introduction, had saddled a horse. The keg had been placed on the saddle and the provisions were placed in the pack-sack. He mounted behind the saddle and off we went. The horses and riders

---

[11] The Schwanensee, an ice-skating spot in Weimar, was made famous by Johann Wolfgang Goethe during the winter of 1775. Günther, et al. (eds.), *Weimar: Lexikon zur Stadtgeschichte*, 395.

were panting and puffing, and the gravel and sparks were flying. On the way back [to the wagon], we met the two Dippelhöfer sisters, who had been compelled by their thirst to follow me, and Tallör with his cart. I described for them how to get to the house where they were being awaited, and hurried on. As soon as my supplies were unloaded, my companion and I went back. I accepted the offer of the *alcalde* to stay in his house, for I had happened before upon the residence of Don Eduardo García, who held that office there. I unloaded Tallör's cart and drove it back [to my wagon], where I loaded my baggage into it and then I fastened under the wagon's broken leg a pole that I had brought with me. Then I hauled the whole mess to town.

I am as tired now from writing as I was then from riding, walking, and talking. Unfortunately, my stay here seems to have been very much extended, and I will probably write you from here a few lines about this place, but until then, . . .

Revilla, August 6, 1834

My inimical fate has unfortunately kept me here until today. If it would have helped me any, I would have certainly fallen into despair several times. But I did not, and failing to take that step has put me in the position of being able to leave tomorrow. I hope that I will not have to stop at another place. In keeping with my promise, before I leave, I am going to recount what has happened since my last report.

The evening of my arrival here my guide from Begades appeared and announced that he wanted to go back home the next day. I did not want to take him with me any further anyway, so I told him to bring the oxen the next morning and he would get his pay. I gave him the four oxen that I had just used and he was to take them with the others out to the prairie, and I kept the horses with me. He appeared the next morning, but without the oxen and claimed that the four oxen I had given to him the day before were not to be found. I was accustomed to hear such as this from him. Too lazy to look for them, he had come to me every day with this complaint. So, we all had to go out ourselves just so we could get underway. But this time I sent him off again with the admonition not to be so lazy. That afternoon he appeared again, but he had still not found the missing oxen and he reported that he had driven the other two to water, that they had swum across the river and that they were now on the other riverbank. The story seemed suspicious to me. I thought that he was trying to play a game with me out of revenge. I ordered him to go immediately to the river, to bring the oxen back to this side, and to find the others. I told him that if some oxen were lost, then I would know how to force him to replace them. Here I must mention a small *rencontre* [confrontation] that I had had with him a few days earlier: After my wagon had tipped over the first time and we were busy unloading it, I caught sight of him sitting on his horse as usual and watching us work. Annoyed by this behavior, I called him a *carajo flaco* (roughly "lazy *canaille*" [scoundrel]). In return, he called me a *carajo* also and insisted that he had been hired only for *servicios a caballo* (working on horseback, tending the cattle, etc. for which he was responsible) and that he did not have to help me. I was in no mood to explore with him the areas of responsibility included within his services. I needed him on his feet and ordered him to dismount, and when he refused, I grabbed my saber and gave him a few blows with the flat of the blade. This, to be sure, got him off his horse, but instead of going to the wagon, he ran to the tree where his musket was hanging. But I had already guessed his intent, and before he reached the tree I had my rifle aimed at him and called out to him that as soon as he reached for his firearm, he would become acquainted with the contents of mine. Then he became peaceable and maintained that it had not been his intent to shoot. He came over and helped. As a result of this, I later always had to keep an eye on him.

This time, as soon as he left, I saddled a horse and rode out too. I sent Tallör and Dippelhöfer out to look for the lost oxen. Thinking that the Rio Grande was flowing nearby and that the oxen had been driven off in that direction, I rode downstream along the Rio Salado, but I did not find the river. But when I realized my error, I returned to camp after a few hours and found the missing four oxen, the same ones that had been very quickly found as I had expected they would. I learned that the other two had indeed swum across the Rio Salado, but they had been driven back by the Mexican [guide]. The German women had been witnesses [to his deed]. Until that evening then I waited in vain for the return of the oxen. Then I thought that he would come in the next morning in order to be able to demand pay for another day. But this day passed also and he still did not come back. This worried me and right away I decided to report the matter to the *alcalde*, my host. But unfortunately, it was Sunday when he spent the whole day strolling around in the town and did not even come home to dinner. Finally, as evening was approaching and he still did not come home, I set out to look for him wherever he was. A tremendous uproar attracted me to the marketplace where I found several hundred inhabitants gathered on their horses. In their midst the *alcalde* was settling a dispute about the victory in a race. After waiting a long time, I finally found an opportunity to tell him about the matter. But he was not in a good mood and did not seem to want to be concerned with it. He claimed that he had just seen the man in the crowd and advised me to look for him. After sending the others out on the same errand, I ran through all the streets, but I did not pick up his trail.

Another attempt that I made the next day to prompt the *alcalde* to action was also fruitless. Since he was leaving at noon for Camargo, he referred me to the second *alcalde*. In him I found a different kind of man. He immediately took some measures, sending messengers out to the surrounding *ranchos* with the order to arrest the thief if he should offer the oxen for sale there. In response to the *alcalde*'s question whether I wanted to have the runaway guide pursued on the roads, for which I would have to pay the man to pursue him one peso per day, I answered in the negative. I had no desire to throw away more money on the matter. It was too unlikely that the runaway would be caught, given the ease with which someone could hide or flee in any direction. I was also afraid that the men I would send after him might be even greater thieves than the one they were supposed to follow, and it could easily cost me more than the value of the oxen, in spite of their excellent quality. Overall, losing them was not such a great loss. The pay that I owed my guide was about ten pesos, and a pair of oxen can be purchased here for twenty to twenty-four pesos. So, I let it go at that.

In the meantime I had placed the other oxen in the care of a man whom I was paying to be responsible for them. Don Francesco, the son-in-law of the *alcalde*, knew the man and had ridden with me to his *rancho* nearby. I had had the animals driven there earlier. But I did not meet the man until we started back to town. Then I made the arrangements with him and indicated to him the place where we had left his charges. Five days later he came to me in the morning and reported that one of the oxen had strayed. I inquired which one it was, to which he answered that it was the yellow one. That one belonged to Tallör. All of our riding around and looking for it was in vain. The ox was nowhere to be found. Finally, Tallör offered five pesos to anyone who found it.

In a conversation that I had with the man [I noted that] he was contradicting himself in the details which made me suspicious. I told him then that he had to replace the ox. He refused to do so, whereupon I took him before the alcalde. Since I did not know the language well enough, I sent for a Mexican who understood some English, but soon I realized that he either wanted to help the other Mexican get out the situation, or he spoke less English than I spoke Spanish. I continued presenting the case by myself. My opponent was handling himself so clumsily and told such bold lies that it was easy for me to expose him completely. For example, he maintained that he had seen only three oxen and had no knowledge of a fourth one until he learned by chance that a fourth one had been there. When I asked then how he could have known to tell me the color of the ox, he could not give an answer.

In the end he was sentenced by the *alcalde* to a fine of sixteen pesos if he could not produce the ox, and to forfeit the finder's fee for telling a lie. Four days later the ox appeared. Another man had found it and he received the finder's fee of two pesos. Out of gratitude to me for getting his ox back for him, Tallör was expecting me to pay the fee out of my pocket. I believe that at times he is delusional. This incident has made me cautious. I have tethered my livestock in the vicinity of the house under some trees and I am feeding them with *rastrojo* (corn stalks), which is of course very costly.

In the meantime I was doing everything to get ready to travel on as soon as possible. But then a number of obstacles conspired against me. At first there were three holidays when the carpenter did not want to work or was not permitted to do so. Then he had a relapse of fever so that he could not work. Now, there were probably other blacksmiths in the town, but none of them understood how to reduce the rims onto the wheels [of my wagon]. They were afraid of ruining everything. After a lot of persuasion and [the promise of] good pay, one of them decided finally to try it. Dippelhöfer and I promised to help him, and after four hours of work the rim was firmly on one wheel, of course, but it had been beaten up badly while we were working on it. However, it could be repaired again. A second wheel was taken off also, and with the lessons we had learned with the first wheel, the second one was made fast somewhat more easily and with less damage. Finally, the carpenter was finished with the wheel and in order to have new spokes inserted, because they were the only things broken, I had to pay eight pesos. Then, as far as all that was concerned, there was nothing more to prevent me from leaving, if my inquiries about the road ahead had not persuaded me to give up the idea of getting through with my loaded wagon. So, I tried to arrange to have my baggage transported by other means and to continue on only with my wagon and the most essential things. To do that the pair of oxen I still had was sufficient. But it was all in vain. There was not a cart to be found anywhere, because everything is transported here on pack mules. Any carts that might have been found on the *ranchos* were already in use during this the harvest time. Also, my attempts to rent some mules were at first fruitless. In part, they were already being used and in part their owners did not want to send just three of them to Matamoros.

As I was strolling through the town in pursuit of this matter, someone showed me a house in which a man lived who owned a number of mules. I entered the courtyard where about fifty pack saddles were set out in the most attractive order. I was just approaching the door when a large handsome man about forty years old came out to meet me. He asked me what I wanted and after I described to him my wishes, he offered me a chair and we sat down in the courtyard. Then a conversation ensued that lasted about an hour. He interrogated me like a German police chief and I was beginning to think that I could accomplish there what I wanted. When he asked me what I wanted to pay for a mule as far as Matamoros, I quoted the cheap price of five pesos, but immediately I offered to pay a bit more. Then he told me that the matter was not convenient for him, but if I wanted to wait until a mule caravan left, which was supposed to take a shipment of wool, then he would send my baggage along with it. But the time of the shipment was indefinite.

He took me into his house where it looked like the home of a Jewish horse trader who deals not only in animals, but in anything else he can talk a farmer into buying or selling. Among all those things there was a boundless disorder. The adjoining room seemed to be his living room and bedroom. Still keeping my objective in mind, I excused myself with the promise to visit him again. This man interested me already at first glance. His intelligent or rather his cunning physiognomy and his wealthy appearance caused me to suspect that there was something special about him. His behavior testified to a degree of education that I have not found in this country before. He was dressed in very fine fabrics and was wearing among other things blue velvet laced boots.

As I was swimming in the river a few days later, I saw him on his horse and in his hand he was holding a white umbrella which he was using against the sun. When he recognized me, he called out to me and asked if I wanted to sell my wagon and whether I had any horse harness. I answered in the affirmative to both questions, and he asked me then to come for him in a half hour at his house. I came at the appointed time, and on the way back to my residence we met a *señorita* who respectfully kissed his hand as he spoke to her, and then she went on. This astonished me quite a bit.

The wagon did not appeal to him, because he wanted a light carriage. On the other hand, he liked the harness very much. In the meantime his horse had been brought. He mounted the horse and in order to show off himself as an experienced rider and his horse's skills to the assembled ladies, he compelled the horse to make all sorts of leaps until he stopped on the other side of the house and removed the saddle. The harness was placed on the horse and it pleased him very much. So, the business deal was concluded that he would bring my baggage for free to Matamoros and he paid me an additional fifteen pesos cash.

After the man left, I was quite astonished to hear from my host and hostess that this *arriero* and *ranchero* was also the chief cleric in the town. Curious to get to know this man better, I visited him the next day and frequently after that. My business with him provided me with the best reason to do so. He led me into his living room where it did not look much better than the room I had already seen. His priestly vestments were lying over riding saddles and pack saddles. A bridle and his scapular were hanging from a single nail. Over there was a pile of corn and next to it lay a book on Latin grammar. A knout had been laid across the Bible so that the pages would not blow about. In short, the instruments he used to keep his spiritual flock and his secular flock on the right path were so mingled that it was impossible to know which flock he preferred to serve.

We sat down [at the table] and a trough [filled] with watermelon was placed between us and we bravely began eating. Following the trough a pack of brown children came running in, in all sizes like organ pipes. They attacked the melon like a pack of little pigs, but their voraciousness seemed to bother my host after a while. When words did not help, he took the knout from the Bible and drove the children out the door with it. In response to my question whether they were his children, he answered "yes" and then hanging on that thought, he complained very much about [the rule of] celibacy. As I remarked with a smile that he knew how to get around the main issue of celibacy, he admitted it laughingly, but maintained that it would be after all more suitable to be able to marry legally. Then I suggested to him to travel to Rome to seek the Pope's permission to marry, which, I added, would not necessarily be refused because many *padres* in Europe had already received dispensation, chiefly in order to prevent the dreaded revolt of clerics against the law.

This [news] made him furious. I had to calculate the expenses [of such a trip] for him which I estimated as low as possible, and this got him in the end so worked up that I assumed he would be going around town soon as a suitor for his bride so that upon his return from Rome he could immediately climb into the conjugal bed.

Another conversation with him in the presence of my host family and several other [of the town's] inhabitants was no less interesting. Probably at the request of the latter I had to submit to a religious catechism and make a confession of my faith. With trepidation I was reminded of the school exam that I once had to endure in my hometown, where the headmaster tortured me to my own aggravation and that of all present with questions about Latin and Greek, which were not my strong suit. The *padre* asked me first of all whether I was a Christian. I was able to answer that question confidently with a "yes," even if not in the same sense as he intended. Then, he asked whether I believed that Maria was the mother of God? My answer was: "The Bible teaches us that." And that seemed to satisfy him. Then he demanded to know how many Gods I prayed to. This question put me in something of a predicament. Then it occurred to me that he meant perhaps the Holy Trinity. At my answer, "three, God the Father, His Son, and the Holy Ghost," he went into such ecstasy that he turned to the others and pronounced me to be one of the best Christians [he knew].

The exam continued on for some time, becoming more and more like a conversation. In the course of our talk it became clear to me that he did not have the slightest knowledge of the distinctions between the Catholic and the Protestant faiths. All at once he broke off the conversation and asked me if I was familiar with the gods of the Greeks and the Romans. Here the tables were turned. In order not to let the conversation lag, I had to assume the role of the catechist. It soon became apparent that the holy reverend knew only three: Jupiter, and as anyone can guess, Venus with her godless son.[12] This exam did not seem to suit him. He assumed his former role again, turning the conversation to the Spanish language. When I revealed some knowledge about [verb] conjugations and [noun] declensions, and that I knew what *masculinum*, *feminimum*, and *neutrum* were, he turned again to the bystanders and described me as an extremely smart man. Meanwhile, I did not say that I considered him because of this description to be extraordinarily dumb, but I wisely kept it to myself.

Today he had my baggage picked up. He came himself, weighed it, and helped pack it on the mules. His name is Don Antonio Penna. In addition to his business enterprises I have already mentioned, he is also in the business of being a physician and, so I am told, the business of being an archrogue.

I had to pass also an exam in philosophy, which turned out well enough for me. A relative of my host family who was about sixty years old had apparently read a philosophical essay about the soul. One of the first days after my arrival he had asked me, "Where is the soul located?" When I answered that I did not know, he asked me whether I had ever thought about it. Then I answered that I believed the soul surrounded the human body. Fortunately, this was also his opinion. Boasting quite a bit, he proclaimed my answer correct, and then he turned to the bystanders and notified them that I knew very much. Later, whenever he saw me, he would call out the same question to me, even from across the street, until I became bored with the game and told him once, "on your nose." That had the desired effect.

I am on a fairly friendly footing with my host and hostess. The *alcalde*, who returned after a few days from his trip, seems to be a very good man. He does not talk much, but he sleeps all the more. His spouse, however, is a true dragon. She kicks up a row all day around the house and strikes the servant girl, and at times even her youngest daughter, a girl of fourteen. I have been able to get along with her quite well. One of her thunderstorms was directed at me only once, but I just ignored her thunderbolts. When she was negotiating with one of the German women once for a hat, I called out to

---

[12] It is unclear to whom Ludecus refers as "the godless son" of Venus. It could well be Aeneas, the son of Venus and Anchises, a mortal. See *Websters New Collegiate Dictionary*, 20. He is unimpressed with the scope of this priest's knowledge of Greek and Roman cultures.

the latter to demand a higher price. The German woman insisted then that the hat box had to be purchased separately, and that without this condition she could not give up the hat. However, her ploy was of no use. My hostess figured out what I had said and called me a *puerco*. I was polite and answered that I did not understand what she was saying. But the furious Circe repeated the incantation and insisted, she knew very well that I knew the meaning of the word.[13]

I have already mentioned the second daughter. She has a very friendly and impertinent face with an unusually white skin tone. One day she will surpass her mother, a seven in meanness, by a few points. I estimate that she will be in her twenty-fifth year at an eight, and in her fortieth year at a ten. Her older sister is very ugly, as dark as her sister is white, with a very unclean skin. She has two children, a dark-skinned three-year old boy and a light-skinned one, about six months old, whom she loves above everything. Since I had never seen her husband about, I asked her once whether he lived on the *rancho*. She denied it, and then I asked whether he was dead. Again, she gave me the same answer with the remark that she had never had a husband. My pale cheeks flushed a bit, and I cast an ambiguous glance at her fat boys. This did not embarrass her in the least. The larger boy, she told me, was by a Mexican and that he was a bad man. But the other one, who seemed to be her favorite and who was known by the name of the "Little American," was by an American. Another time she was showing me her dresses, which resembled the misplaced items from a theater wardrobe. Her servant girl, who was standing nearby, called out to me that they were all gifts from the woman's lovers.

The Mexicans spoil their children in a scandalous fashion. The youngest son of the *alcalde* and the oldest son of his daughter are the most ill-mannered rascals that I have ever seen. All day long they never stop screaming, "*agua, madre! sandías, madre!*," and if their demands are not immediately met, they begin screaming and stomping their feet. I said once that one should give them the *sandías* on their head. But they answered, "they are only *muchachitos*." In Germany someone would have given those brats a sound thrashing.

The customs in Revilla differ from those in San Fernando in many respects and in each respect I much prefer the latter. The routine here is approximately as follows: Early, about an hour before sunrise, the people arise and at six or seven o'clock, they eat breakfast, usually grilled meat, and about two o'clock they eat again. They prepare their meals with a lot of fat and with so much red pepper which grows abundantly here, that I cannot

---

[13] Again, Ludecus likens an angry woman to the enchantress Circe. See the twelfth letter, Note 1.

eat them. They do not know vegetables. Then they have their *siesta*, which lasts probably until five o'clock. At nightfall they lie down again, and at ten o'clock they eat supper, and after that they sleep for the rest of the night.

Their leisure time is spent lying about on their beds while they eat fruit and in pursuit of their most important and favorite occupation, catching lice. So that one's hands do not lie idle in one's lap, divine providence has created this creature in such numbers and allowed it to prosper so well in the thick hair of the Mexicans that in the absence of combs, it might be impossible to eradicate them if one wanted to, which I have good reason to doubt. As frequently as I have walked through the town, I have rarely looked into one of the houses where there was not a devotee of the hunt busy in the pursuit of game. Mostly they sit in the doorway or in front of the house where there is better light. It appears that the first words of affection that a young couple have for each other are uttered during this exercise. A shy suitor asks the girl he loves to perform this odd act of kindness or to allow him to remove her lice. If the request is accepted, then he can be certain that he will not be languishing in vain. Dippelhöfer's sister was the recipient of such a proposal by one of the *alcalde*'s sons, a handsome boy with black hair who had come from the *rancho* to visit for a few days. When she refused his overture, he did not speak another word with her.

Another diversion and one that is just as necessary is bathing. When I went down to the Rio Salado the first time for that same purpose, I was quite astonished to see women and men in the water, all mingled together. While the old people remained nearer to the riverbank, the younger people amused themselves swimming. Several señoritas had become really quite advanced in this skill. The Mexican swims by beating at the water with his hands and feet, which is very tiring and noisy. They seemed to grasp right away that my movements were more advantageous and many of them tried to imitate me. Most of the women and girls kept their dress on, but they had pulled it down from their upper body and fastened it around their waist. With them their bosom is not an object of shame that their sense of modesty prohibits baring. On warm days they allow their dresses and shirts to hang far down over their shoulders.

My female compatriots here once had to pay dearly for their vanity. It was on a Sunday and in order to dress up just once, they had put on their best things and under it all there had to be a corset. Their altered figure did not go unnoticed, and soon a whole crowd had gathered around them. Our house was constantly under siege by the curious anyway. At first the women and then the men investigated from outside and inside the cause of this metamorphosis. There was nothing more for the German women to do than to stand still for it. The Mexicans liked the style, which I had not expected, but corsets were not worn again.

The Rio Salado is a beautiful, clear river. It is about two hundred paces wide, but it contains salt, which spoils the taste somewhat. It is deep and it flows over and among stones, which here and there form waterfalls. Once, as I was riding downriver, I found a fall that was about twenty feet high. Divided by [a barrier of] rocks into two parts, it was very picturesque. It was a very hot day and I jumped into the water to cool off a bit. Soon I saw two men swimming toward me who, probably in order to frighten me, spoke to me in an Indian language, or at least they were imitating the language quite convincingly. Although they had a very dark skin color, I had no doubt for a minute about their ethnicity. I told them in Spanish that I was a Tonkawa and did not understand the language of the Comanches. At this reply, they went away laughing.

A canoe and a ferry carry people and goods for a fee across the river. However, the ferrymen have to serve the town's inhabitants for free. Around noon the riverbanks are so hot that I have to put on my boots in the water. It is impossible to place one's bare feet on the hot earth.

During the holidays, one of which I witnessed in San Fernando and two of them here, the streets are filled with male and female riders on horseback. In spite of the heat and the dust, young and old riders chase from morning until evening back and forth in the streets. But the ladies do not come out until the afternoon. While the ladies in San Fernando sat alone on a saddle with a backrest and a footrest, here they are placed alone in the saddle and are held by a rider who sits behind them. Their apparel resembles that of a horseback-riding tightrope walker. I have not heard anything here about any dances. Perhaps it is due to the [approaching] harvest time when all the young people will be busy working on the *ranchos*. They do not farm anything there but corn, peppers, and melons. However, they keep large herds of cattle and swine, and they breed also good mules and horses. My host owns five to six hundred head of cattle. He is also fattening twenty hogs, and I do not know the number of mules he owns. I have never seen fatter hogs than in these regions. In a short while they are fattened so well on corn and leaves from the corn stalk that they literally become too fat to walk. Horses are even cheaper here than in Texas.

Like all the newer Mexican towns, Revilla has been built according to a very regular plan. All the streets intersect each other at right angles. The houses are constructed mostly of stone which is available in abundance in the surrounding area. It is brought here on mules, and yet one finds also many huts here. There must be probably two thousand people living here.

My health has noticeably improved and I believe that I am out of danger now. The change has been wrought completely by better foodstuffs because my diet has consisted every day of coffee and goat's milk, beef soup with rice, and beefsteaks. The latter were often inedible, of course, because the

Mexicans slaughter only old, unserviceable oxen and cows. In addition, I had every day one or two *sandías* and a [honeydew] melon. These fruits are extraordinarily large and delicious here. A melon can be peeled like an apple and the rest of it is edible, sweet and soft. *Sandías* are so juicy that one must consider them to be more like a beverage. But I could not eat the thing I desired the most, wheat bread, for any less than eight and a half *Groschen* a day of our money. As in Laredo, it is made with sugar and fat. Wheat flour and oat flour come from the southwestern regions of Mexico where these grains are grown.

This is just about everything that I have to report from here. Tomorrow afternoon I am going to go across the river and in the company of Padre Penna I am going to Matamoros, and from there I will send more news.

SEVENTEENTH LETTER
Proposal to Settle Down in Revilla and Marry There. Departure via
Mier. Crossing Over the San Juan, Camargo, and Reynosa Rivers.
Plagued by Ants *and* Prickly Heat. *Ranchos on the Rio Grande.*
Arrival in Matamoros.

Matamoros, August 30, 1834

Before I say anything about this place, I first want to bring all my friends to whom these letters are directed and who take the trouble to read them up to date from Revilla where I last left them. My thoughts were already outside the door, in the saddle, and ready to leave. I was [standing] in front of Don Eduardo's house (The *alcalde* is my namesake.), where, after concluding my last letter to you all, I received a very tempting proposal. It consisted of nothing less than settling down in Revilla. I could have land in abundance. A house could also be built quickly, and I was supposed to choose a wife, as I very clearly understood it, from the two available daughters of the *señor alcalde*. I could have either the ugly, young one or the chaste, old one.[1]

I was quite embarrassed. What should I do? A hundred head of cattle, a dozen hogs, some land, and most important of all, a woman who had already two uncouth boys was not a bad offer. One does not get such an offer every day. The older daughter with the two offspring appeared to have reserved for herself the first claim to me. The matter as she presented it to me was very plausible. I believe that she has in mind nothing less than to form a union with [individuals from] a hundred and eighty nations in the world with or without the blessing of the church. But such a kinship was too extensive for me.

In order to give the ladies at least some hope, I did as my good girlfriends in Germany do who out of curiosity stroll every Sunday afternoon through each fashion shop and finally they promise the sweetly smiling and obliging simpleton of a salesman that they will be back. The ladies of Revilla, who are not yet acquainted with the tricks of the European ladies, seemed satisfied with that promise. As souvenirs I left them some portraits that I had sketched in pencil. My work had been done to the accompaniment of the constant laughter of the onlookers who seemed to be very much amused probably by the serious face that I was trying to elicit from my sitting subjects. I had the good fortune to achieve a recognizable likeness in each of the sketches that I produced in a few minutes. When I was asked about the price, and I answered, "Nothing," I had the pleasure of seeing the whole crowd sit down

---

[1] Ludecus seems surprised (and possibly amused) that the *alcalde* would offer his daughters in marriage to a stranger.

instantaneously in order to have a sketch made of themselves. I told them all to come back on another day when I was sure I was not going to be found.

On August 2, I bade a fond farewell to my friends, and from my purse which had been filled from the sale of several of my personal belongings, I paid two *pesos* rent for the doghouse where I had been living. Then I fetched my *amigo*, the *padre* and muleteer, and got myself and all my belongings across the river. There we found all of the well-trained followers of my friend already assembled in order to carry quietly their earthly burdens. To our displeasure we learned that one of them had already disobeyed the commandment: Thou shalt not run away. Soon the riders came back without having found the fugitive. You should have seen our Moses, the way he cursed and ranted. His *"diabolo* of a *mula"* resounded through hill and dale. Finally, the fugitive was brought back, but it was by then too late to go on, and our departure was postponed until the next morning.

The next day, already an hour before sunrise, I saw the *padre* and his white umbrella on the opposite bank and soon I saw him walking about among his followers. There were thirty of them, and with them there were five *arrieros* (muleteers). The pack saddles were set out in a straight line and behind each one of them lay its respective load. Each animal carries about three hundred pounds of weight. The mules assembled in a row like a troop of cavalry, so that each one of them had a saddle in front of him. Two *arrieros* quickly placed a halter on each mule and tied him securely to his neighbor with a short rope. As soon as this had been done, a band attached to the halter was pulled over the mule's eyes. Then the saddle and the bales [of wool] were placed on the mule's back. The load is placed on the mule's back in two halves. A wide strap that has a rope on the end is tied around the load and the two muleteers, which stand on either side of the animal, grasp it and, bracing one leg against the animal's body, they pull it tight with all their strength and tie it fast. Each time they pull, the animal groans as though it were going to die. As soon as this is done, the band is removed from the animal's eyes and that mule waits until the others have had their turn. The lazy ones sometimes lie down and then have to be helped to stand up.

This work held us up until nine o'clock in the morning. I saw immediately that it was going to be impossible for me to ride along [each day] with the caravan. I decided not to wait for them again, but to get underway early every morning. I would first inquire about the road to take and then I would stop at the designated place for our camp. Finally, the signal to start was given and the caravan was set in motion, the lead horse with the bell at the point.

The first half hour the caravan made very slow progress. First, a mule lay down and had to be helped to his feet again. Then, a girth strap broke, and then another strap had not been tied securely enough and the bales slipped down under the animal's body. Another animal fell and came to be lying on his back. For the *arrieros* and their leader, who was riding with us, there was nothing to do but spring quickly from their horses and back on again in order to put everything back in order. Finally, everything seemed to be moving along well and the *padre* took leave of us.

Just as the mules had earlier lagged behind, now it became my turn. The caravan was soon out of sight ahead of me. Fortunately, I had made the decision not to travel with my baggage [in my wagon]. It is impossible to travel over the road through these hills with a loaded wagon. After sunset we reached the camping place only after having overcome a number of obstacles. At the camp there was an abandoned hut where, as the *arrieros* told me, all of the inhabitants, ten altogether, had died of the cholera within two days. There was no water there. Earlier a well had been there, but in it there was only bad, salty water. Our animals had to be driven to the Rio Grande that was two hours away. We did not get back until eleven o'clock in the evening. Grazing for the animals was out of the question. The next morning we found them resting at the same spot where we had left them the evening before. That day we got underway very early in order to reach Mier possibly before noon. The road was good except for two places that held us up for several hours. Both of them were deep ravines that were more difficult to cross than all of the previous ones. Our oxen had to literally climb down the ravine and back up again with the wagons while they were being held.

That day we bade farewell forever to the bad roads, for we had been told that beyond Mier the road was very good and we found that we had not been deceived on this point. This last day brought us also somewhat nearer to the Rio Grande, which offered us a much better image of the country. The road led most of the time through [a region that was like] a beautiful garden in which a lot of oxen, cows, and horses belonging to the *ranchos* situated along the river were grazing under the shade of trees. The day was terribly hot, and we would have liked to stop just to get out of the sun but thirst compelled us onward. My watermelon supply had become exhausted very early and the oxen had not eaten since the previous evening. Consequently, we were very happy to come upon the Cualco, a small river, about three o'clock in the afternoon.[2] We crossed the stony bed of the river with ease and a half hour later we arrived in Mier. I immediately inquired there about a blacksmith who turned out to be a native of Switzerland who had left his homeland as a boy and who did not speak a word of German. That same evening he repaired the tires on the wheels of my wagon that had become loose again, and then he took us into his house. But we set up our overnight

[2] Neither Cualco River nor Cualco Creek could be located, but since Revilla is on the Sabinas Hidalgo River, it was likely a tributary of that river.

accommodations in the street as we had done the whole time in Revilla. Mier could be somewhat larger than the latter town and it looks wealthier. The surrounding area is also very rocky.

The next day at noon we stopped at [a cluster of] six or eight huts standing on the bank of the Rio Grande. The inhabitants of the huts appeared to be very poor and in general they had a very suspicious appearance. I found there my old friend Antonio, the jokester.[3] As he explained to me, he was about to go to Matamoros where he was supposed to deliver a letter. He offered to accompany me there if he received the horses soon enough that he was expecting to come from the other side of the river. Soon after that another Mexican came to me to ask whether he could ride along with us. He added that there was a lot of bad riffraff along the road who attacked travelers there. His face and his whole demeanor caused me to suspect that he was one of this riffraff himself. I told him that my horses were already being used and that the women were riding in the wagons. As for the robbers, [I told him that] I knew how to rid myself of them, and I showed him my firearms. I let him know too that we kept watch the whole night through. The sight of my firearms caused him some obvious displeasure, but he promised to follow after us the next day. I promised him that I would be traveling only a short distance, but I went even further [than usual]. At sunset we got underway and I noticed that both of those fellows were carefully watching us surreptitiously from behind the houses and trees. I had distributed the firearms and we cautiously continued our march. That night at two o'clock we stopped at a very attractive *rancho*. For a little money I bought a lot of feed there for my poor animals which had had little or nothing to eat in the last few days. I bought also a lot of pretty melons larger than any I had ever seen before.

Since we set out again very early, we reached the San Juan River about nine o'clock. It is quite wide and deep. A ferry took us across the river to Camargo. I sent the wagons on ahead while I rode through the town to buy some flour, bread, coffee, and rice. Camargo is larger than Mier and it has also a much better appearance than the other town. I would have liked to reach that day a *rancho* that the *arrieros* had designated as the assembly point for everyone. I had not seen them again since the second day after we left Revilla. In the vicinity of Mier they had taken another road in order to avoid Camargo and paying the fees for the ferry. But the heat forced me to stop at the first watering hole for the sake of the oxen. At any minute one of them seemed about to fall down. When I rode out ahead I discovered several huts a short distance from the road and I led the wagons there. I tried

---

[3] Ludecus uses the term "Spaßmacher" to describe Antonio. A *Spaßmacher* can be a clown, wag, joker, or a prankster—that is, one who deceives. See Ludecus, *Reise*, 322.

unsuccessfully to exchange my weakened ox for another one. The people saw my predicament and made a shameless demand for one, also for feed. I refused their demands and spent the night there in the expectation that some rest would restore the animal's strength, because the march of recent days must have fatigued the animals a great deal. As the outcome proved, I had not been wrong.

No longer fatigued from our labor on the bad roads, we resolved to get something for the animals to eat ourselves. By burning the spines off the nopal cactus at the [camp] fire, we prepared a very nourishing and refreshing meal for the oxen. Only the horses had to be fed with feed that we purchased. I made the acquaintance of an honest old man there also who introduced himself as the son of a Swiss [immigrant]. He was the *alcalde* in the vicinity and lived in a miserable hut. He did not know anything of his ancestors' language. His father also, who had left Europe when he was very young, had not known the language. He led me around his small piece of property and treated me to the best food that he could find. In return, I treated him to a good rice soup. That evening we went swimming together in the lake that adjoins his field. The lake receives its water from the Rio Grande when it rises. I was quite astonished to see that this old man with his white hair could swim and dive much better than I. He warned me also to be on my guard against the *ladrones* who customarily attack travelers and murder them.

My fellow travelers I mentioned earlier have not been seen again. Our shotguns obviously did not appeal to them. The next morning we had to make only a short day's march before reaching the *rancho* that I mentioned before. It consisted of six or eight huts. In response to my inquiries I learned that the mules I was looking for had not yet passed that way. When they did not arrive that evening, I decided to continue on the next day. It was still dark when we were already traveling on the road. Unfortunately, because of this early start my small hatchet, the only one we had and which we sorely needed, was left behind with a beautiful knife. Of course, this does not seem remarkable, but in this territory such a loss is difficult or impossible to replace immediately. But that day I had very good luck hunting. In a short time I had shot five rabbits and that evening I gave two of them to a team of *arrieros* who had caught up with us with two hundred mules. At that time I was devoting a few hours every morning and evening to hunting by riding out ahead of the wagons. By pushing doggedly onward, we reached Reynosa during the night of the fifteenth [of August], and after traveling through the town, we stopped on the other side.

Early the next morning I mounted my horse and rode into town to buy some meat. I went into a courtyard where I saw the item I required hanging outside. Since the owners immediately recognized me as a stranger there, they tried to swindle me. Since I did not want to pay right away what they were asking, they let me know very clearly that I should leave. In retaliation I called out to them that they were all *carajos* and galloped away. I have observed that the nearer I came to civilization, more and more the people have become uncivil and wicked. It is like that everywhere, so why should Mexico be the exception? When I returned [to the wagons], I learned that someone had been there, had produced a piece of paper, and demanded money. Since no one understood the man, they had told him to come back later, but no one showed up.

Reynosa is situated on a hill a quarter-hour away from the Rio Grande from which the town gets its water. The houses are built of the same material as the houses in San Fernando. In size and appearance the town is very inferior to Camargo. In order to obtain better nourishment for myself and my livestock, I hurried ahead and stopped at a *rancho* an hour outside of the town to await the [arrival of the] mules, for there had been no sign of them yet. There we took shelter from the blazing sun under some beautiful large trees.

The next morning I rode back to the town to purchase some meat. This time I happened upon some more polite people. An American was living in the house who, when he heard that a compatriot was at the door, invited me in to see him. I dismounted and was led into the house. A voice behind the curtain asked me to come nearer. I stepped closer and saw a young, very handsome man kneeling in front of a bed and holding his wife who a half hour ago had given birth to his son. A boy was just bringing the calendar to him so that he could look up the day's date while a couple of old women were arguing about the name the boy should have. He recognized immediately from my pronunciation that I was not from his country. But he was happy to hear his mother tongue being spoken again. From him I received confirmation that the demands for money of the day before had been an attempt to cheat me. After a brief conversation I departed, but I left for the new mother a rabbit that I had shot on the way there. On the way back I was rewarded with two more rabbits.

Upon my return, I found that Tallör had already departed. He had joined several Mexicans who were also going to Matamoros. I was very happy about that, for this person behaved constantly in such a way that he would have been abandoned to his fate by anyone else. Only the thought that he could meet with some misfortune kept me from treating him as he deserved. Following one of his acts of rudeness toward the other Germans I had rebuked him the evening before, which he now did not believe that he, as a *gentleman*, had to endure any longer.

At this point I must mention two other nuisances from which I have not yet been liberated. They are 1) the ants, and 2) the *prickly heat*. The latter is a skin disease that everyone gets who is not native to the torrid zone. Even natives are said to be not always immune. It is caused by the heat. A rash with pustules covers the entire body, especially the back, the chest, the body, and arms. A constant stinging as if by a hundred needles keeps a person moving about night and day, and nothing helps all the itching. I have often jumped out of bed at night and run to the water in order to get a little rest for a quarter-hour. But even this remedy gives one relief for only the time that one is in the water. One can hardly bear to wear clothes, even a shirt on one's body. At night I usually wore the clothing of an Indian just to be able to get some sleep. In this climate one can dare to do that without harm to one's health.

The other nuisance, a species of ant, is no less troublesome. Notwithstanding the larger species of ants, all the [Mexican] states I have traveled through are populated by a very small type of these insects. They immediately cover the traveler who is forced to lie on the ground to rest and they rob him of the little peace that the *prickly heat* allows him to have. There is absolutely no means of protecting oneself from them. If I had slept in the wagon, I would have been subjected to this pest less, but there was no movement of air there. The warmth caused my body to sweat and that made the *prickly heat* unbearable. Some medications that cool the blood might cure the disorder.

After waiting in vain for the mules, I set out that evening and drove through the whole night. I stopped only for a few hours at a spot where there was some grass for the animals, the first grass they had eaten for about three weeks. We stopped about nine o'clock in the morning at a *rancho*, and soon afterwards Tallör arrived there also. I had passed him during the night and he had already left his new companions. The road from Camargo, but chiefly, the road from Reynosa, runs continuously along and near the Rio Grande. Its banks are covered there by a series of *ranchos*. The huts are situated on the high bluff of the riverbank and the planted fields are below. When the river rises, the fields are subject to flooding and their soil is therefore very rich. Of course, the areas suitable for planting are extremely small. I have noticed an odd thing that probably deserves to be mentioned. No matter what time of the day or night I may be traveling, I never come to a *rancho* without being alerted long before to its existence by the crowing of roosters. This happens even at high noon when people and animals are usually sleeping.

The road went off then for some distance again from the Rio Grande and the *ranchos* that we encountered were situated on small lakes that contained extremely muddy water. Near one of them I found one day a copperhead snake that must have been twelve feet long. It is the only one I have seen here and it is just as poisonous as the rattlesnake. But since it does not rattle, it is even more dangerous than the rattlesnake. I broke off a tree branch to kill it, but it did not wait for my attack and withdrew into its hole.

All of my subsequent efforts to shoot the snake were fruitless because as soon as I raised my shotgun, it pulled its head back again.

These *ranchos* are inhabited by a lot of suspicious people, and the inscriptions on the increasingly numerous crosses along the road indicate that murder does not appear to be a great sin here. I have seen a lot of these crosses since leaving Camargo. On the morning of the twentieth, after marching all night for fourteen or fifteen hours without finding water, I reached Guadalupe, a small village on a lake three miles from Matamoros. Of course, there was a small well and a house located along the first quarter of the distance we covered where one could purchase water, but enough for the animals is only rarely available and rarely for a good price. Consequently, I had made arrangements accordingly. Tallör, who again had traveled on ahead without any knowledge of the situation, had not only come into distress over lack of water, but had been forced to spend a lot of money for some and had also been robbed. As the people there told me, someone had driven off his oxen, which were not returned to him until he had paid a good finder's fee for them.

I remained in Guadalupe until four o'clock in the afternoon. Then I searched through my traveling bag in order to do my toilette, but I found nothing there but a clean shirt, some trousers, and a vest. My other clothes were back with the mules. The only jacket I had kept with me was only partially intact. The other half of it was hanging in a hundred different parts on the thornbushes along the route. So, for better or worse, without a jacket I mounted my horse, put on my felt hat, which I fortunately had with me, and trotted happily ahead to Matamoros. I left orders with the others to follow me in a few hours with the wagons.

Even from a distance I could see the beautiful houses built in the American style jutting up over the roofs of the Mexican huts. In a short time I had ridden through several streets filled with huts and then I came to the more refined streets with the attractive houses. I inquired there about the Germans, for I knew that a lot of them lived there, and I was directed to a corner house on the market plaza. As I entered the building, I saw a young man sitting inside and I asked him in Spanish whether a German lived there. He answered me in the best German that he was, to be sure, not German, but that he had lived a long time in Germany. Then a *conversation* ensued in which I introduced myself to him and to a young German who came in. I told them how I came to be there in my strange getup. I asked them for their advice about where I and my companions could find some accommodations. These gentlemen, I soon noticed, seemed to be afraid that I was getting around to my chief objective, namely to ask them for money. They could not give me the information I wanted and directed me to another building where some Germans lived also and who would certainly help me.

I found there in fact two young compatriots, the gentlemen Heim and Wagner who jointly owned a *liquor store*. There the reception was very different. No arrangements could be made for us that day, and so that night I took the road back to Guadalupe where I found my wagon among the gardens there. I brought also the bad news to the Germans [with me] that the passage to New Orleans cost thirty-five pesos, and that the ship's captain would very seldom agree to take on steerage passengers. The next morning I immediately sold my oxen and horses. I would have also had the opportunity to get rid of my wagon for a good price, but I did not want to be too quick to let go of something that was not costing me money to keep.[4]

Now I am living outside of town in a house facing the garrison. The German businessman, Herr Habenstreit, has been kind enough to direct me to this house.[5] Of course, there is only half a roof on it, and my trunks and boxes that finally arrived yesterday are my furniture. The buffalo hide is still my bed, but compared to my earlier accommodations, I am very comfortably situated here. I still have not formulated a definite plan whether I am going to continue on my journey or not. For the moment there is no ship being loaded for departure to New Orleans.

Here I received confirmation of the sad news that the four ships that came after us and tried to enter Aransas Bay had met with accidents. With this news I am concluding this letter, etc.

---

[4] Attempts at identifying Heim and Wagner, have been unsuccessful. Heim was possibly Johann Georg Heim, an earlier associate with the firm of Spitta, Hagedorn, and Co. in Tampico. See Heinrich Dane, "Die wirtschaftlichen Beziehungen Deutschlands zu Mexiko und Mittelamerika im 19. Jahrhundert" *Forschungen zur internationalen Sozial-und Wirtschaftsgeschichte*, I, ed. Hermann Kellenbenz (Köln: Böhlau Verlag, 1971), 16.

Neither the price of passage from Matamoros to New Orleans nor the policy of ship captains concerning steerage passengers could be confirmed.

[5] Attempts at identifying Herr Habenstreit have been unsuccessful.

EIGHTEENTH LETTER
Sojourn in Matamoros. Culture of the Region. General Observations and Warnings for Emigrants. A Festive Ball and Pastimes of the Inhabitants. Preparations for Departure to New Orleans.

Matamoros, October 12, 1834

The above date shows clearly that I am still lying at anchor here. The reason is the complete calm that was reigning in me and the fact that [for some time] I still did not quite know the direction in which I should steer my ship. I am making preparations now to depart for New Orleans. The schooner *Louisiana* is lying [at anchor] ready to sail, and my place is reserved. I am expecting any minute the order to depart. The actual cause of my stay here was, with my health being not yet restored, to avoid rushing into the mouth of the lion, [that is,] the city of New Orleans and America's sepulcher.[1] Consequently, the conditions here seemed to me to be of such a nature that they were worth careful consideration as to whether they could perhaps persuade me to set up my *wigwam* here.

In respect to its climate, Matamoros is an exceptional place among all the other cities on the Gulf of Mexico. Even the cholera did not do a good business here and therefore, when it visited this coast a second time, it did not come here again. Of the ten thousand inhabitants who live here, probably half of them are foreigners, Americans, British, French, Italians, and Germans. The latter, as well as the French, seem to have become somewhat coarse, especially through the example of the North Americans who really can be held up as models of crudeness. Only fifteen years ago one is said to have been able to see nothing more here than a *rancho*, and now one sees buildings here which might adorn the most attractive plazas of Europe's capitals, and the city is still growing in size every day. The surrounding area offers the farmer a sufficient amount of good land. To be sure, the best land has already been taken, but perhaps a lot of good land can be purchased cheaply. To do so, the foreigner must obtain the permission of the state, but it is not denied even though the conditions under which it is granted (there is a colonization law) are not the most liberal.

The best and rather expensive land is on the banks of the Rio Grande. Of course, it is subject to flooding when the river rises, but the long succession of *ranchos* on the river demonstrate that one does not fear the floods. The sale of [farm] products is as easy here as it is difficult at other places where the land is somewhat cheap. The export of foodstuffs is absolutely

---

[1] Ludecus probably called New Orleans "America's sepulcher" because many Americans and European immigrants died of cholera there the previous year. See the fourteenth letter, Note Five.

forbidden. The Mexican is too lazy to plant more than he needs for himself and he understands nothing at all about horticulture. But this would be the most advantageous endeavor to pursue here. The prices for everything except meat are high; for some items they are outrageous. I cite the following: Corn is six times more expensive here than corn [grown] in the United States on the Missouri River. A month ago an onion cost a half s[hilling] and now one is not to be had at all for any price. A pound of butter costs one *Thaler*. Good cheese would have such a high price also, since the bad stuff that is made here is not fit to eat. And yet, I do not want to assert that this climate allows good things to be produced. Potatoes and every kind of vegetable cost very dearly, and the small number of these various foods that are produced do not meet even one hundredth of the demand. Only a small number of Americans have gardens where a beginning has been made to grow products native to the northern regions and to acclimatize the plants to this region. These attempts have likely been successful. The autumn is the season when gardens are planted here. A chicken costs from two to four *florins*, and a dozen eggs cost three *florins*. Geese and ducks, etc. cost proportionately the same, except in the autumn when flocks of wild birds cover the river and the lagoons. If one then has a farm located near to a sandbank in the river where these birds customarily rest at night, one can send geese to town every day [and sell them] for several pesos. An old musket, fully loaded with large shot and fired a couple of times, will yield a sufficient number of birds. A wild goose costs now only two *florins*. Beef tallow from oxen was costing two *florins,* and pork fat was two and a half *florins*. Pigs themselves are expensive and they thrive extremely well, but miserably poor specimens are selling for a half *florin* apiece.

But on the other hand there are also enough difficulties here, for how can one have a little confidence in a country where laws are made and broken at will? No matter how enlightened and political the government may be, given the Mexicans' jealousy of foreigners and their aversion to them settling in their country, I am convinced that foreigners will encounter all kinds of difficulties and intolerance in the execution of a colonization plan, and finally, after considerable expense of one's efforts, time, and money, the foreigners will gain no security for their property. Moreover, one must consider also the following: one's lack of knowledge about the influence of the climate on the goods one wishes to produce, the lack of good workers (the Mexican is too lazy and given to thievery), the difficulties caused by the authorities, and the lack of trust that one can place in the government and in the general population. In addition to these considerations, there may be other difficulties that catch the eye only during an extended stay in the country, for usually the advantages are more easily discerned than the disadvantages.

After all the things that I have experienced in Mexico, as everyone will probably easily see, I do not have any special liking for the country. My decision to return to the United States was an easy one. I am sure that when my reports from New York brought you news of my decision to go to Mexico, many of you did not approve of it. To be sure, it is evidence of a rather unsettled character for a person to allow himself to be deflected from already formulated plans by the first opportunity that presents itself without that person having tried in the slightest to bring one of those plans to realization. I freely admit this, but I note in this regard that it is very impractical to make plans in Europe at all and expect to carry them out in America without having a thorough knowledge of the country, for of what value are all the reports that we read in books measured against the reality? Of the hundred [emigrants] who come over here from Europe, probably only two will bring to realization the plan that they had concocted sitting before the stove at home. In general, my advice is to concern oneself as little as possible with such thoughts. Here in America the moment matters. One must seize it, and even though one does not always seize the right moment, with perseverance and some acquired experience, that moment will certainly come along. A great obstacle and the most difficult moment [for the emigrant] is when he arrives. Say, he arrives in New York, Baltimore, or New Orleans, and on the ship he has made a hundred plans for what he wants to do when he gets to utopia. Once arrived, he stumbles out of pure fearfulness over all the small obstacles, in order not to collide with them, and ends up falling on his face. That has happened to hundreds of emigrants. I was no exception, and so it will be with hundreds more [in the future]. The most dangerous things for the newly arrived emigrant are the people who give him advice, and the suggestions they make to him. A man needs only to ask a dozen people and each one of them will spout at him twelve warnings and eleven of these will be contradicted by other people. Of course, this creates mistrust toward everybody and everything. Taking it all into account, however, I do not regret even now that I participated in this cross-country crusade. To be sure, it cost me some time and money and much more than I had anticipated, but the experiences I had are worth twice as much to me. But now I want to return to the city [of Matamoros]. I wanted to give you a brief description of it.

With the variety of nations that are [represented by the people] living here, of course a great deal of segregation takes place. Consequently, there is nowhere a sign of social life. Whoever comes here wants to earn money—as much and as quickly as possible. So, all day they work and in the evening everyone goes to the coffee houses and the billiard salons. Besides faro and roulette, billiards is the only game played here. The North Americans are the most numerous of the foreigners here. When these gentlemen play, they segregate themselves somewhat more from the others and one has very little good to say about them. Then come the French, the Germans, the British, etc. I have heard that only two Americans are heads of households here. The others are all bachelors since none of them can make up his mind to marry a Mexican woman. Probably among the women of the lower class there may be marriages with these men. There are also several American families here. The lack of beauty, education, and virtue of the native women provides sufficient reason for the reluctance of these foreigners to become seriously involved with these ladies, who are incidentally too obliging, although they are said to often enough press for such a relationship with the men.

I had the opportunity to admire the upper crust here at a ball given by the trades council. I arrived there at nine o'clock in the evening dressed in European ball attire. A small stairway led up into a long, narrow room, where I saw a lot of combs moving around in rhythmical movements. A breastwork of men permitted nothing more to be seen of the dancers than these tasteless adornments which the Mexican women wear, and they are larger than any I have ever seen before. Such a comb often costs from ten to twenty pesos and lends the woman's appearance, especially when a *mantilla* is hanging over the comb, an unattractive profile because it makes her head appear twice as tall. Then the dance ended and everyone began moving about in the narrow room as well as one could. The ladies were sitting around the room on chairs and had small slender Spanish cigars in their mouths. The gentlemen were busy supplying the ladies with fresh cigars or lighting the cigars that had gone out. The music was provided by two violins, two guitars, and one flute. The fee paid for the evening's music was a hundred pesos. In order to look the place over, I wandered around in the room and found only three ladies who were worthy of my notice. The others can be grateful to me that I will refrain from describing them here. I will call those three ladies Juno, Pallas, and Venus. I want to make mention of the first one only to note that she was a native of Spain, and had a tall, proud build, although she was somewhat skinny. She had a very fine physiognomy. The second one had an attractive figure and a pretty face as well, and a particularly white and much too pale skin color. Otherwise there was nothing agreeable about her. On the contrary, she had something cold and repellent in her features like all warring characters, although as someone softly whispered in my ear, she was brave at the attack, but not very *courageous* in the defense. Now I come to the third one, the Venus who was indeed somewhat too short and corpulent. Perhaps the heat may have been to blame, for as Ovid tells us, the goddesses on Mount Olympus also did not wear belts in the hot summer months.[2]

---

[2] This reference to the apparel of the goddesses on Mount Olympus could not be confirmed. A careful search of Ovid's works uncovered no remarks like the ones Ludecus recalls.

Otherwise, she had beautiful dark brown hair, black eyes, an elegant nose, and a mouth, ah yes, a mouth—now I feel like many a good speech maker when he comes to his main point—words fail me. I cannot presume to describe this sweet little devil, for it is so difficult. In contrast, Hannibal's journey over the Alps would seem like child's play. To make a long story short, my decision not to dance staggered and fell. I had myself introduced to her and I asked her for a waltz which she granted. We took our places for the dance and she began to speak. If her mouth was pretty to look at, it was even prettier to hear form words. Really, she spoke her language in such a charming manner that my ears distracted my eyes, and my eyes distracted my feet so much that out of pure delight and confusion, I stepped a few times on her (God forgive me my transgression here) rather large feet. The music changed then. The second part was a jig and she explained to me that she did not know how to dance to it. All of my pleas were fruitless. Her *absolument* put an end to them. Then I led her back to her seat. Her "*mil gracias*" sounded to me like a swan song, and almost devastated, I took a seat opposite her on a bench. When I had recovered somewhat, I began to draw comparisons between her and the beautiful girl who lived on the bank of the Rio Grande near Laredo, where incidentally, a piece of my heart still lies buried and stewing in the hot sand. I was almost of a mind to go looking for that lost piece of my heart, so that I would not have to offer the beautiful girl sitting *vis à vis* a piece of it that was much too small. But just then an acquaintance took me by the arm and led me to the dining room, and a piece of turkey erased the whole business from my memory. Overall, the meal was quite good, and the wines, among them some champagne, were not spared either. I left about two o'clock completely satisfied. This ball costs the sponsors about eight or nine hundred dollars. It was just as boring as our balls in Germany, but by far not as glamorous. Altogether there may have been a hundred and fifty people in attendance, among them a very few Mexican gentlemen. They came dressed in white trousers and jackets made of the finest linen or of batiste. Everyone was smoking as much as he wanted.

Matamoros is said to have been diminished a great deal since the last revolution, for it forced a lot of wealthy Spanish families to leave and that, with the withdrawal of the army, did grave damage to the city.[3] In addition, the [Stephen F.] Austin colonies have delivered a serious blow to the commerce

---

[3] Throughout Mexico, in cities and on rural estates, the withdrawal of Spanish families (and in the case of Matamoros, the removal of the Spanish army) led to declines in population, commerce, agriculture, and mining. See Michal C. Meyer et al., *The Course of Mexican History* 7th ed. (New York: Oxford University Press, 1003), 289, and Newton R. Gilmore, "British Mining Ventures in Early National Mexico," (Ph.D. thesis, University of California at Berkeley, 1956), 38–47.

of the inhabitants here, for after the custom officials and the soldiers had been driven away by the American immigrants, a large portion of the imports from New Orleans were lost that used to continue on their way into the interior on [the backs of] mules.[4] Even the larger local merchants now send their goods shipments to those ports [in Texas]. A few weeks ago, of course, the army returned, which has brought more life into the city and even more is expected. The few dragoons which made up the garrison here before the arrival of the other troops resembled a band of robbers more than soldiers. Some of them had no uniforms and were running around here in rags; some others were half naked. The new arrivals have quite good uniforms with French styling. Now in the summer they are completely white, including the shako, which does not look bad.[5]

A few weeks ago the festival of freedom or independence was celebrated here with a lot of cannons being fired. The drills of the artillery are very slow and if these soldiers went to battle against European artillery, they would probably have to strike their sails in a short time. On this day there were several celebrations such as for example the dedication of a school. All day long and during the following two days people were gambling at booths set up on the market square. Besides the private gambling houses there are two public ones where roulette is played, but they are not patronized much by decent people. I find more confirmation here of what I have said before: the nearer one comes to civilization, the more wicked the people are. Acts of murder are so common here that one hardly talks about them. For example, no one would dare carry anything on the street in the darkness [of night]. Any moment one would have to expect a couple of *ladrones* to tear it from his hands, and the first movement indicating any resistance to them would earn the owner a few stabs with a knife. Consequently, one goes out at night only if one is armed. One must keep a sharp eye as well on the members of the elegant and richer class, for if any of them sees a chance to make off with something, it is said, they are rarely able to resist it. Merchants who visit the

[4] During and immediately after Mexico's war for independence from Spain, Matamoros lost importance as a port for shipping goods from the U.S. and Europe. Later, it gained in importance. In 1827, German and Prussian goods valued at 200,000 pesos were received and further expedited there. By 1829 the value of German and Prussian goods is reported to have increased to a million dollars. The Mexican peso and the U.S. dollar were roughly equal in value. Dane, *Die wirtschaftlichen Beziehungen Deutschlands*, 16.

[5] As early as 1826 (eight years before Ludecus arrived in Mexico) the Mexican infantry wore white warm-weather uniforms during the summer. In January 1832, the Mexican government contracted for 10,000 new infantry uniforms. These uniforms probably had the long coat tails that were fashionable in France at the time. Ludecus probably perceived this feature as French styling. See René Chartrand, *Santa Anna's Mexican Army 1821-1848* (Oxford: Osprey Publishing, 2004), 27, 29.

rich cities of the interior such as Saltillo, Durango, Zacatecas, etc. with their wares and whose words I have reason to trust have told me that they must constantly keep a watchman standing in their stores who keep an eye on the fingers of their customers. I was told also that they have caught the culprits several times, but they had not been able to achieve anything with the *alcalde* who had responded with the excuse that the accused were some of the most distinguished people of the city. He had said that he could not proceed against them and had rejected the merchant's charges. In general one must exercise a great deal of caution in becoming involved with the courts here. The *alcaldes*, I am told, are for the most part open to bribery. Whoever has the most money gets the most justice.

A few weeks ago Mr. Egerton and Mr. Addicks arrived here from San Fernando. They were quite surprised at finding neither money nor news from Dr. Beales here, and so they are going to wait for something. Since then they have visited Troy, our abandoned settlement, again with a military escort. They claim that the crops have developed splendidly, but I have good reason to be suspicious of the veracity of this allegation. Again they found traces of Indians who are still moving about in the vicinity. They told me too that a few days after my passing through Begades our friends, the Lipans, attacked four Mexicans and murdered three of them. The fourth one is still alive with seventeen wounds and with a scalped head, but everyone doubts that he will recover. And so I can say that I was lucky to slip through the fingers of these brown devils! I was tormented so much more by their countrymen, the fleas. These beasts live here in such horrific numbers that in every house the people have to sprinkle water three times a day and sweep out the house. That is the only way to keep the creatures at least from gaining the upper hand if one wants to protect oneself from them. What amazes me is that even here, where the population has already grown so large, that the larger pests have not yet been exterminated. Behind my quarters four rattlesnakes have been killed, and in the house itself I found a scorpion. Once a skunk polluted the house so badly that I had to stay away for several hours.

A few weeks ago the rainy season began and with it the second springtime of the year. Everything is turning green again and it breathes new life into every creature. As the rain began falling, the streets were filled with people who were making a game out of letting themselves be completely drenched by the rain. All the children came out dancing and jumping around naked in the mud. Women and girls swim here in the lagoon without any timidity, and I used to bathe there twice a day. It is very salutary to one's health. Several times I came upon a group of young *señoritas* there who were swimming together across the wide lagoon. After every stroke of their arms they disappeared under the water's surface, then resurfaced just to disappear again, and like undines [female water spirits], they swam the whole watery course that way. Their dark naked bodies with their long raven hair appearing and disappearing in the water provided quite a pleasant spectacle. [Christoph Martin] Wieland would have certainly told some very cute things about it. But I do not have Wieland's flair for writing; so, I will not say anything.[6]

My health has been completely restored now, but that is unfortunately not the case with most of my fellow travelers. Marzelino, who came down here with Mr. Egerton, will probably not leave town again. Since the time when he came down with a serious illness in [San Antonio de] Bexar, he has not been able to recuperate, and now his condition is getting worse from day to day. Peter Dippelhöfer, Schwartz, and some others are growing more miserable every day. Their health has been compromised too much by the strain and deprivation of this trip.

This would be about all that I have to report from here. So, now I appeal to the god Neptune to grant me safe passage through his realm. I do not know yet what his answer will be, but I expect to report it to you with my next letter from New Orleans.

Accept my last farewell from Mexican soil!

---

[6] Christoph Martin Wieland (1733–1813) was the author of several didactic and satirical novels, as well as epic poems. Ludecus appears to have enjoyed Wieland's works, many of which were written while the author lived at the court in Weimar. Weiland, who was not at all provincial in his views, would likely have admired the naive innocence of the dark-skinned señoritas swimming in the lagoon. Garland and Garland (eds.), *Oxford Companion*, 938-939.

NINETEENTH LETTER
Departure for Boca del Rio. Aduana. Embarking for New Orleans. A Party of Travelers. Lagoons. Survey of the Journey Here and Back. A Stormy Voyage. Arrival at the Mississippi and in New Orleans. End of the Journey.

New Orleans, November 19, 1834

My appeal to the god of the sea does not appear to have found him in a good mood, for we did not enter [the mouth of] the Mississippi until October [November] 15. But all's well that ends well! So, I do not want to complain about him anymore. On the fifteenth of last month I packed all my belongings together, loaded them the next morning onto a cart, and had them transported to the steamer that was going to Boca del Rio (mouth of the river), where the ships drop anchor at the mouth of the Rio Grande. As I was walking along behind the cart, I came to the outskirts of the city where there are only wretched huts. A dog came rushing out of one of them and grabbed me by the leg. I was hardly able to defend myself from the dog, but finally I laid hands on a rock, and since the animal's owner, who was standing in the hut and observing the spectacle with amusement, was not showing any inclination to call off his dog, I hit the animal in the back of the head with the rock so hard that it dropped dead. Then his master began cursing, rushed back into the hut, and came back with a shotgun. He threatened to shoot me if I did not replace his dog. In answer to his threat, I pulled my own, albeit unloaded double-barreled shotgun from the cart and aimed it at him. As swiftly as the wind, that *poltrón* [lazy lout] ran back inside his hut and nothing more was heard from him. His neighbors, who had watched the affair, were laughing themselves half to death. When I went back by [later] to have the *capitano del puerto* examine my passport, I ran into the man again, but he acted as if he did not know me. I wanted to narrate to you this unimportant event only in order to let you get to know the character of the inhabitants of this town better. After I had finished that business [with the *capitano del puerto*], I bade farewell to my acquaintances there [in Matamoros]. I expressed special thanks to Herr Dörien, a native of Braunschweig, and Richter, Heine, and Wagner for their many gestures of friendship demonstrated to me during my stay there.[1] Then I returned to the steamboat which left immediately. The trip was very entertaining. The banks [of the river] are covered by a succession of *ranchos* and are bristling with vegetation. They are adorned also by a lot of beautiful tall palm trees.

Shortly before nightfall we reached Boca del Rio, which consists of eight or ten wooden houses built on piles. When there is a strong northeast or an

---

[1] None of these German gentlemen could be identified.

easterly wind they all become flooded and seem to be standing in the sea itself, for they are located directly on the water. The officers of the *aduana maritima* came on board immediately in order to conduct the inspection for money. There is an export duty only on money. However, the inspection was very superficial. I showed the officials only my money bag with about ninety pesos in it and declared that this was all the cash I had, and they moved on. Sums under a hundred pesos are duty-free and for larger amounts one must pay three percent duty. That same day I went on board the schooner, a very clean and elegant vessel. The food was excellent. The high fare for passage, thirty-five dollars, entitles the passenger, however, to demand such fare, since it is a high price for a voyage that can be completed with a good wind in four or five days. For every extra day that the ship remains in port, one dollar extra is charged, which often can go on for months.

The company of people on board was quite pleasant, consisting of a Pole who had been a colonel in Mexican military service. There were two Frenchmen who were very fine people as are all people from that country. One of them, a somewhat older man, ate almost nothing but sugar, and never any meat. And then there was a tanner from Matamoros who was a pettifogger and a most peculiar phenomenon. He spoke English, French, and Spanish with great fluency, and he claimed that he could speak also Italian and Portuguese. Before long he had picked up a few German words which he used probably a hundred times a day. He sang and whistled probably over a couple of dozen French and Italian operatic airs. He would lie behind a large barrel full of Porter beer from Philadelphia, which was our gathering place for aesthetic pleasures, and recite a few Spanish tragedies with all the characters and all the gestures. He had been in a lot of different countries and had learned a lot of different trades. He was always finished with the calculation of our latitude sooner than the helmsman, and he was for sure the most malicious scoundrel on God's green earth. In direct contrast to him there was another man whom I must call the Trappist monk. I never heard a single syllable come from his mouth. However, he seemed to understand English, because he demonstrated some interest when this language was being spoken nearby.

In addition, I must mention also an old Frenchman who had left his homeland after the revolution and who was now living on the Missouri River. He began a conversation probably twenty times a day with the words, *"I tell you that Missouri is the best country in the world."* He continued on in French after that and promised me that there were golden mountains there. That phrase seemed to be the only one he had learned in the English language during his entire thirty-year stay there. That seems quite excessive, although the French are famous for not learning foreign languages. One evening he bored me so much with his story of the French revolution and the history of Napoleon that, after telling him in vain that I knew everything quite well and far better than he did, I corrected him several times in his confused narrative. Then I lay down and pretended to go to sleep. That had the desired effect—he spared me from his oratory.

The rest of the passengers consisted of three young Americans. Two of them could do nothing but swear and curse, and the third one could speak some German. He had been raised among Germans in the state of Pennsylvania. When he was eating for the first time at our table (He had come on board a few days late.), his build and spatial economy caught my eye because he took up only half as much space as every other flesh-and-blood person.

The [Polish] colonel who greeted me sometimes in the morning in German and to whom I remarked once that another gentleman must be a tailor, answered me in Spanish that he did not understand me and that I ought to speak Spanish or French to him. At that I became confused, for I did not know whether he understood either of those languages. Suddenly, the person *en question* answered me in fairly good German: "Yes, I am a tailor. How did you know that?" I was quite amazed [at his response] and told him the truth. At that he began to laugh loudly. Then I explained the joke to the others present, and at that they demanded that I make a full apology to the gentleman concerned. Then everyone laughed when I insisted that an apology was not necessary, for a tailor was the most respected profession in the United States and that General [Andrew] Jackson, himself the son of a tailor, had said that it took nine men just to make one tailor.[2] The gentleman really was a tailor, and a very well-bred and educated one at that.

During our stay in port and later on during the voyage, the captain was lying in bed all the time suffering terribly from the gout. It was due to this that we were held up on the river for seven days longer than was necessary. The helmsman missed the opportunity one morning to put out to sea, claiming that the sea was too *roff* [rough] to be able to get across the bar. When he had gone out in a boat to investigate it, he had not gone out far enough. We disagreed with him and in order to show him the proof, I got into the boat with three other passengers and we passed right through the breakers. By the time we returned to the ship, however, the ebb tide had already commenced and the best time [to sail] was already past. The captain did not appear to have gotten his smuggling business in order yet. So, he did not want to sail. Perhaps he was too fearful to investigate the matter properly because he could not swim. In any case, all seafaring people should learn to swim, because there are too many instances where this skill is indispensable. Because of his negligence he was dismissed from service in New Orleans.

---

[2] This remark by General Jackson could not be corroborated.

We passed the time [aboard ship] as well as we could. Sometimes the tanner would sing a ballad and we played whist, but hunting was our chief pastime. Like the hunting at Aransas Bay the year before, it was very productive. Countless waterfowl covered the beach that was partly under water and I spent the whole day in pursuit of them. The Rio Grande there played a couple of jokes on me again too. Several times I sank so deeply in the mud that some men had to throw me a rope from a boat so that I could be pulled out. Another time all the passengers were gathered on the bow of the ship when the talk turned to bathing and swimming, etc. The suggestion was made to go bathing in the water, but several people thought that no one should dare to go into the river because there was a risk of being bitten by an *alligator gar*. I had been in the river several times, but I had always considered the matter to be just idle talk and so I jumped overboard, intending to swim around to the rope hanging down in the water from the stern of the ship and then to climb back on board. When I came back up, I was quite surprised to find myself being swept along by the current. A few minutes of laborious swimming convinced me that it was useless to swim against such a [strong] current. I called out for someone to send the boat for me, but it was not even on board. So, I had no choice but to steer a different course and I began swimming toward the shore. In the meantime, the current had continued to sweep me along and only by applying all my strength was I able to reach the point of land safely where the Rio Grande empties into the sea. I rested there for a while and then I walked back along the shore and swam out to the ship.

Here I must mention an error, albeit understandable, that I committed perhaps in one of my earlier letters where I made mention of alligators. In Matamoros people claimed that they did not live in the Rio Grande, but only alligator *gars*. I have already written about them. They are the same size and have the same appearance [as alligators], but the alligator gar has no feet. Recently, while he was bathing, a young Mexican lost a leg from a bite by one of these animals.

From time to time I hike also along the coastline, and at one place I discovered the wreck of a ship that had been driven up on land. It seemed to have been a type of cutter or some similar vessel. Usually I brought back a load of mussels from these outings. On them I have seen also for the first time the sea spider and they were very numerous too. Their repulsive appearance could not prevent me from observing them and laughing at them as they scurried about. You see, this animal moves in any direction, backward or forward, to the right or left, with the same ease and speed, but always in a straight line. One can approach one of them only very rarely because the slightest noise causes it to flee. A wave washing in to shore usually drives a number of them out in front of it, and then, as the water recedes, they follow it back again in order to look for the food it has left behind. They have holes that they have dug in the sand, and they are almost like crabs. Only their bodies are smaller, their legs longer, and their eyes are at the end of small stalks that protrude out from their head.

These lonely hikes along the seashore have a great allure for me, although in most cases I must agree with the English poet who said:

"That the best works of nature improve
When we see them reflected from looks that we love." [3]

This situation is for me an exception, for in the absence of another living being before me, and without hearing or seeing something of that person's actions and influence on me, standing on a small spit of land with the raging sea before me and beside me is the most sublime spectacle of nature.

Almost six or eight miles north of Boca del Rio is another port called Brazos [de] Santiago, which has a safer and better, that is, a deeper harbor entrance. At low tide the bar is said to have a depth still of seven to eight feet.[4] During our stay [here] a Mexican pirate sea captain was captured there and thrown into chains. The pirates had been careless enough to allow a woman to go ashore and she had divulged the infamous business of the ship. She revealed among other things that the passengers who had been on the ship the pirates had looted had been cast overboard into the sea.

All of the pirates that have been captured in America in recent years have been Spaniards or their descendants. Faithlessness seems to be in them an innate quality. The crew of one pirate ship is now in prison in Baltimore and some of them have already been condemned to death.

I have made the acquaintance of the customs officers in Boca del Rio. Their commanding officer (*el commandante*) is a very amiable and fine man. However, he is completely true to his Spanish heritage. He never puts aside his pompous demeanor. The subordinate *commandante* once provided us with a rather ridiculous spectacle. The matter went as follows: Captain Lafontaine from the steamboat was on board our ship when we heard suddenly the commanding voice of that officer coming from the steamboat, saying that Captain Lafontaine should come back on board. Lafontaine paid no attention to him. Then the order was repeated, but with no more effect, and Lafontaine told us that the officer only wanted to show off the authority he thought he had in front of the passengers on the steamboat. Then the Mexican [officer] shouted that he was ordering Lafontaine in the name of the Mexican nation to appear, but he received no response [from the captain]. Lafontaine stayed on board another half hour and then I accompanied

---

[3] The source of these two lines could not be identified.

[4] No official records from 1834 concerning the depth of water at the port of Brazos de Santiago could be found to corroborate Ludecus's information.

him to the steamboat, expecting to witness an interesting scene. Once we were on board, the Mexican, with a face as red as a turkey's, confronted Lafontaine and asked him angrily, why he had not obeyed the order. Captain Lafontaine, a small but determined Frenchman, answered him very dryly: "Because you have no authority to give orders. The *capitán del puerto* gives me orders, not you." Then the other man went on more vehemently: "But I gave you an order in the name of the nation." To that Lafontaine replied: "You could just as well have given me an order in the name of the devil." By then the officer was furious: "You would not say that to me if I had soldiers here with me." Lafontaine: "Of course I would." The other man: "Then I would have you put in chains." Then Lafontaine, as he drew a pistol from his pocket and held it under the nose of the Mexican officer: "But first I would shatter your skull." At this remark the red cheeks of the officer grew pale and his pompous demeanor had been diminished so much that he withdrew as quickly as possible.

During the day these officers are occupied by nothing more than games of chance. The considerable income that they have, coupled with the bribes they receive aboard the ships and which can run into thousands, enables them to gamble for high stakes. However, they gamble respectably and without overt signs of passion and, I believe, honestly.

Finally, on the twenty-eighth [of October] the direction of the wind changed to the south-southwest and the pilot came aboard. He had been ordered by the captain to get us out to sea the next morning if it was at all possible. It happened too, even though it was done with some difficulties and dangers. The wind was blowing somewhat too strongly to keep the ship in the channel, so it had to be stabilized by towing it by the anchors that were cast overboard and which the boats then pulled this way and that. The masts of a ship that had recently sunk right in the mouth of the river and which were jutting up out of the water were a sufficient reminder to be careful. We were cast up on the bar three or four times with such force that we were afraid the ship would be shattered any minute. (Every river cuts for itself a channel through the land that gradually emerges from the sea as the current carries away the sand or whatever the ocean bottom consists of there. The point where the force of the current is equal to the force of the advancing sea is called the "bar" and is the shallowest spot [in the channel]. The channel and the bar move frequently, especially during storms which blow in from a direction contrary to the river's flow at its mouth.) Nevertheless, our ship suffered no great damage, although we were obliged to keep the [bilge] pumps going during the entire voyage.

The first day was beautiful and brought us along a good distance. But on the second day, around noon, we ran into a calm and then the wind turned and began blowing from the opposite direction, and then there came a storm. So, we were blown about for seventeen days instead of three, as we had hoped. During that time our provisions became completely exhausted. Except for the first and last day, I was seasick the whole time, but only to a slight degree, so I slept on deck during the entire voyage.

Before I take final leave of Mexico, I want to give you a brief survey of the provinces through which I traveled. I want to do this even more because I am sure that much incorrect information has been broadcast by the different *empresarios* or by owners of the grants in order to persuade people to migrate there.

The land is generally level or there are undulating *pampas* (prairies) that on the coast down to about ninety-eight degrees western longitude contain good fertile land. Adequate rain falls there and makes irrigation unnecessary. This is true in the north even more so than in the south, but as the land rises toward the west, it loses this feature and the lack of water makes any cultivation of these large tracts impossible. There are narrow strips of good land to be found only directly along the rivers and creeks where the land is low enough to be flooded when the waters rise, but then irrigation systems still have to be constructed. The country's greatest deficiency is the lack of timber for construction. However, the colonies in the north along the Colorado and Brazos rivers are an exception. The Rio Frio is an exception also.

There are few mountains and they hardly deserve the name. They are covered only with low-growing thorn bushes. On the other hand, the higher elevations of the English[?], the western, and the southern provinces Coahuila, Chihuahua, Santa Fé, and Nuevo Leon are barren, grotesque stony peaks. I have seen the latter ones only from a distance. As I have already mentioned, water is very scarce and almost all rivers and creeks contain some salt.

Corn, sugar, cotton, tobacco (which in these provinces is not permitted to be grown), rice, pepper, aniseed, etc. either thrive here or they would thrive extremely well, if they were planted—especially Mexican cotton, for it is considered to be the best. As far as fruits are concerned, the country produces chiefly figs and peaches. The climate is not suited to oranges, lemons, pineapple, etc. and they do not have a good taste.

I have already described the people as well as the animals. The great multitudes of wild horses and buffalo, which used to roam over the land in such large herds that wagon caravans traveling through the country had to send riders out ahead to clear a way, have almost disappeared. As settlement has advanced, these animals have retreated into the wild country out west.

The climate is unhealthy on the coast and in the northern regions bordering on the United States. It becomes healthier, however, the further one travels to the west into the higher elevations. In that regard it might be counted among the most agreeable climates in the world. As regards the political situation in Texas, it is very precarious and sooner or later it will perforce furnish provocation for differences between Mexico and its powerful neighbor [to the north]. For although Mexico is much too weak to be able to hold its own against its giant neighbor, it will nevertheless not willingly allow these provinces to be snatched away. That will of necessity result in terrible consequences for their inhabitants. The matter is complicated even more by the fact that it is in the interest of many of the [holders of] grants and will be in their interest to remain under Mexican authority as long as they can preserve a certain degree of independence from the Mexican government as Austin's colony has done. Such empresarios would embrace this choice rather than to be absorbed into the United States. On this point I have questioned Dr. Beales and found him to be very much against annexation to the United States. One must wonder also whether the question of slavery will not soon come up for debate in Texas, especially in the northern regions where the population may consist chiefly of North Americans. There the encroaching civilization of the southern and western states of the United States is one that embraces a policy of slavery, which is forbidden in Mexico, and it may invite imitation [in Texas].

On the fifteenth of this month we finally reached the Mississippi River. We sailed up to Fort Jackson where [the direction of] the wind did not allow us to pass a curve [in the river]. We went ashore and looked over the small fortifications of the battery, which would be a better name for the fort. The mosquitos were tormenting us terribly. So, we were delighted when the towboat, the *Lion*, came during the night and in sixteen hours brought us, together with three three-masted ships, two brigs, and one schooner, altogether with ours, seven ships, up to New Orleans. From this example one can imagine the power of these steamboats.

The weather was bad. We passed the time by admiring the banks of the river, the beautiful sugar plantations and orange groves, and by eating oysters. We were being observed very keenly by a number of ladies on board the Havre packet boat ahead of us.[5] As I have just now learned, they were French actresses. They were all wearing rubber rain apparel and in spite of the rain they were wandering around all day long on the deck. Our colorful *frazadas* that we had thrown on also as protection from the rain seemed to attract their charming attention to us. That evening at six o'clock, to the

---

[5] According to the "Marine Journal" in the newspaper, *The Bee*, the towboat *Lion* brought the schooner *Louisiana* (from Matamoros) and the ship *Ruthetia* (from Havre) to New Orleans on Monday, November 17. Two other schooners from Matamoros, the *San Luis* and the *Harriet*, arrived at New Orleans the same day but no passengers on either of those ships are mentioned. *The Bee*, New Orleans, November 17, 1834.

accompaniment of cannon fire, we ran up to perhaps three hundred three-masted French ships and dropped anchor.

Here I am concluding the first packet of my letters and I will send them to you. I hope to find enough material here in the United States to let a second one come later. Until then think of me in good friendship and receive herewith my fond greetings!

EPILOGUE

While Eduard Ludecus waited in Matamoros to set sail for New Orleans, John Charles Beales was still in New York City recruiting a second contingent of settlers for his colony on the Rio Grande. In October 1834, he wrote to the colonists in Dolores that a vessel had sailed from New York in August with more settlers. Upon receiving this news, Addicks rushed to Copano Bay to meet the new colonists and lead them to Dolores. When he arrived, however, he learned that the colonists, about twenty of them, had been told by the Texans living in Copano Bay that the inhabitants of Dolores had been massacred by Comanches. The new colonists, he was told, had either returned to New York or scattered to other settlements.[1]

A third group of colonists sailed from New York, probably about the end of January 1835. Their vessel landed in early spring at Live Oak Point where it was met by Egerton with oxen and carts to transport them to the colony. In the meantime, Beales had sailed to Matamoros where he was met in March by Addicks. There he purchased oxen for the new colonists to use on their journey from Copano Bay to the Rio Grande. He left Matamoros immediately with his brother and his brother's family to join the other immigrants at Copano Bay. This third contingent of settlers included three families, five heads of families, and ten unmarried men.[2]

Instead of taking the long, round-about route from Copano Bay via Goliad and Bexar to Dolores as the first group of colonists had done, Beales decided to forge a new route directly from Copano to Dolores. This new roadway—which the colonists cut through the mesquite, chaparral, and cactus—took three months of arduous labor to complete.[3]

After the new colonists arrived at Dolores, the colony thrived for a few months. Under Beales's leadership they built houses, gristmills, and sawmills, cultivated fields, and planted crops. But Beales did not remain long in the colony. In September 1835, he left once again for New York to bring his own family and another group of colonists who were anxiously awaiting his return. In New York, he recruited a group of sturdy farmers with substantial

[1] Rister, *Comanche Bondage*, 89; Dickson, "Speculation," 98–99.
[2] Rister, *Comanche Bondage*, 89-90; Dickson, "Speculation," 99–100.
[3] Rister, *Comanche Bondage*, 90-91; Dickson, "Speculation," 100–101.

experience, but their return was delayed because of a large fire in New York City that winter. Once again, circumstances seemed to conspire against the success of Beales's colony.[4]

By the end of March 1836, the agricultural colony of Dolores on Las Moras Creek seemed doomed. The eruption of the Texas Revolution—Santa Anna and his six thousand troops crossing the Rio Grande to suppress federalism, the assault on the Alamo, and Santa Anna's threat to "exterminate every white man in Texas"—seemed to put an end to Beales's dream, a dream that had cost him dearly in cash, labor, and time.[5]

When news of Santa Anna's approach reached the colonists at Dolores, they dispersed. Some traveled east to the other Anglo colonies; others set out for Matamoros to return to New York; still others fled to Copano. The John Horn family was traveling with the second group of colonists to Matamoros when they were attacked by Comanches. Mrs. Sarah Ann Horn was captured by the Indians, but survived her captivity to recount her experiences as a Comanche captive.[6] Meanwhile, Beales, Addicks, and Egerton buried machinery (and other immovable comapny property) to keep it safe. Then they left for San Fernando with the cattle and tools. From San Fernando, Beales evidently returned to New York. By early June 1836, all but about eight settlers had abandoned the colony. Egerton and Addicks stayed on for awhile to look after Dr. Beales's property, but they were detained by the locals and charged with conspiring with the Texans. It is reported that the equipment they had wanted to secure was confiscated and sold, and the buildings in the village were burned.[7]

During the remaining forty-two years of his life, John Charles Beales made several attempts to receive compensation—from the Republic of Texas and then from the United States government—for his land in Texas and his expenses as empresario. However, none of his attempts were successful. The only wealth he received had been paid to him by the Rio Grande and Texas Land Company for a portion of his interest in several grants. Because Beales was not a careful keeper of records, the exact amount he received remains unknown.

Beales practiced medicine in New York during the last years of his life and became a respected physician. He also became a fellow of the New York Academy of Medicine. He died in New York City on July 25, 1878.[8]

---

[4] Rister, *Comanche Bondage*, 91; Dickson, "Speculation," 101–102.

[5] Dickson, "Speculation," 105; Lewis W. Newton and Herbert P. Gambrell, *Texas; Yesterday and Today* . . . (Dallas: Turner Co., 1949), 139 (quotation).

[6] Rister, *Comanche Bondage*, 92–93.

[7] Dickson, "Speculation," 111.

[8] Ibid.; Raymond Estep, "Beales, John Charles," *The New Handbook of Texas*, ed. Ron Tyler, et al., I, 435.

SELECTED BIBLIOGRAPHY

MANUSCRIPT COLLECTIONS

Archives and Records Division, Texas General Land Office, Austin.
Genealogical Division, Texas State Library, Austin.
John Charles Beales papers in the Private Manuscripts collection of the
Texas State Archives, Austin; also in the Center for American History at
the University of Texas at Austin.

PRIMARY SOURCES

Baptismal Register of the Evangelisch-Lutherischen Hofkirche in Weimar,
1798–1808, Jahrgang 1807.
"Descendants of Theodoricus Ludicus of Germany: Eduard Broeckmann
Ludecus," typescript, 2 pp. Courtesy of S. Stemmons.
"Document granting Knighthood in the Holy Roman Empire to Johann
August Ludecus (July 6, 1792)," translation in typescript, 6 pp. Courtesy
of S. Stemmons.
Loch, Ed. Archivist, San Antonio Archdiocese. Letter to the author,
December 5, 2005.
Loch, Ed. Archivist, San Antonio Archdiocese. Telephone conversation
with the author, Dec. 5, 2005.
Marriage Register of the Evangelisch-Lutherischen Hofkirche in Weimar,
1801–1821, Jahrgang, 1805.
Record of Interments, City of Montgomery, Alabama Department of
Archives and History.
"Reminiscences of Wilhelm Ludecus," dictated in July, 1849, translation in
typescript. Courtesy of S. Stemmons.
United States Seventh Census (1850), Population Schedules, Georgia District 13, Chatham County.
United States Eighth Census (1860), Population Schedules, New York District, Fourteenth Ward.
United States Sixth Census (1840), Population Schedules, New York City,
Sixth Ward.
United States Ninth Census (1870), Population Schedules, State of
Alabama, County of Montgomery.

Published Works

Allgemeine Deutsche Biographie, Historische Commission bei der königlichen Akademie der Wissenschaften, reprint, 56 vols. Berlin: Duncker and Humblot, 1967.

Austin, Stephen F., comp. *Map of Texas,* . . . Philadelphia: H. S. Tanner, 1831.

The Bee, New Orleans, November 17, 1834.

Beilage zum Frankfurter Journal, Dec. 14, 1832.

Braunschweigisches Adreß-Buch für das Jahr 1828. Braunschweig: Johann Heinrich Meyer, [1828].

Hecke, Johann Valentin. *Reise durch die Vereinigten Staaten von Nord-Amerika in den Jahren 1818 und 1819* . . . 2 vols. Berlin: H. Ph. Petri, 1820–1821.

Ludecus, Eduard. *Reise durch die Mexikanischen Provinzen Tumalipas, Cohahuila und Texas im Jahre 1834. In Briefen an seine Freunde*. Leipzig: Johann Friedrich Hartknoch, 1837.

Racknitz, Johann von. *Vorläufer für Auswanderer nach dem Staate Texas, an dem Flusse S. Marco, oder der Colorade, auch de la Cannes im Gebiete Neu-Mexico in Nordamerika*. Meersburg: [n. p.], 1832.

Secondary Sources

Barker, Eugene C. *The Life of Stephen F. Austin, Founder of Texas, 1793–1836; A Chapter in the Westward Movement of the Anglo-American People*. Austin: University of Texas Press, 1990.

Berlandier, Jean Louis. *Journey to Mexico During the Years 1826 to 1834*. trans. Sheila M. Ohlendorf, 2 vols. Austin: The Texas State Historical Association, 1980.

Brister, Louis E. "Eduard Ludecus's Journey to the Texas Frontier: A Critical Account of Beales's Rio Grande Colony." *Southwestern Historical Quarterly*, 108 (January, 2005), 368–385.

Brister, Louis E. "Johann von Racknitz: Ein Württemberger an der Spitze der deutschen Auswanderung nach Texas, 1832–1841." *Zeitschrift für Württembergische Landesgeschichte*, 53 (1994), 227–261.

Brister, Louis E. "Johann von Racknitz: German Soldier of Fortune in Texas and Mexico, 1832–1848." *Southwestern Historical Quarterly*, 99 (July, 1995), 48–79.

Brockhaus. *Die Enzyklopädie*. 24 vols. Leipzig: F. A. Brockhaus, 1996.

Chartrand, René. *Santa Anna's Mexican Army 1821–1848*. Oxford: Osprey Publishing, 2004.

Collingham, H.A.C. *The July Monarchy: A Political History of France 1830–1848*. London: Longman, 1988.

Dane, Heinrich. *Die wirtschaftlichen Beziehungen Deutschlands zu Mexiko und Mittelamerika im 19.* Jahrhundert, Forschungen zur internationalen Sozial-und Wirtschaftsgeschichte, I, Hermann Kellenbenz, ed. Köln: Böhlau Verlag, 1971.

de la Teja, Jesus F. "Seguin, Juan José María Erasmo." *The New Handbook of Texas* (hereafter cited as *The New Handbook of Texas*), eds. Ron Tyler et al. 6 vols. Austin: The Texas State Historical Association, 1996, V, 966.

Dickson, Lucy Lee. "Speculations of John Charles Beales in Texas Lands." M.A. thesis, Austin: University of Texas, 1941.

Donkin, R.A. "Spanish Red: An Ethnogeographical Study of Cochineal and the Opuntia Cactus." *Transactions of the American Philosophical Society* . . . , vol. 67, Philadelphia: The American Philosophical Society, 1977, 11–12.

Earle, Thomas. *Life, Travels and Opinions of Benjamin Lundy.* 1847; reprint, New York: Arno Press, 1969.

Ehrenberg, H[ermann]. *Der Freiheitskampf in Texas im Jahre 1836.* Leipzig: Otto Wigand, 1844.

Estep, Raymond. "Beales, John Charles," *The New Handbook of Texas*, ed. Ron Tyler, et al. (6 vols.; Austin: The Texas State Historical Association, 1996), I, 435.

Gilmore, Newton R. "British Mining Ventures in Early National Mexico." Ph.D. thesis, Berkeley: University of California, 1956.

Günther, Gitta, Haschke, Wolfram, and Steiner, Walter, eds. *Weimar: Lexikon zur Stadtgeschichte.* Weimar: Verlag Hermann Böhlaus Nachfolger, 1998.

Habig, Marion A. *The Alamo Chain of Missions: A History of San Antonio's Five Old Missions.* Chicago: Franciscan Herald Press, 1968.

Hatcher, Mattie Austin. "The Opening of Texas to Foreign Settlement 1801–1821." *University of Texas Bulletin*, no. 2714. Austin: University of Texas, 1927.

Henderson, Mary Virginia. "Minor Empresario Contracts for the Colonization of Texas, 1825–1834." *Southwestern Historical Quarterly*, XXXI (July, 1927-April, 1928), 295–324; XXXII (July, 1928–April, 1929), 1–28.

Huson, Hobart. *Refugio: A Comprehensive History of Refugio County from Aboriginal Times to 1953*, 2 vols. Woodsboro, Texas: The Rooke Foundation, Inc., 1953–1955.

Holley, Mary Austin. *Texas: Observations, Historical, Geographical and Descriptive in a Series of Letters,* . . . Baltimore: Armstrong and Plaskitt, 1833.

Hyman, Carolyn. "Iturbide, Agustín de," *The New Handbook of Texas*, III, 880-881.

Jenkins, John H., ed. *Papers of the Texas Revolution 1835–1836.* 10 vols., Austin: Presidial Press, 1973.

Johns, Christopher M.S. *Antonio Canova and the Politics of Patronage in Revo-lutionary and Napoleonic Europe*. Berkeley: University of California Press, 1998.

Kennedy, William. *The Rise, Progress, and Prospects of the Republic of Texas.* 1841 reprint, Fort Worth: The Molyneaux Craftsmen, Inc., 1925.

Meyers Konversations-Lexikon: Eine Encyklopädie des allgemeinen Wissens, 4th ed., 19 vols. Leipzig: Verlag des Bibliographischen Instituts, 1889–1892.

Newcomb, Jr., W.W. *The Indians of Texas; From Prehistoric to Modern Times.* Austin: University of Texas Press, 1961.

Newton, Lewis W., and Gambrell, Herbert P. *Texas: Yesterday and Today . . .* Dallas: Turner Co., 1949.

O'Conner, Kathryn Stoner. *The Presidio La Bahía del Espiritu Santo de Zuñiga, 1721–1846.* Austin: von Boeckmann-Jones, 1966.

Peters, Richard, ed. *Public Statutes at Large of the United States of America . . .* Boston: Charles C. Little and James Brown, 1850.

Rister, Carl Coke. *Comanche Bondage: Dr. John Charles Beales's settlement of La Villa de Dolores on Las Moras Creek in Southern Texas in the 1830's . . .* Lincoln: University of Nebraska Press, 1955, 1989.

Roell, Craig H. "La Bahía," *The New Handbook of Texas*, III, 1179.

Rubio, Manny. *Rattlesnake: Portrait of a Predator.* Washington: Smithsonian Institution Press, 1998.

Taddey, Gerhard, ed. *Lexikon der deutschen Geschichte. Personen Ereignisse Institutionen . . .* Stuttgart: Alfred Kröner Verlag, 1979.

INDEX

COLOPHON

This book is set in Adobe Bembo (text) and Chizel Solid (display). Bembo is the name given to an old style serif typeface based upon a face cut by Francesco Griffo, first printed in February 1495. The typeface Bembo we see today is a revival designed by Stanley Morison for the Monotype Corporation in 1929. Printed by Sheridan Books, Inc., of Ann Arbor, Michigan, on 50# House Natural paper, in an initial run of 1,000 books.